5TH INFANTRY BRIGADE IN THE FALKLANDS

Also by Nick van der Bijl

PEN & SWORD MILITARY BOOKS
Nine Battles to Stanley
Victory in the Falklands
Confrontation; the War with Indonesia 1962-1966
Commandos in Exile; The Story of 10 (Inter-Allied) Commando 1942-45
Operation Banner; The British Army in Northern Ireland 1969-2007
The Cyprus Emergency; The Divided Island 1955-1974
The Brunei Revolt 1962-1963
Sharing the Secret; The History of the Intelligence Corps 1940-2010

OSPREY
Argentine Forces in the Falklands
Royal Marines 1939-1993
No. 10 (Inter-Allied) Commando 1942-1945

HAWK EDITIONS
Brean Down Fort and the Defence of the Bristol Channel

5TH INFANTRY BRIGADE IN THE FALKLANDS

NICK VAN DER BIJL & DAVID ALDEA

Pen & Sword
MILITARY

To the officers and men of 5th Infantry Brigade
without whose patience, persistence and courage the
Falklands Campaign would not have been successful.

First published in Great Britain in 2003 by Leo Cooper
Republished in this format in 2014 by
PEN & SWORD MILITARY
An imprint of
Pen & Sword Books Ltd
47 Church Street
Barnsley, South Yorkshire
S70 2AS

Copyright © Nick van der Bijl, 2003, 2014

ISBN 978 1 78346 263 6

The right of Nick van der Bijl to be identified as Author
of this work has been asserted by him in accordance with the
Copyright, Designs and Patents Act 1988.

Printed and bound in England
By CPI Group (UK) Ltd, Croydon, CR0 4YY

Pen & Sword Books Ltd incorporates the Imprints of Aviation, Atlas,
Family History, Fiction, Maritime, Military, Discovery, Politics, History,
Archaeology, Select, Wharncliffe Local History, Wharncliffe True Crime,
Military Classics, Wharncliffe Transport, Leo Cooper, The Praetorian Press,
Remember When, Seaforth Publishing and Frontline Publishing

For a complete list of Pen & Sword titles please contact
PEN & SWORD BOOKS LIMITED
47 Church Street, Barnsley, South Yorkshire, S70 2AS, England
E-mail: enquiries@pen-and-sword.co.uk
Website: www.pen-and-sword.co.uk

Contents

Acknowledgements

Our wide variety of sources includes published books as well as and unpublished sources, interviews and personal experience.

Considerable reference is made to Michael Clapp's *Amphibious Assault Falklands,* Ewen Southby-Tailyour's *Reasons in Writing* and Nick Vaux's *March to the South Atlantic.* It gives us much pleasure to thank the following, in their current ranks and their contribution in 1982.

From the Royal Navy, Commodore Michael Clapp, Commodore Amphibious Warfare, for his honest evaluation of his role in the campaign, and Rear-Admiral Peter Dingemans of HMS *Intrepid.*

From the Army, Brigadier Christopher Dunphie at Northwood; Major-General Jeremy Moore, General John Waters and Major-General David Pennefather, both HQ Land Forces Falkland Islands; Brigadier Brendan Lambe and Lieutenant-Colonel Will Townend of Headquarters 5th Infantry Brigade; Major-General Michael Scott and Danny McDermid of the Scots Guards; Brigadier Johnny Rickett of the Welsh Guards; Brigadier David Chaundler and Lieutenant-Colonel Chris Keeble of 2nd Battalion, The Parachute Regiment; Brigadier David Morgan, Colonel Bill Dawson and Colonel Mike Kefford of 1/7th Gurkhas; Lieutenant-Colonel Chris Davies of 9 Parachute Squadron, Royal Engineers, and Edward Denmark, Tony McNally and Tim Ward of T Air Defence Battery.

From 3rd Commando Brigade, Major-General Julian Thompson, Chris Pretty of 40 Commando; Major-General Nick Vaux of 42 Commando; Captain Steve Nicholls of the Mountain and Arctic Warfare Cadre, Royal Marines; Lieutenant-Colonel Ewen Southby-Tailyour , Royal Marines, and finally Bob Hendicott of 59 Independent Commando Squadron, Royal Engineers.

Others we must thank are those who wish to remain anonymous and those with whom Nick chatted at such functions as the South Atlantic Medal Association (82) Annual General Meeting before the annual Army versus Navy rugby match at Twickenham and the annual San Carlos Dinner nights at Commando Forces Officers Mess in Plymouth, usually over a pint.

So far as our Argentine acknowledgements are concerned, we are grateful for the assistance given by the former Argentine Ambassador in Australia, Enrique Candiotti, and his secretary, Gerardo Buompadre; Colonel Alberto Gonzalez of the Argentine Army Historical Services Branch, who unearthed documents and first-hand accounts; the prominent historian Isidoro Jorge Ruiz-Moreno of the Argentine Army General Staff College, for putting up with endless questions and pestering by telephone and letter, and finally Colonel Felix Roberto Aguiar, the former Chief-of-Staff of the Argentine 10th Mechanized Infantry Brigade in the Falklands, for allowing the authors to quote from his personal account, *La Brigada de Infanteria Mecanizada 10 'Teniente General Nicolas Levalle' en accion en Malvinas*. Their contribution in balancing this history has been invaluable.

The one notable absence is Brigadier Tony Wilson, who commanded 5th Infantry Brigade. For reasons which we respect, he declined to contribute. However, we both hope that there will be a time when, in Far East terms, he will daub the dragon's eyes and tell his contribution to the defeat of the Argentines.

Our thanks to Neil Hyslop, who produced the maps, to Chris Davies, Steve Dock of *Soldier* magazine, Will Fowler, Barrie Lovell, who served with 81 Intelligence Section, Alex Manning, who served with Commander Amphibious Warfare, Steve Nicolls and Will Townend for supplying photos. Finally and most important, two more people, my editor Tom Hartman and the managing editor at Pen & Sword, Brigadier Henry Wilson. We must also thank whoever invented E-mail!

Not to be forgotten are Nick's wife Penny and their daughter Imogen van der Bijl for their patience and understanding.

I Will Go

A song by the Scottish folk band *'The Corries'* and adopted by
Lieutenant Robert Lawrence's Scots Guards platoon as
the platoon song.

I will go, I will go
When the fighting is over
To the land of the MacLeod
That I left to be a soldier.

When we landed on the shore
And saw the foreign heather,
We knew that some would fall
And some stay for ever.

When we came back to the glen
Winter was turning,
Our goods lay in the snow
And our houses were burning
I will go, I will go.

The Malvinas March

A song sung by Argentina referring to its claim of
the Falkland Islands.

Behind a fog mantle, we must never forget them!
The Malvinas!
Argentina! Cries out the wind, roars out the sea.
Nor of those horizons, shall they rip our Standard, for its
White is on its mountains and its blue the sea is dyed.
By absent, by defeated they are under a strange covering;
There is no land more loved, of the Fatherland in the growth.
Who speaks here of forgetting, of giving up or forgiving?
There is no land more loved, of the Fatherland in the growth.
Break the fog like the sun, our symbol! The Malvinas, Argentina,
In already immortal dominion! And before the Sun, of our Banner, pure,
Clear and triumphant; Shine oh Fatherland,
In your jewelled headdress - the lost Austral pearl.

(Chorus)
For the honour of our Emblem, for National Pride, shine,
Oh! Fatherland in your jewelled headdress - the lost Austral pearl.

Author's Preface

It is often the case in military history that the activities of one unit overshadows another, the 8th Army and 1st Army in North Africa being a fine example. So it was during the Falklands War. The story of 3rd Commando Brigade has been well told by Major-General Julian Thompson in his excellent *No Picnic*, but no one has yet picked up the mantle for 5th Infantry Brigade. This book is designed to go some way to breaching that gap.

Stripped of two battalions and left with its Gurkha battalion, when the Ministry of Defence warned 5th Infantry Brigade for deployment 8,000 miles from the United Kingdom, the Brigade, which had no amphibious capability, was hurriedly cobbled together with several units with whom the Headquarters had never worked. It is, therefore, not surprising that after a shakedown exercise in Wales there was doubt that the Brigade should be sent south. When it was, it did so in the golden carriage of the *Queen Elizabeth 2*. Denied a stopover at Ascension Island to sort out its landing plan, the Brigade landed at San Carlos, which had recently been vacated by most of 3rd Commando Brigade. Some of its officers felt that the arrival was not wanted. How often is the latecomer ignored, particularly if not known and from another culture, in this instance an Army brigade in an amphibious environment in an operation commanded by Royal Navy officers determined to show that the defence cuts of the previous year were ill-judged. Vigorously encouraged to join the party at the gates of Stanley, the Brigade leapt forward to Fitzroy and Bluff Cove in a brave move but lost a shoe at Fitzroy, not Bluff Cove, where the Welsh Guards suffered a high casualty list before it had fired a shot, as a consequence of a combination of events, the most influential being the Argentine Air Force. However, the Brigade picked itself up and the Scots Guards, without the benefit of the days of preparation afforded to the Commando Brigade, carried out a difficult night attack against the toughest of the Argentines, a marine infantry battalion, and drove them from Mount Tumbledown in a battle far more strategically important than Goose Green. When the campaign was over, while the Royal Navy and Commando Brigade returned to a heroes' welcome, 5th Infantry Brigade returned with barely a fanfare. Those opinionated journalists, authors and military men who have argued that the Brigade was not combat ready have undermined the resolution and courage of the soldiers involved.

Recrimination is not the substance of this book although we have allowed ourselves the privilege of brief examination, admittedly in hindsight. Apportioning responsibility and culpability is left for future historians to pick over and draw their own conclusions but with one flaw, they were not there - tired, hungry, cold, wet and having to make rapid decisions in the heat of the moment, not in the comfort of some desk in a warm office.

Nick van der Bijl   David Aldea
Somerset   Sydney
United Kingdom   Australia

Maps

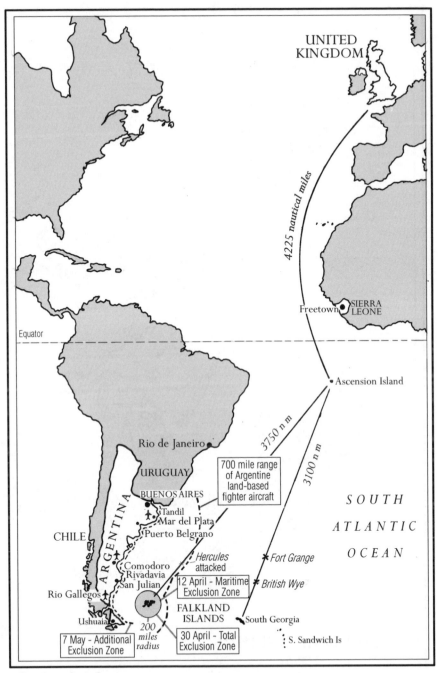

The South Atlantic

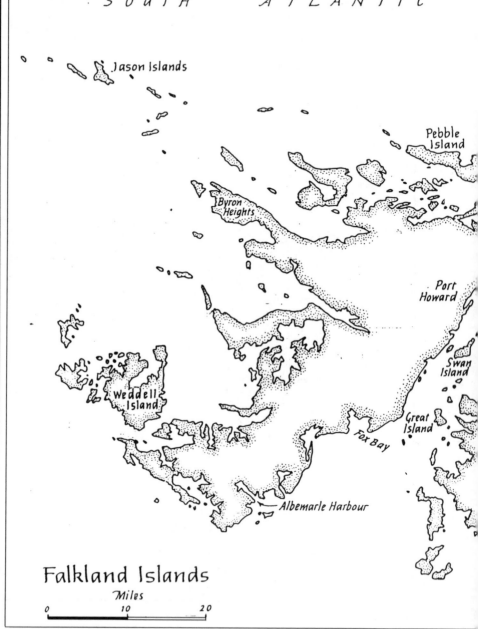

SOUTH ATLANTIC

Jason Islands

Pebble Island

Byron Heights

Port Howard

Swan Island

Weddell Island

Great Island

Fox Bay

Albemarle Harbour

Falkland Islands

Miles

0   10   20

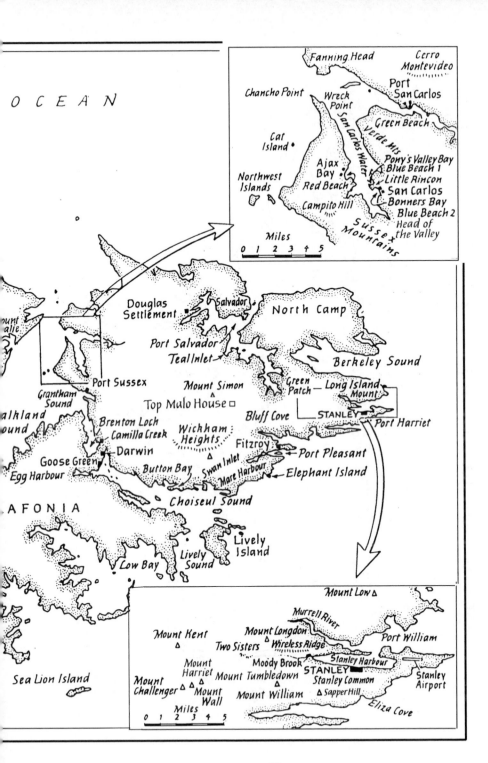

OCEAN

Inset (top right):

Fanning Head
Cerro Montevideo
Chancho Point
Wreck Point
Port San Carlos
Green Beach
Verde Mts
San Carlos Water
Cat Island
Pony's Valley Bay
Blue Beach 1
Ajax Bay
Little Rincon
Northwest Islands
Red Beach
San Carlos
Bonners Bay
Campito Hill
Blue Beach 2
Head of the Valley
Sussex Mountains

Miles
0 1 2 3 4 5

Main map:

Douglas Settlement
Salvador
North Camp
Port Salvador
Teal Inlet
Berkeley Sound
Port Sussex
Mount Simon
Green Patch
Long Island Mount
Grantham Sound
Top Malo House □
Falkland Sound
Bluff Cove
STANLEY
Port Harriet
Brenton Loch
Wickham Heights
Camilla Creek
Fitzroy
Darwin
Swan Inlet
Port Pleasant
Goose Green
Button Bay
Mare Harbour
Elephant Island
Egg Harbour

LAFONIA
Choiseul Sound
Lively Island
Low Bay
Lively Sound

Inset (bottom):

Mount Low △
Murrell River
Mount Kent △
Mount Longdon △
Wireless Ridge
Two Sisters
Port William
Mount Harriet
Moody Brook
Stanley Harbour
Mount Tumbledown
STANLEY
Stanley Common
Stanley Airport
Mount Challenger △ △ △ Mount Wall
Mount William △ Sapper Hill
Eliza Cove
Sea Lion Island

Miles
0 1 2 3 4 5

xv

ESTIMATED ENEMY LOCATIONS ON 3 JUNE 82

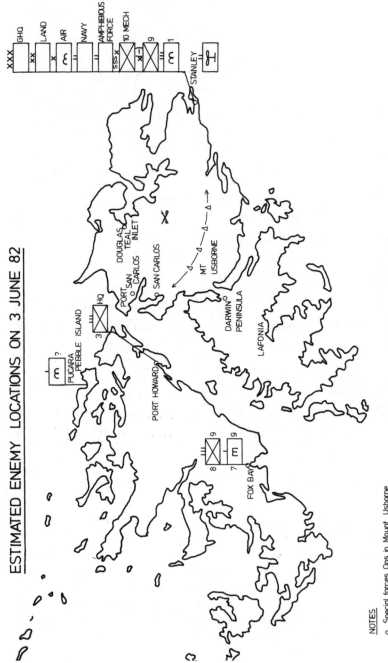

NOTES

a. Special forces Ops in Mount Usborne

b. 601 Commando company group neutralised by Mountain and Artic Warfare Cadre at Top Malo House thus ✕

Remnants of Argentinians from Goose Green loose in Lafonia

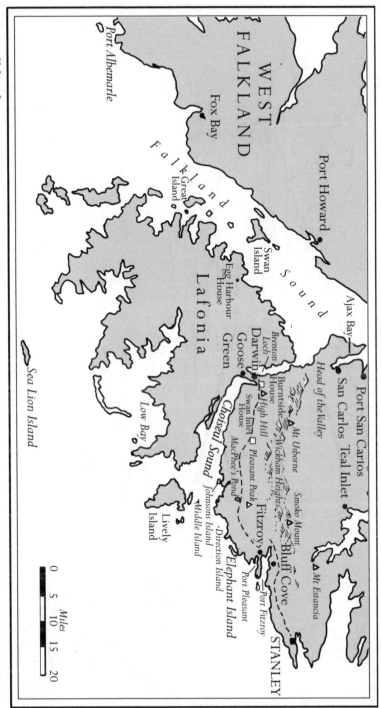

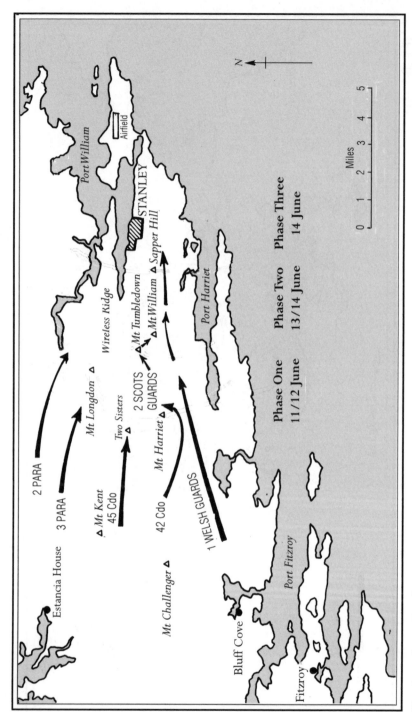

The Assault on Stanley

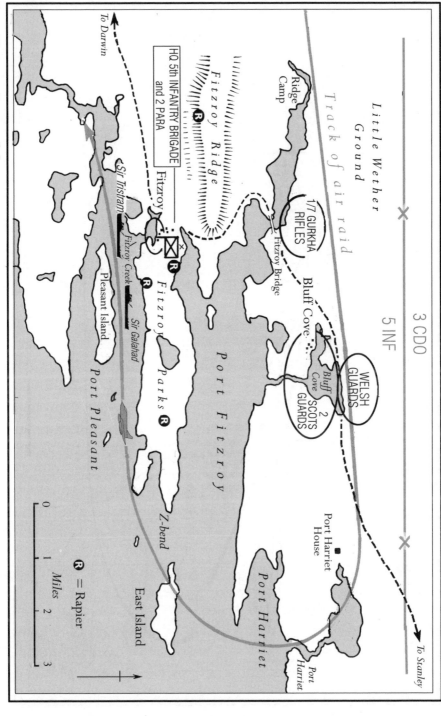

Port Pleasant Sector, 8 June

To Darwin

HQ 5th INFANTRY BRIGADE
and 2 PARA

Little Wether
Ground

Track of air raid

3 CDO

5 INF

Ridge
Camp

Fitzroy Ridge

1/7 GURKHA
RIFLES

Fitzroy Bridge

Bluff Cove

Sir Tristram

Fitzroy

Fitzroy Creek

Sir Galahad

Fitzroy Parks

Bluff
Cove

WELSH
GUARDS

Pleasant Island

Z-bend

Port Fitzroy

2
Cove
SCOTS
GUARDS

Port Harriet
House

Port Pleasant

East Island

Port Harriet

To Stanley

Port
Harriet

0   1   2   3
Miles

Ⓡ = Rapier

xix

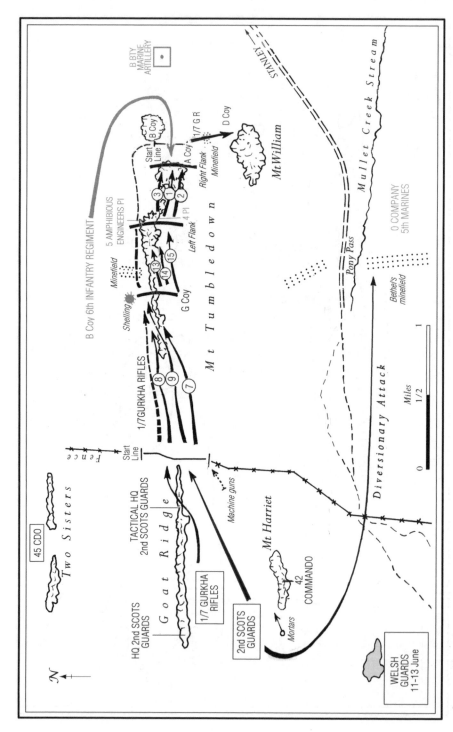

The Battle of Mount Tumbledown

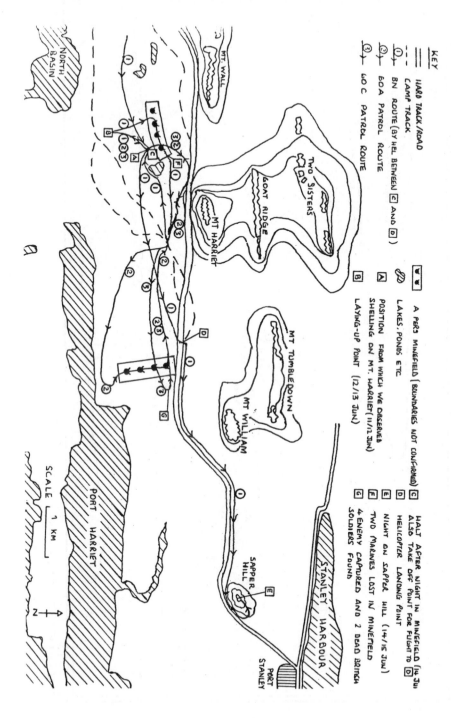

ADVANCE ROUTE OF ONE TROOP UNDER COMMAND OF 1st BATTALION WELSH GUARDS

xxi

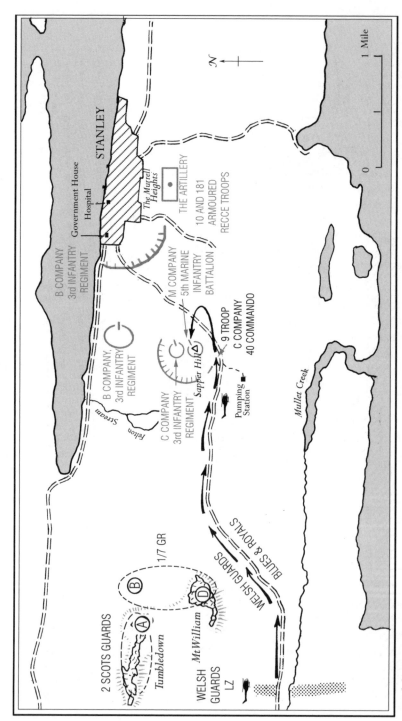

Welsh Guards and 40 Commando Attack on Sapper Hill

5th Infantry Brigade

Politically embarrassed and militarily humiliated at being caught out by a country that, apparently, posed no major threat to its national sovereignty or reputation and was a friend in the South Atlantic region, Great Britain was quick to react to the audacity of the Argentinian invasion.

In a tense Cabinet meeting on Friday 2 April Prime Minister Margaret Thatcher, her ministers and civil servants considered the pros and cons of recovering the Falklands Islands and its Dependencies. National morale was low and virtually everything weighed against recovery – the distance, no British bases in the region and the immediate unavailability of forces.

An airborne operation was out of the question, not only because of the great distance, lack of bases and uncertainty of the weather but also because during the late 1970s Great Britain had effectively dismantled its parachute capability. In spite of the heavy casualties suffered by German airborne forces in Crete in 1941, the British had developed a credible airborne capability through 1st and 6th Airborne Divisions. Post-war, these were whittled down to 16th Parachute Brigade and the Territorial Army 44th Parachute Brigade, both with combat and service support. Apart from a drop during the Suez crisis in 1956, the British had not jumped into combat since 1945. By 1977, the Labour Government decided that Great Britain had no further need of airborne forces and 16th Parachute Brigade, in Aldershot, was converted to a conventional role as 6th Field Force. During the early 1980s the Services underwent yet more reorganization, usually in pursuit of severe cost-cutting. Much of the focus centralized British strategy on Priority One, the North Atlantic Treaty Organization (NATO) and home defence, while main-taining a presence in overseas garrisons such as Hong Kong, Cyprus and Belize. A consequence of the defence reorganizations was that some brigades were renamed 'field forces', a term reminiscent of Queen Victoria's armies. Retained in 6th Field Force as a small airborne capability was the Leading Parachute Battalion Group, which consisted of one of the three parachute battalions as the Leading Parachute Battalion, the conventional 29 (Corunna) Field Battery from 4th Field Regiment, Royal Artillery, 9 Parachute Squadron, Royal Engineers and a Field Surgical Team from 23rd Field Ambulance, Royal Army Medical Corps.

The First Sea Lord, Admiral Sir Henry Leach, then joined the meeting and, when asked by Thatcher what could be done, he replied that a naval Task Force could be ready to leave within forty-eight hours and would include 3rd Commando Brigade. Next day the Prime Minister announced to the House of Commons, in a tense Saturday morning debate, that 'A large task force will sail as soon as preparations are complete'. So was born Operation *Corporate*, the name given to the naval and military operation to recapture the Falkland Islands and its Dependencies. It was hoped that a positive show of naval and military strength by the British, as the aggrieved nation, would persuade Argentina to abandon the territories she had occupied. The previous year the Royal Navy had taken the brunt of the defence cuts and senior naval commanders were determined to show that the nation could not do without a strong maritime capability. By 9 April the Task Force order of battle was as follows

❐ *Commander Task Force 317 (CTF 317) for the South Atlantic operation was Admiral Sir John Fieldhouse, who was Commander-in-Chief Fleet, with his headquarters at Northwood.*

❐ *Appointed as Deputy Land Forces Commander was Major-General Jeremy Moore MC*, who was then Major-General Commando Forces at Mount Wise in Plymouth. Great Britain's response to the crisis was principally naval, and since Moore was virtually the only Royal Marine of sufficient rank available, the Commandant-General Royal Marines, Lieutenant-General Steuart Pringle, had extended his service. Moore, who was nearing the end of an illustrious career, was initially based at Northwood.*

❐ *Combined Task Unit (CTU 317.0) was commanded by Commodore Michael Clapp ADC, the in-post Commander Amphibious Warfare at Plymouth, as Commander Amphibious Task Force. An experienced officer with sea-going command and a navy pilot, he had seen active service in Korea, Aden and Borneo. His responsibility was the transportation of the troops and implementation of the landing plan. Initially he had a staff of seven but during the next weeks this grew to twenty. He had no Intelligence Officer and was therefore reliant upon Headquarters 3rd Commando Brigade for assessments.*

❐ *Combined Task Unit 317.1 was the Landing Group, which was commanded by Brigadier Julian Thompson OBE and consisted of his 3rd Commando Brigade reinforced by several units including the Spearpoint Battalion, which was 3rd Parachute Battalion, from 5th Infantry Brigade, and T (Shah Sujah's Troop) Air Defence Battery from 12th Air Defence Regiment. The British Army always had a United Kingdom-based 'fire brigade' battalion on immediate notice to move to a crisis involving Great Britain; this is known as the*

2

Spearhead Battalion. Along with 40, 42 and 45 Commandos, the brigade now had four major manoeuvre battalions.

❏ Combined Task Group (CTG 317.8), the Carrier Battle Group, was commanded by Rear-Admiral John 'Sandy' Woodward. He commanded 1st Flotilla and had just finished exercising in the Mediterranean. The Carrier Battle Group centred on the aircraft-carriers HMS Hermes and Invincible, each with Sea Harrier and anti-submarine warfare Sea King helicopter squadrons. They were joined by a formidable array of destroyers and frigates; all supported by fleet tankers and replenishment ships. Woodward was entrusted to dominate the South Atlantic to ensure that Thompson's brigade arrived at their destination in one piece and then keep the sea lines of communication open to the United Kingdom.

A Task Force organization issued on 2 April had Woodward in command of South Atlantic operations until superseded on 9 April. However, it has rather perpetuated the myth that Woodward was in overall command of operations in the South Atlantic, when, in fact, he commanded only the Carrier Battle Group. It does seem that, on occasion, Northwood was one of a number of organizations that ignored, or forgot, this.

The organization did cause some confusion. Under normal amphibious warfare principles Clapp would have been Commander Amphibious Task Force with 3rd Commando Brigade under his command, the latter until it landed. Technically, although both had their headquarters on the same ship, HMS *Fearless*, on the voyage south Thompson and Clapp should not have conferred without referring to Moore's headquarters. But this was an impractical arrangement and, both men being of equivalent rank, they and their staffs disregarded the philosophy but were never really certain what was expected of them. Their fruitful relationship ensured that problems and difficulties were resolved amicably.

Immediately available to Commodore Clapp were the only amphibious warfare ships the Royal Navy had – the Landing Platform Dock (LPD) ships HMS *Fearless* and *Intrepid*. Also in support were six Royal Fleet Auxiliary Landing Ship Logistics (LSL). HMS *Fearless* became the headquarters for amphibious operations.

HMS *Fearless* and *Intrepid* were also often known as assault or command ships. Designed in the 1950s to accommodate an armoured regiment, they had a displacement of 12,000 tons and could comfortably accommodate a battalion of 400 troops, plus twelve tanks and about twenty-five light vehicles. Amphibious operations were directed from the

Amphibious Operations Room, which was capable of handling a battalion command post, not a brigade headquarters, as was now anticipated for HMS *Fearless*. The flight deck could comfortably handle two support helicopters simultaneously. A Royal Marines Assault Squadron provided coxswains to handle the four LCUs and four LCVPs and man a beach assault group. Both ships were armed with two 40mm Bofors anti-aircaft guns, four Seacat surface-to-air missiles and whatever small arms could be assembled from the Embarked Force.

LCUs are Landing Craft Utility, also known as Landing Craft Marine. Weighing 100 tons, they are designed to carry two main battle tanks or about 150 fully equipped troops in short fair-weather voyages. Carried in the dry tank deck of their parent assault ship, they were skippered by a Royal Marine colour-sergeant or sergeant and a crew of seven, with the Royal Navy usually providing two engineers. The navigation fit is rudimentary and in 1982, there was no shelter for passengers. LCVP are 10-ton plywood Landing Craft Vehicle and Personnel, which can carry either two Land Rovers or four tons of stores or thirty fully equipped troops. A Royal Marine corporal is usually the coxswain, supported by two marines. The assault ships each have four hoisted on davits. The landing craft on HMS *Fearless* were painted in grey and black camouflage and their radio callsigns were prefixed by *Foxtrot*, while those on HMS *Intrepid* were painted green and black and prefixed by *Tango*.

LSL is Landing Ship Logistic of the *Sir Lancelot* class. In 1982 there were six in service, all named after Knights of the Round Table and crewed by the Royal Fleet Auxiliary. With a full displacement of 5,500 tons, these ships could carry sixteen tanks and over 500 troops, admittedly in Spartan conditions, and were designed to land vehicles and equipment straight on to beaches through a bow door. At the rear was a ramp for unloading on to jetties and other vessels. Landing ships could also carry two Army Mexeflote ferries flat against the sides of the ship. Two flight decks were available for support helicopters. All were lightly armed, most with two 40mm Bofors anti-aircraft guns. *Sir Percivale* and *Sir Galahad* both had one Bofors. The landing ships each had a Port Operating Detachment from 17 Port Regiment, Royal Corps of Transport, to man the Mexeflotes and associated handling equipment such as cranes. The Roll On/Roll Off ferries also each had a Port Operating Detachment to assist with loading and unloading of men and material.

A Mexeflote is a versatile three-part (bow, centre and stern) multi-purpose pontoon specifically designed for salt-water port operations. They can be converted into rafts, as was done during the Falklands campaign, or joined together to form jetties, causeways and breakwaters and were transported by being fitted to the side of a logistic ship. Each Mexeflote has its own specialized diesel engine. During the campaign, men of 17 Port Regiment, Royal Corps of Transport, operated them.

This was the sum total of Great Britain's amphibious capability – two assault ships, six landing ships and sixteen landing craft supported by helicopters but no amphibious tracked vehicles. The Royal Corps of Transport also had several landing craft of various sizes, but these were designed for port work. Argentina's capability mirrored the US Marine Corps in organization, equipment and tactics, but was stronger than that of Great Britain.

The Task Force quickly converted from its Priority One NATO role to preparing to fight a conventional war 8,000 miles from British shores. No other country, in recent years, had undertaken such an expedition and many in the Task Force, and indeed in the country, had no idea where the Falklands Islands were. For some units conversion was a relatively simple matter, but the issue for smaller ones was finding men. The preparations reported in the media reinforced Britain's military intent.

Critical to the venture was Intelligence, but, considering the threat that Argentina had posed to the Falklands for over a century, there was remarkably little information available. Earlier in the year Captain Will Townsend, an Operations planning officer in Headquarters 5th Infantry Brigade, had attended a high-level Intelligence briefing in which every threat was evaluated – from republican movements in Northern Ireland to Guatemala's claim to Belize, to the Warsaw Pact threat to West Germany and so on. The only one missing was Argentina's long claim to the Falkland Islands Dependencies, in spite of the fact that, only five years before, Argentina had sabre-rattled Prime Minister Callaghan's Labour Government and was now occupying South Thule. One wonders if this omission was because the Falkland Islands was a Royal Marine responsibility and not an Army remit. In any event, Royal Marine interest in Intelligence was well down the priority list and it was not a specialist qualification.

In an early operational assessment of the crisis, Northwood calculated that another brigade would be needed to tackle the Argentinian forces. This would bring the ground forces up to weak divisional strength. If the Argentinians were ejected, then a force of brigade size would be needed to provide a strong garrison. But the Army was fully committed to NATO, had nearly 20,000 men in Northern Ireland and had several over-seas garrisons. In the event of hostilities in Europe, Great Britain was a critical staging post and rear base for American and Canadian forces and consequently thirty per cent of the Army's strength, including Reserve Forces and training establishments, was devoted to the home defence against the threat of Warsaw Pact Special Forces prior to and during hostilities. But two formations were available, both of which had just been reroled, 1st Infantry Brigade at Tidworth and 5th Infantry Brigade at Aldershot.

5th Infantry Brigade was commanded by Brigadier Matthew Wilson OBE MC and had its headquarters at Aldershot. When Wilson had arrived in mid-1980, it was known as 8th Field Force and was a mixed Regular/Territorial Army home defence formation with its headquarters at Tidworth. Its Regular Army elements included 1st Cheshires, 2nd Royal Irish Rangers, 2nd Parachute Battalion and 205 Signals Troop. It had the Leading Parachute Battalion Group role. Its Territorial Army complement included 2nd Wessex (V), 6th Light Infantry (V), 55th Signal Squadron (V), and an Ordnance Company. In January 1982 8th Field Force was renamed 5th Infantry Brigade but still with a home defence role. It became an all Regular formation and took over several 6th Field Force units including 3rd Parachute Battalion and 1st Battalion, 7th (Duke of Edinburgh's Own) Gurkha Rifles (1/7th Gurkha Rifles), which was based at Church Crookham. After India won independence in 1947 four Gurkha regiments (2nd, 6th, 7th and 10th Gurkha Rifles) joined the British Army and, although serving mostly in the Far East, for several years one battalion was based in this small Hampshire town. Except for 29 (Corunna) Battery, the Brigade lacked artillery. The Reserve Forces units joined their regional District Headquarters, 2nd Wessex (V) and 6th Light Infantry (V) going to South-East District and South-West District respectively on home defence.

6th Field Force had been renamed 1st Infantry Brigade and was assigned as the United Kingdom Mobile Force with its own logistic support group. Brigade Headquarters moved from Aldershot to Tidworth. 1st Cheshires and 2nd Royal Irish Rangers were transferred from 8th Field Force and joined 1st Queen's Own Highlanders, which was equipped and trained in winter warfare. Well-suited to contributing to the defence of NATO's Northern and Southern Flanks, the Brigade had a secondary role reacting to 'out-of-area' contingencies, such as the crisis in the South Atlantic, but the Ministry of Defence felt it would be politically and militarily unwise if it was so deployed.

Born in October 1935 into a titled family and preferring to be known as Tony, Brigadier Wilson was commissioned into the King's Own Yorkshire Light Infantry (KOYLI) in October 1956, the fourth generation of the family to serve in the Regiment. He had seen active service in some capacity in every rank he had held – Aden, Borneo, Cyprus and Northern Ireland. In 1968 the KOYLI was amalgamated into the Light Infantry. Promoted to major in 1970, in 1973 Wilson held a two-year

Operations staff appointment in Headquarters Northern Ireland during a difficult time for the Army and was awarded the MBE. Returning to his Battalion, he was awarded the Military Cross as a company commander in Northern Ireland. Promoted to lieutenant-colonel in 1975, he commanded 1st Light Infantry in Northern Ireland and Hong Kong. His MBE was later upgraded to OBE. Promoted to full Colonel, Wilson was appointed Colonel General Staff (Military Operations) at the Ministry of Defence. A colleague was Lieutenant-Colonel David Chaundler of the Parachute Regiment. On 30 June 1980, Wilson was promoted to Brigadier and appointed Commander 5th Infantry Brigade. He had imagination and soon gained a reputation for doing the un-expected, which certainly kept his staff on their toes.

According to one of his staff officers, Brigadier Wilson was perceptive and, realizing that Great Britain would, one day, be expected to provide troops in periods of international tension, he identified an out-of-area role for 8th Field Force, that of hostage rescue and disarming indigenous forces. In 1978 the United Kingdom had been unable to contribute para-chute forces to the rescue of civilians held hostage in Kolwezi in Zaire; it was left up to the French Foreign Legion and Belgian para-commandos. Apart from the Special Air Service action at the Iranian Embassy, the last time that British Forces had rescued hostages was during the December 1962 Brunei Revolt when Captain Jeremy Moore MC led L Company, 42 Commando to rescue several at Limbang at the cost of five Royal Marines killed and several wounded. Moore was awarded a bar to his Military Cross. The naval officer who provided naval crews for the Limbang operation was Lieutenant-Commander Jeremy Black, who was now commanding HMS *Invincible*. During Operation *Aghuila* in 1980 1,100 British troops joined the Common-wealth Monitoring Force to supervise disarming indigenous forces during the ceasefire in Rhodesia.

In January Major Brendan Lambe, a Royal Artillery officer, arrived at Headquarters 5th Infantry Brigade as the Brigade Major, fresh from a two-year course at the Staff College at Camberley. A firebrand who had served with the Airborne and Commando Forces, he knew many Royal Marine officers, including Major-General Moore and Brigadier Thompson. Lambe was not best pleased with what he found. During a short command post exercise at RAF Abingdon, he found Brigade Headquarters operating from Land Rovers reversed into small 9-foot by 9-foot frame tents and two senior offices running a battle from the front of a Land Rover. When he asked why red lights were being used in preference to white lights, he was told this had been on the instructions of the 55th Signal Squadron (V) Regimental Sergeant Major. As far as

Lambe was concerned, what happened in the Command Post was none of any Regimental Sergeant Major's business and white light was used thereafter. On his return to Aldershot, Lambe ordered a large purpose-made frame tent for Brigade Headquarters

His first brigade exercise with troops, Exercise *Green Lanyard*, was in February at Thetford and was designed to practice the two parachute battalions and one Gurkha battalion in hostage rescue in a Middle Eastern setting, except that it rained almost the entire fortnight. It does seem that the first seeds of the distrust between Brigade Headquarters and some Parachute Regiment officers emerged when a debate developed on how parachute battalions should be used. There was also a lively discussion as to whether 2nd Parachute Battalion should carry out a drop. It did and without undue difficulty.

On the morning of 2 April, the day that Argentina invaded, after the redesignation parade at Borden for the transfer of 10 Field Workshops to 5th Infantry Brigade, Major Lambe heard from a colleague in the Special Air Service asking if it was likely that the brigade would be mobilized for deployment to the South Atlantic. So far the official response by 5th Infantry Brigade to the crisis was that, since 3rd Commando Brigade had joined the Task Force, there was no need to raise the 'ready to move' stakes. But Lambe wisely insisted that contingency plans should be dusted, just in case. The same day 3rd Parachute Battalion was warned for deployment with 3rd Commando Brigade. Brigadier Wilson despatched Captain Townsend to attend Commanding Officer's Orders. He returned to Brigade Headquarters with the assessment that the battalion not only lacked sufficient machine guns and cameras but its *Larkspur* fit of tactical radios was not compatible with the *Clansman* range used by the Royal Marines. Arrangements were hurriedly made to equip the paras with *Clansman*.

Over the next weeks 5th Infantry Brigade carried on as normal until Major Lambe took a telephone call from the Ministry of Defence wanting to know what the square footage of the brigade was. No one had any idea, but Lambe, suspecting the rationale behind the question, told the caller, 'Give us the ships and we'll get on'. Captain Townsend was then asked by Lambe to calculate the staff tables for the Brigade in heavy, light, manpack and come-as-you-are roles. He estimates that from 2 April until 12 May, when he embarked on the *Queen Elizabeth II*, he drew up a dozen different staff tables while Lambe believes that he signed off at least thirty contingency staff requirements.

Shortly after the crisis broke out a high-level conference was held at Headquarters United Kingdom Land Forces at Wilton to identify additional forces for the war. Among the delegates was Major-General

Sir Desmond Langley KCVO, MBE, General Officer Commanding, London District. Even with the opportunity of a real war, there were very few offers, so stretched was the Army. Nothing changes. The only spare troops were in London District and so Langley volunteered two of his three available battalions, which were the 1st Welsh Guards at Pirbright and the 2nd Scots Guards and 2nd Grenadier Guards in London. Very few members of the Welsh and Scots battalions, their families or the public imagined that within ten weeks they would travel south in a luxury liner and land on windy rainswept beaches at San Carlos, still bearing the scars of battle, for instance the buoy marking the spot where HMS *Antelope* lay beneath the waves. One battalion would suffer a long casualty list without firing a shot and the other would storm, at night, a well-defended hill held by one of Argentina's toughest units.

The unreasonable and unjustified controversy that emerged over the deployment of the Guards battalions was largely inspired by the media and others, who felt that it would be a more sensible option for a 1st Infantry Brigade battalion, in particular the Queens Own Highlanders, to join the Task Force and for the Guards to be attached to 1st Infantry Brigade in the unlikely event of hostilities against the Soviet Union. The problem was that since the Guards were usually seen on ceremonial parades and guarding Royal palaces, they somehow seemed less efficient and fit than county battalions and Light Infantry. The fact is that the Household Brigade is expected to be at the same level of fitness and training as any other military unit. The Guards have a long history stretching back to the formation of the Regular Army and wear the bearskin and red tunic with the same *esprit de corps* as the Parachute Regiment wear their red beret and the Royal Marines their green beret, both of which emerged during the Second World War. Guards' military culture may be different but that is not a benchmark for combat effectiveness. If there is an insistence to judge a unit by its special duties, the Guards have a long history – the Guards Patrol of the Long Range Desert Group in the Western Desert. G Squadron, 22 Special Air Service, which deployed to the South Atlantic, owes its inheritance to the 1st Guards Independent Parachute Company. Indeed the commanding officer of Special Air Service, Lieutenant-Colonel Michael Rose OBE, was commissioned into the Coldstream Guards. Captain Aldwin Wight of the Welsh Guards led a Special Air Service patrol during the campaign. Three former Welsh Guards serving with the Special Air Service were killed when their Sea King suffered a bird strike on 19 May. Those who painted an inaccurate and unsubstantiated myth about the wisdom of sending the Guards to the Falklands have done the Guardsmen a major disservice.

9

With the departure of 3rd Parachute Battalion, 5th Infantry Brigade was now left with two infantry battalions, 2nd Parachute Battalion and 1/7th Gurkha Rifles.

2nd Parachute Battalion was formed in 1941 and was quickly blooded when C Company, which contained mainly men from Scottish regiments, raided Bruneval to remove a Wurzburg radar. It then served in North Africa, dropped at Sicily and took heavy casualties attacking Nijmegen Bridge at Arnhem in 1944. Post-war, the battalion saw service in Borneo and Northern Ireland. In April 1982 2nd Parachute Battalion was at Bruneval Barracks in Aldershot. One company had recently returned from an exercise in Kenya and another was providing actors for a film about the battalion's first operation, the raid on Bruneval. It had recently completed a two-year tour in Northern Ireland during which it had suffered seven killed when a bomb exploded alongside a column of vehicles at Warrenpoint, an ambush that adversely affected morale. Since Kolwezi, the Battalion had a hostage rescue role. On its return, Lieutenant-Colonel Hubert 'H' Jones took command.

On 4 April Jones was returning from a ski-ing holiday in Meribel, France, when he heard of the crisis in the South Atlantic. Next day he went into barracks and found that the scheduled deployment of 2nd Parachute Battalion to Belize still stood; indeed the advance party had departed. Jones was determined that his battalion should join the Task Force and, using his knowledge of the way the unit tasking system worked from his posting with Headquarters United Kingdom Land Forces between 1979 and 1981, he telephoned and visited key contacts and unscrambled the Belize plot. Jones's principal argument for joining the Task Force was that it made sense for 3rd Commando Brigade to have two identically equipped and organized parachute battalions as reinforcements, as opposed to the airborne-organized 3rd Parachute Battalion and infantry of 1st Queen's Own Highlanders. The argument against such a proposal was that with 1st Parachute Battalion in Northern Ireland, the United Kingdom would have no airborne capability to which Jones countered that, with 2nd Parachute Battalion in Belize, it would not have one anyway. Coincidentally, Headquarters 3rd Commando Brigade, on their way to Ascension Island, had calculated that it would need another battalion and on 15 April 2nd Parachute Battalion was placed on three days' notice to move to join 3rd Commando Brigade and the Royal Anglian Regiment was instructed to send a battalion to Belize. Jones recalled the advance party. Major Tony Rice of 29 (Corunna) Battery and two Forward Observation Officer parties, 2 Troop, 9 Parachute Squadron, Royal Engineers and three Scout helicopters from 656 Squadron, Army Air Corps, joined the battalion.

Jones, who knew Brigadier Thompson from Northern Ireland, and a small headquarters flew to Ascension Island to wait for the Royal Marines. After some frustrating delays, during which the paras each night managed to convince several pub landlords to serve free ale on the pretext that this would be the last night in the United Kingdom, the battalion finally embarked on the P&O North Sea ferry MV *Norland,* which sailed on 26 April, eight days after the 3rd Commando Brigade had arrived at Ascension Island. 2nd Parachute Battalion remained on the ship until it landed at San Carlos on 21 May.

This left 1/7th Gurkha Rifles on its own in 5th Infantry Brigade and for a period it looked as though it would be left behind. However, diplomacy with the King of Nepal through the Defence Attaché in Kathmandu ensured that permission was given for the battalion to join the Task Force. When told about this, Prime Minister Thatcher is said to have commented 'Only one *(Gurkha)* battalion?' As soon as the media cottoned on to the Gurkhas going south, there was the inevitable rush to photograph them charging across green fields waving their famed kukris.

Lieutenant-Colonel David Morgan MBE, a career Gurkha officer, had taken command of 1/7th Gurkha Rifles in October 1981. Like many of his senior officers and other ranks, he had seen active service in the Confrontation with Indonesia in the mid-1960s and had been Brigade Major of 48 Gurkha Infantry Brigade/Gurkha Field Force when thousands of Chinese illegal immigrants flooded into Hong Kong in the late 1970s. Throughout the Falklands campaign Morgan carried a thick stick hacked from a King Bamboo shoot and topped by a silver knob, which had been given to him by his grandfather when he was a missionary doctor in China and had been carried by him during the Boxer Rebellion. Morgan described the stick as 'a monstrous ferrel weighing a ton which could still do a lot of damage to anyone stupid enough to get too close!' By the end of the war the silver top was dented in several places when Morgan was thrown or fell down, particularly during the shelling of Tumbledown. On his return to the United Kingdom, Morgan had two silver bands made for the top; one inscribed 'Boxer Rebellion 1900' and the other 'Falkland Islands 1982'. The stick actually achieved a legendary status. When asked by helicopter pilots how they could find his headquarters, Morgan replied, 'Look for the prick with the stick!' On an occasion when Morgan was putting on his boots, he fell over and dislocated his shoulder and asked his orderly, Lance-Corporal Dilbahadur Rai, to fetch the medical officer. Dilbahadur, schooled in the jungle warfare, rushed to the Battalion Command Post asking for the doctor because the 'the commanding Sahib had been bitten by a snake'!

7th Gurkha Rifles was raised in 1902 and recruited from the Rai and Limbu clans in the foothills of East Nepal. Gurkha literally means 'defender of cows'. Its soldiers had first been absorbed into the British Army in 1816 after the East India Company, in a particularly difficult war against the Nepalese hill men, were impressed by their military qualities. 1/7th Gurkha Rifles fought in Mesopotamia (modern Iraq) and Palestine throughout the First World War. During the Second World War it served with distinction in Burma Corps when it took part in the longest retreat the British Army has ever undertaken through the jungle from Rangoon to India. It then returned to Burma as part of 14th Army and contributed to the defeat of the Japanese. Its sister battalion, 2/7th Gurkha Rifles, had the unusual distinction of being captured twice, first by the Turks at Kut-al-Amara in 1916 and then by the Germans at Tobruk in early 1942, and each time raising a new battalion to fight in Palestine and Italy respectively. Among other battalions raised during the war was the parachute 3/7th Gurkha Rifles, which, as 154th Gurkha Parachute Battalion, carried out an operational jump during the advance to Rangoon in May 1946. When the Regiment was absorbed into the British Army, it did so as part of the Royal Artillery until the outbreak of the Malayan Emergency in 1948 when it reverted to infantry. In 1963 1/7th Gurkha Rifles deployed to Sarawak during Confrontation. By 1967 it was in Hong Kong and involved in the troubles on the border with China. When the battalion arrived in the United Kingdom, it was part of Aldershot Garrison and regularly had a company in Cyprus and another in a jungle camp in the southern district of Toledo in Belize. On the formation of 5th Infantry Brigade, the Gurkhas were allocated an airlanding role, but, since this was relatively new to the Army, it largely organized its own training programme. Like other Gurkha battalions, 1/7th Gurkha Rifles had nearly 1,300 British officers, Queen's Gurkha Officers (QGOs) and soldiers on its books, but with men on leave in Nepal, on extra regimental duties and courses, it usually had a combat effective strength of about 750 all ranks. Stronger than the average British infantry unit by about 100 men, the battalion was divided into four rifle companies, each commanded by a British officer. In 1982 Support Company was commanded by Captain (QGO) Khali Rai and consisted of Mortar Platoon, Anti-Tanks, with Milan missiles and Wombat anti-tank guns, Reconnaissance Platoon and the Assault Pioneers.

When Argentina heard that Gurkhas were to be sent south, she lost no opportunity in accusing Nepal of supplying mercenaries to the British Army. It so happened that the United Nations Ad Hoc Committee was considering a draft definition that a mercenary

❐ *Not be a member of the regular armed forces of a country.*

❐ *Be paid more than a member of the regular forces of that country.*

❐ *Are not bound by treaties between two countries.*

Since the Gurkhas are paid members of the British Army, and had been so since 1816, they are no more mercenaries than the Papal Swiss Guard. In Security Council debates, Argentina was instructed to stop accusing the Gurkhas of being mercenaries. Nepal also was quite happy for her soldiers to be deployed to the South Atlantic because she saw the recovery of the Falkland Islands and its Dependencies as a matter of self-determination. Having failed through diplomatic channels, Argentina continued its black propaganda campaign in the international media by accusing Gurkha soldiers of barbaric warfare, of going into battle high on drugs, of eating their prisoners and using their kukri to chop up the enemy. Their efforts were discredited almost from the start because, if there is one British Army organization that is widely respected, it is the Gurkhas. In Argentina, when many conscripts became genuinely frightened at fighting Gurkhas, attempts were made to compare the Argentinian machete favourably with the kukri, but this failed, such was the renown of the Gurkha blade.

Lieutenant-Colonel Johnny Rickett had lobbied Major-General Langley hard that, in the event that troops were required for the South Atlantic, his battalion, 1st Welsh Guards, should be selected. At full strength and, having handed over Spearpoint Battalion duties to 3rd Parachute Battalion on 1 April, it was packed and ready to go. It had not been on Royal Duties since it had exercised in Kenya the previous autumn. When 3rd Parachute Battalion joined 3rd Commando Brigade, Rickett got his way and on 4 April the Battalion joined 5th Infantry Brigade to bring it back up to three battalions. The Prince of Wales later donated a quad-bike, which would prove a valuable vehicle for a despatch rider. 1st Welsh Guards joined 5th Infantry Brigade.

Of the Household regiments the Welsh Guards is the youngest. Formed in 1915, at the express wish of King George V for a Welsh battalion to complete the national line-up in the Guards Division, it was pitched into the muddy fighting on the Western Front and remained in the trenches until Armistice Day. During the Second World War it retreated to Dunkirk in 1940 and then in 1944-45 was heavily involved in North-West Europe. Post-war the Battalion saw service in Aden, with the United Nations in Cyprus and, in between rotating with tours in Northern Ireland, was part of the British Army of the Rhine as mechanized infantry. In 1982 the Welsh Guards were based at Pirbright and had good access to ranges and exercise areas. The late 1970s/mid-1980s was a period when aircraft hijacking by armed quasi-military Palestine organizations was relatively common. In response, the Pirbright battalion were on stand-by to give military counter-terrorist support to Heathrow in Operation *Trustee*. The battalion had a fine tradition in rugby and was one of the few military units to have its own choir.

On 7 April, after a commanders' briefing at Brigade Headquarters, 5th Infantry Brigade went on Easter block leave. With the imminent departure of 3rd Commando Brigade and the probable need for another brigade, the Ministry of Defence reduced the Brigade's ready-to-move status from the standard seven days to three days. Leave recall codewords were despatched to cancel the two-week Easter leave. On 9 April, the same day that SS *Canberra* sailed south to Ascension Island with 40 and 42 Commando and 3rd Parachute Battalion from Southampton, Brigadier Wilson held a planning conference at Brigade Headquarters where he explained that the Brigade had been warned for probable deployment to the South Atlantic either to support 3rd Commando Brigade or provide the garrison for the Falklands Islands and South Georgia for six months. Otherwise information was scarce. Lieutenant-Colonel Rickett wasn't so clear:

5 Infantry Brigade's role was never spelt out. We were just another brigade sent south probably with the intention of using it as a garrison in due course. However, it must have been obvious to anyone from the start that, given the number of Argentinian forces on the islands, one brigade would not have been enough to have won back control on its own. Our understanding was that we were going to fight from the outset and we carried out countless appreciations during the voyage south on what would be our initial tasks. Why spend an awful lot of money and time on exercising the brigade in South Wales prior to actual notice to move unless it wasn't going to be used to fight?

With 5th Infantry Brigade still a battalion short, London District was again instructed to transfer one of the two remaining Guards battalions. The Grenadier Guards had just returned from the British Army of the Rhine and were therefore still in an armoured frame of mind and consequently on 14 April Major-General Langley selected 2nd Scots Guards to join the Task Force.

Commanded in 1982 by Lieutenant-Colonel Michael Scott, the Scots Guards' ninety battle honours reflect the regiment's distinguished history. Tracing its history back to 1642 when King Charles I raised the Argyll Regiment, a year later, on the Restoration of Charles II in 1660, it was renamed The Regiment of Scottish Footguards. As the Scotch

Guard, it took part in the last battle on English soil at Sedgemoor in 1685 on behalf of the Catholic King James II against the Protestant Duke of Monmouth. In 1712 it was renamed the Third Regiment of Foot, the First and Second being the Grenadier and Coldstream Guards. In the wars against France it served in all the major campaigns. During the Crimean War the bearskins of its guardsmen were at Alma and Inkerman. In 1877 Queen Victoria renamed the Third Regiment of Foot the Scots Guards. It then saw service in Egypt with Lord Kitchener, battled with the Boers, endured the misery of the Western Front in the First World War and saw service in Norway, the Middle East, Italy and Europe during the Second World War. Post-1945, its two battalions were engaged in the Malayan Emergency and in Borneo in between Royal Duties and as mechanized infantry in West Germany. Cut to a company as part of Prime Minister Edward Heath's Conservative Government's ill-timed defence cuts in March 1971, when Northern Ireland was becoming difficult, it was reformed as a battalion on 15 June 1971. It had its fair share of Northern Ireland tours and had two young soldiers convicted, many think most unfairly, after a shooting incident at a vehicle check point. In 1982 2nd Scots Guards were providing the Queen's Guard at Buckingham Palace, St James's Palace and the Tower of London, a ceremonial duty but with the operational twist of providing a robust military presence in answer to the threat from Irish Republican terrorists in London. A Blues and Royals troop and a Light Infantry band had already been subjected to Irish Republican Army bomb attacks in Hyde Park.

To convert the battalions into a wartime establishment, Lieutenant-Colonel Scott reorganized his battalion. Major the Hon Richard Bethel MBE, who, after about twelve years with the Special Air Service, was commanding Headquarters Company, was instructed to form Reconnaissance Platoon from the Drums Platoon and volunteers. When asked, eighteen years after the war, what was the role of 5th Infantry Brigade, as he understood it, Scott replied:

Interestingly, our role did, of course, change as the days went on, really up to the very last minute when it was ultimately decided that the Commando Brigade could not do it all entirely by themselves. However, I am convinced that, initially, we were going to be the garrison when the war was won. We would be there for a 4-month tour when everyone else had left for home and glory. But what a perfect role for Foot Guards – guarding things. You can almost see the Staff thinking how clever they had been. So it probably didn't matter that we weren't brilliantly trained, straight off the gravel of the Forecourt of Buckingham Palace. At the last conference down at Aldershot Field Marshal Bramall came to give us words of encouragement and I asked him point-blank whether we were to be the

15

garrison and, of course, wily old bird, he denied it. Naturally, I made absolutely no mention of my concerns to the Battalion. As far as they were concerned, they were going to get stuck in.

Scott's comments are not isolated. There was what appears to have been a perception in 5th Infantry Brigade that the Royal Marines were out to win the war by themselves in order to avenge the largest ever mass surrender of Royal Marine Commandos. This tension sometimes affected the relationship between the two brigades and there is no doubt that 5th Infantry Brigade believed they were second fiddle to 3rd Commando Brigade. There seems to have been a belief at Northwood that the Royal Marines could have defeated a division of Argentinians on their own, but in reality this was nonsense, as was an even more fatuous suggestion by a Special Air Service corporal that its D Squadron could have beaten the Argentinians. There was also a perception among some in senior military, political and official circles that the war was just against a few 'dagos', who would give up at the sight of a gun, an assessment based on the misconception that the South Americans would not fight. As 2nd Parachute Battalion found out at Goose Green, the Argentinians were prepared to fight for the honour of their nation just as some Italian units had done in the Western Desert.

When 5th Infantry Brigade was formed, it absorbed several units. 205 Signal Squadron was renamed 5th Infantry Brigade Headquarters and Signals Squadron. Consisting of two radio and support Troops, it was commanded by Major Mike Forge. He had just completed a two-year tour in Oman and, although on disembarkation leave when the crisis erupted, responded to an appeal from Brigadier Wilson to return to duty. He was also a freefall parachutist. When the ready-to-move status was dropped to three days, Forge issued instructions for radios to be tested, vehicles thoroughly inspected and kit checked. Sergeant Larry Little and his 566 Rear Link Detachment were already at sea with 3rd Parachute Battalion.

A major problem immediately faced by the brigade was to replace its obsolete *Larkspur* radios with *Clansman*. By coincidence, on 30 March, Captain Townsend had submitted a case to the Ministry of Defence that, with its new role, the brigade should be equipped with *Clansman*. When it became clear that 5th Infantry Brigade had a role of some sort in the South Atlantic, Major Lambe demanded the new range and was astonished when some radios arrived from several sources, including Army Cadet Force units. Some for Brigade Headquarters arrived from the Southampton University Officer Training Corps. Captain Colin Meredith, the Squadron Quartermaster, led a team to re-equip the entire brigade with *Clansman*, a quartermaster's worst nightmare!

Designed as a lightweight system, *Clansman* had one Ultra High Frequency, three High Frequency and five Very High Frequency radios. Using the PRC 349 with its throat microphone, an infantry section commander had, for the first time, direct contact with his platoon commander and his fellow section commanders. Previously orders were shouted or, more usually, delivered by runner. The PRC 350 and PRC 351 linked company commanders with their platoon commanders. Battalion Headquarters used the PRC 352 to communicate with its companies. All could be manpacked. Of the High Frequency variants, the PRC 320 was a manpack while the PRC 321 and 322 were vehicle-mounted. Using 'Skywave', its minimum range of 25 miles could be extended, particularly over water. 'Skywave' is essentially a wire aerial strung between two high poles, posts or trees with a coaxial connection to the rear of the set. The High Frequency variants were used as rear link, for instance from battalion to brigade headquarters or brigade headquarters to division. When Lambe asked the Ministry of Defence for vehicles for the Brigade Headquarter radios, he was asked 'What do want them for? There is only a mile of tarmac'. True, but the Brigade needed vehicles to mount its rear link *Clansman*. Later, Brigadier Wilson remembered that he had seen a few obsolescent Snocats during a visit to the Ludgershall vehicle depot and had several assigned to 5th Infantry Brigade. In any event, restrictions on loading meant that 5th Infantry Brigade could only take eleven Land Rovers per battalion, which was insufficient for effective command and control. The Ultra High Frequency PRC 344 manpack radio is used for ground-to-air aircraft and helicopter communications and has a range of up to 100 miles. It allows forward air controllers to direct fighter ground attack and also enables pilots to give 'real time' briefings of the situation to the ground forces, for instance, events on the reverse slope of a hill.

Generally *Clansman* stood up well to the rigours of the campaign although the antenna was prone to snapping in battle as radio operators scuttled from one position to the next. Keeping the batteries charged also presented administrative problems. 2nd Parachute Battalion later reported that without *Clansman* their communications would have failed. Communications developed into an issue for 5th Infantry Brigade, largely because radio operators were not familiar with *Clansman,* which is hardly surprising considering they did not have much opportunity to test its functions until they landed at San Carlos. Some equipment never arrived, in particular drums of cables that enabled users to operate remotely from the radio.

Intelligence support was provided by 81 Intelligence Section, which was commanded by Lieutenant Whipple with the experienced Staff Sergeant Andy Peck as his deputy.

As we have seen, the home defence role of 5th Infantry Brigade meant that there was no requirement for artillery. Stationed in Aldershot was 4th Field Regiment, whose role was Priority One to NATO with 1st Infantry Brigade. Its 29 (Corunna) Battery was attached to the Leading Parachute Battalion Group. Had it not been for the intense lobbying of its highly respected Commanding Officer, Lieutenant-Colonel Tony Holt, 5th Infantry Brigade might well have sailed south without any guns. Indeed one armchair general is said to have commented there was no need to take field artillery because the Royal Navy could provide naval gunfire support. Holt's persistence paid off and when, on 15 April, the Regiment was earmarked to support 5th Infantry Brigade, the decision had to be kept from the Supreme Allied Commander, Western Europe (SACEUR). Historically the Regiment had been consistently refused permission to train with the brigade as a unit. When training was undertaken, it was usually only with 29 Battery because of its role with the Leading Parachute Battalion Group. In terms of successor management, the Gunner commanding officer usually assumed command of formations in the event that the brigade commander went missing or was killed. This arrangement, initially, did not exist in Headquarters 5th Infantry Brigade.

Of its other two batteries, 88 Battery had just returned from six months in Belize and was therefore left behind, leaving 97 Battery available for deployment. To ensure that 5th Infantry Brigade had sufficient direct artillery support, two teams of a battery commander and Forward Observation Officer parties, commanded by Major Roger Gwyn from 49th Field Regiment and Major Fallon of 132 Field Battery, Support Regiment, Royal Artillery at the School of Artillery at Larkhill respectively, joined 4th Field Regiment. Neither had ever worked with 5th Infantry Brigade. 29 Commando Regiment already had Forward Observation Officer teams attached to 40, 42 and 45 Commandos, but could not provide any to support 3rd Parachute Battalion. On 22 April Holt helped out by forming a team of a battery commander and two Forward Observation Officer teams from his Regiment. Unofficially known as 41 Battery but without guns, it was commanded by Major J. Patrick. Air defence was provided by the Blowpipes of 43 Air Defence Battery from 32nd Guided Weapon Regiment. That 4th Field Regiment went to war with such a hotchpotch of organizations must be unusual for such an important asset. Its post-combat report briefly mentions the inability of the Regiment to train with 5th Infantry Brigade, but thereafter nothing further is said except to comment, pointedly, that the

Brigade was not 'only unfamiliar with 4th Field Regiment but with regimental gunnery as a whole, having no precedent for a gunner tactical headquarters and its services within the headquarters'. The report also says that the failure 'to train (with the infantry) was a disadvantage on operations'.

29 Commando and 4th Field Regiments were both equipped with the 105mm Light Gun. Light, manoeuvrable and versatile, it fired the same ammunition as the Abbot self-propelled gun to a maximum range of 17,500 metres, which is well in excess of comparable artillery. The gun is towed, barrel first, by a 1-tonne Land Rover, can be underslung from a helicopter or loaded into a Hercules. Crewed by six gunners, it has a rate of fire of six rounds per minute. In comparison, the 105mm Pack Howitzer, with which the Argentinians Marine, 3rd (Field) and 4th Airborne Artillery Groups were equipped, had a maximum range of 10,575 metres. Crewed by five gunners, it had a maximum rate of four rounds per minute and eight rounds on rapid fire. The Argentinians also deployed four 155mm CITEFA Howitzers as D Battery, 3rd Artillery Group, and it was these that caused some concern to the British because they outranged the Light Gun.

Brigadier Wilson had a full engineer squadron. Consisting of a headquarters and four field troops, 9 Parachute Squadron numbered 172 all ranks and has a long association with the Airborne Forces. Major Chris Davies RE was in command. 3 Troop usually supported 3rd Parachute Battalion and, although warned to join 3rd Commando Brigade, no room could be found on the ships, so it deployed with 5th Infantry Brigade. When 2nd Parachute Battalion departed, Lieutenant-Colonel Jones insisted on taking 'his troop', 2 Troop, which was commanded by Captain Robbie Burns. To make up for the lost troop, Captain David Foxley's 20th Field Squadron, a dark blue beret unit among red berets, joined the Squadron as 4 Troop. Whatever the colour of their beret, the sappers had a wide range of skills ranging from laying and lifting mines, building and demolishing bridges, building water points and field defences, track and road repair, watermanship and diving, quite apart from honing infantry skills. A key asset was the Combat Engineering Tractor, a remarkably efficient amphibious general-purpose tracked vehicle equipped with a large bucket and which could fire a rocket and chain to help haul itself up steep banks. It could also ford rivers, dig pits, prepare riverbanks and recover disabled vehicles.

For light helicopters, 5th Infantry Brigade was supported by a flight of six Scouts, some fitted with SS-11 anti-tank guided missiles and a flight of six Gazelles. Like most of the Brigade, helicopter deployment was also confusing. Under normal circumstances, 658 Squadron, at Netheravon, was the Brigade Air Squadron; however, it was below strength. On discovering that an Air Army corps detachment was to accompany 2nd Parachute Battalion, Lieutenant-Colonel Jones specifically asked for 656 Squadron, the 1st Infantry Brigade Air Squadron, with whom his Battalion had established a close relationship in the United Kingdom and on exercise in Kenya in 1981. The squadron provided an advanced detachment of three Scouts, each with a pilot, an aircrewman and maintenance team, commanded by Captain John Greenhalgh. It was initially absorbed into 3rd Commando Brigade Air Squadron. The remainder of 656 Squadron and its Air Maintenance Group were transferred to 5th Infantry Brigade at the expense of 658 Squadron.

16th Independent Parachute Brigade had pioneered the idea of a logistic regiment, but this had disappeared when the formation was disbanded, only for the concept to be adopted by the Royal Marines into the Commando Logistic Regiment. This consisted of a mix of Royal Navy, Royal Marines and Army grouped into the Medical, Ordnance, Transport and Workshop Squadrons and was ideally suited for the self-sufficient role of 3rd Commando Brigade on NATO's Northern Flank. The Regiment was also well practiced in amphibious operations. 5th Infantry Brigade's service support was typical of an Army brigade and relied on several autonomous units. To deal with casualties was 16th Field Ambulance and elements of 19th Field Ambulance, Royal Army Medical Corps. Having had more time to prepare, the medical order of battle included an Advanced Dressing Station, three casualty-collecting stations and a hygiene section. A Parachute Clearing Troop was already attached to 2nd Parachute Battalion.

81 Ordnance Company, reinforced by 91 Ordnance Company, Royal Army Ordnance Corps, provided logistic and ordnance support. Like 4th Field Regiment, 81 Ordnance Company was a Priority One NATO unit and its deployment also had to be kept discreet. 10th Field Workshops, Royal Electrical and Mechanical Engineers, provided repair and maintenance support for transport, weapons and electrical and electronics equipment. The Brigade did not have an integral transport unit and was supported by 407 Troop, Royal Corps of Transport, which was commanded by Lieutenant Paul Ash. It arrived from 27 Logistic Support Group Regiment with Eager Beaver forklifts. Not to be forgotten was 160 Provost Company, Royal Military Police, and 6th Field Cash Office, Royal Army Pay Corps, which played a critical role in the non-medical administration and notification of casualties.

While Major Lambe was preparing 5th Infantry Brigade for war, he encountered entrenched Ministry of Defence bureaucracy and close adherence to peacetime procedures. Asking for windproof clothing, he was told that there was none and was offered reversible white/brown winter warfare waterproofs. Lambe reminded the logistics staff that, with Europe about to enter summer, the United Kingdom Mobile Force would not require their winter warfare clothing until at least October. No one seemed to appreciate that winter was approaching in the South Atlantic. He also acquired 4,000 pairs of warm overboots and, as a result, not one member of 5th Infantry Brigade suffered trench foot, which is more than can be said of 3rd Commando Brigade. Lambe also managed to acquire several M79 grenade launchers but only with first-line ammunition scales; he was told resupply could be obtained from the Special Forces – some hope!

Knowing the Argentinians had M2 .50-inch Browning heavy machine guns, which outranged the British General Purpose Machine Gun by nearly 1,500 metres, Lambe successfully obtained several Brownings and 112,000 rounds of Korean War vintage, which were distributed to the three infantry battalions. Most of the guns had been in storage for years. Lieutenant-Colonel Scott converted Captain Jeremy Campbell-Lamerton's Wombat-equipped Anti-Tank Platoon into the Machine-Gun Platoon. Since British tanks used .50-inch Brownings as ranging guns for the tank main armament, several Royal Armoured Corps gunnery instructors from the Bovington training school accompanied the Battalion as far as Ascension Island. Scott would later claim, 'It was extremely comforting to have them (.50s) firing overhead and then to a flank in the assault with one-in-one tracer'. The Welsh Guards centralized their six .50 Brownings into the Machine-Gun Anti-Aircraft Platoon, which was commanded by Drill Sergeant Evans (33). 1/7th Gurkha Rifles converted their Motor Transport Platoon into the Heavy Machine-Gun Platoon. The Gurkha drivers were delighted to have a combat role until they realized they would have to carry these heavy weapons, the ancillary spares parts and ammunition. Lambe also demanded doubling the number of General Purpose Machine Guns per platoon, which allowed the normal eight-man infantry sections to break down into two 'fire teams' each built around one machine gun, as opposed to the classic of one machine gun providing fire support to an assault force of six.

Since Headquarters 5th Infantry Brigade had recently been formed and now had unfamiliar faces and unfamiliar equipment, Lieutenant-General Sir Richard Trant, a gunner and the commander of South East District, organized a shakedown exercise at Sennybridge, Exercise *Welsh Falcon*. Invited to a black tie formal dinner by Trant was Colonel Christopher Dunphie MC, a Royal Green Jacket then undertaking a 'turgid logistics study', and his wife. No sooner had Dunphie walked through the front door when he was whisked by Trant to his study and told to plan, within the week, a five-day shakedown exercise at Sennybridge followed by a week of live firing. Trant gave him several criteria – to mirror that which 5th Infantry Brigade might have to do on the Falklands, to exercise logistics and an element of live-firing including fighter ground attack. The directive was every trainer's dream and Sennybridge became 'Falconia', an occupied British territory. An invasion was mounted from three barracks in Wales representing a ship, for instance HMS *Crickhowell*. In addition to a RAF squadron of Puma support helicopters and a flight of Army light helicopters, 4-ton lorries represented landing craft, all of which played real time with correct loading, transit and unloading schedules. Intelligence was to be played for real, i.e. not always correct and collateral needed for confirmation. Lieutenant-Colonel Bill Marchant-Smith's 1st Green Howards represented the enemy, admittedly using British tactics, weapons and organization. Another unit was used to simulate casualties and civilians, although not, it seems, prisoners-of-war.

From 10 to 18 April 5th Infantry Brigade prepared for operations in the Falklands and practiced working together as a team. Since it had been stripped of several units, this would be the first time and only time that Brigadier Wilson exercised the Brigade he led to war. The basic military principle of training in peace for war was ignored. The Sennybridge training area is infamous among British soldiers for the generally unfavourable weather conditions and can be relied upon to produce cold, wet and miserable conditions at all times of the year. Throughout the first week it lived up to expectations and helped remind soldiers of conditions that would be encountered in the Falklands. The first few days were spent on basic military training, weapon handling and field firing. Captain Tim Daplin, of the Light Infantry, brought a team from the School of Infantry to help units become familiar with *Clansman*. The Gurkhas carried out a live-firing night exercise and gained more valuable experience in the art of night fighting, at which the British excel. Lieutenant-Colonel Holt brought his Regimental Headquarters and, after more intense lobbying, also was able to deploy 97 Field Battery. With 29 (Corunna) Battery already with 2nd Parachute Battalion, this meant that 5th Infantry Brigade had twelve 105mm Light Guns, as opposed to the normal eighteen in an artillery regiment.

The second week was designed to simulate brigade operations on Falkland-type terrain. Unfortunately an unseasonable and unexpected heat wave wrecked the plan as temperatures soared into the seventies. Lance-Corporal Barrie Lovell was with 81 Intelligence Section when Brigade Headquarters deployed to its exercise location:

Once in position it was noted that the dark green and brown camouflage nets, used to camouflage the tents and vehicles, stood out vividly amongst the pale yellows and browns of the dry grass. We were therefore ordered to use the grass to camouflage the camouflage nets, weaving handfuls of grass into the nets themselves. All went well for a time until one of the staff officers, a cavalry officer, began cooking himself a meal on one of the small solid fuel hexamine cookers. The officer failed to clear a suitable area around his cooker and, having lit the hexamine fuel block, he managed to set fire to the nearby grass. The grass burned rapidly and, fanned by a light breeze, soon spread out into the surrounding area. The officer tried to stamp out the flames but only succeeded in spreading them still further. In a matter of moments the fire was out of control and blazing across the hillside. Fortunately, due to the number of troops available, the conflagration was soon brought under control although several combat jackets, used to beat out the flames, were ruined. Although there were no casualties a number of soldiers had left their rucksacks and webbing outside the headquarters and the flames had swept across these, destroying personal equipment and sleeping bags.

The threat of fire was also discovered by at least one other unit. Several days after the first fire I saw a cloud of black smoke emanating from a point about a mile from our location. Later that day I drove past the scene of the fire and saw that the 4th Field Regiment had also lost some equipment and in the centre of a blackened circle, some 100 metres in diameter, stood the remains of a 9' by 9' Command Post tent. The canvas material had all burnt off, leaving the aluminium frame standing like a shiny skeleton. Still inside the frame were the remains of a table, chairs and miscellaneous equipment.

The exercise continued, with the grand finale taking the form of an all-out attack by the infantry battalions, supported by artillery and air strikes. The press were invited to watch and the whole show, particularly the firepower demonstration, was giving a great deal of publicity in the world's media. Considerable attention was also focused on the Gurkhas, who were invariably shown on television sharpening their kukris, the curved, heavy-bladed fighting knife which is their trademark.

From several accounts, it does seem that the exercise did not go terribly well. This was hardly surprising – new communications equipment, two new battalions, new artillery and the first time that Brigadier Wilson had exercised his brigade in a conventional war setting. One unit commander found Brigade Headquarters 'poorly communicated' and another exasperated commanding officer commented on the Brigade radio net, 'Who the f*** is running this shambles anyway?' It is not the sort of transmission one would expect from anyone; however, it does illustrate frustrations within the Brigade Headquarters, which is hardly surprising since the Staff were working with units only recently blistered into the Brigade. Another participant recalled that there were also far too many staff officers, instructors and others, no doubt all well meaning, dictating how 5th Infantry Brigade should complete a task.

When a promise by Royal Air Force helicopters to ferry the bergens of one of his Gurkha companies failed to materialize, Lieutenant-Colonel Morgan ruled that his men would never again be separated from their equipment and kit. It turned out to be a wise decision. The Scots Guards found the exercise very useful and spent a few more days at Sennybridge. Like all units involved on Royal Duties, they were under command of London District, which had an administrative role, and thus field training was usually only at company level and only when the Guardsmen could be spared. When the Battalion did get away, Battalion Headquarters ran the exercise and rarely put itself under pressure. Tactical Headquarters, let alone Main, had not been exercised for several years. Lieutenant-Colonel Scott:

We did not even have a current set of Standard Operating Procedures. Major Iain Mackay-Dick, the Second-in-Command wrote them overnight. This is no reflection on my predecessor, Johnny Clavering, who was a superb and much loved CO, and the battalion was brilliant under him in Northern Ireland where the scene was entirely different. I do not think the battalion had done a set-piece night attack on its feet for years. Apart from the armoured version in Germany, my own experience was as a lieutenant in Kenya in 1963! But perhaps that is nothing to be proud of. However, of course, Tumbledown, once the wheels were running, was a Company (individual) battle. The Guardsmen were fit enough for what we had to do, could shoot reasonably straight and had the well-known Scottish aggression to crack on.

It was hardly the best preparation and there was some debate whether 5th Infantry Brigade was ready for deployment. Shortly before the traditional climatic final attack, Brigadier Wilson was summoned back to Sennybridge and advised by Headquarters United Kingdom Land Forces that his Brigade was to embark for the South Atlantic on 12 May. As an observer commented after the exercise, 'They've a hell of a way to go', implying that the Brigade was not yet ready for combat. This is hardly surprising – a home defence formation cobbled together with several units completely new to its order of battle. No other brigade in modern times could have been so badly prepared and the blame should not be levelled at Brigadier Wilson. Some very strange decisions are made at the Ministry of Defence, anyway.

In comparison, the deployment of 3rd Commando Brigade had gone smoothly. In the closeted world of their Corps, Royal Marine officers and men moved within the Brigade and knew each other well. Thompson had been Brigade Major to Brigadier Jeremy Moore. 40, 42 and 45 Commandos were thoroughly integrated with each other and the Army commando gunners, sappers, signallers and naval medics supporting their needs. A close *esprit de corps* had developed around the culture of the Green Beret and the role of the Brigade as an independent formation. It was the most stable of brigades. Although defence cuts had curtailed the Royal Marines' annual full winter deployment to Norway in 1982, they were experienced in winter warfare.

Exercise *Welsh Falcon* finished on 29 April and by 1 May most units were back in barracks and receiving an Aladdin's Cave of supplies as peacetime constraints on stores issues was lifted. Previously frequently refused requests for equipment, material and clothing were willingly met by a mere signal or a telephone call. Trucks rolled into barracks from Royal Army Ordnance Corps logistic depots loaded with supplies. Virtually every solder received a set of windproofs and a 'Mao-Tse-Tung' quilted jacket and trousers and windproof combat kit. For units without ski-march or parachute bergens, about 2,000 were purchased from the travel and outdoor retailers Blacks of Reading, but, even so, some units went short. The distribution of all this clothing and equipment meant that the soldiers of 5th Infantry Brigade were far better clothed than those of 3rd Commando Brigade, whose departure had been much less leisurely.

Since potentially two brigades of eight battalions were now earmarked for the South Atlantic, there was the need for a divisional headquarters and Major-General Moore was appointed as Commander Land Forces, Falkland Islands or CLFFI. This was the first time that a Royal Marine had commanded the equivalent of a division since the Second World War and, although there were Army officers with experience in one of the four armoured division headquarters in West Germany, his appointment reflected the amphibious nature of the campaign. To many in the Task Force and virtually everyone in the Falkland Islands, Moore became a hero in an age when few military men acquire such esteem and stature. Assembled so quickly from a wide variety of officers with equally wide experience, for Moore it was not an easy command. Arriving from the Royal College of Defence Studies, as his deputy, was Brigadier John Waters, of the Gloucesters, who was described by one senior naval officer as 'a total brick' – steady, reliable and robust. He was also the reserve 5th Infantry Brigade commander. Colonel Brian Pennicott, who had commanded 29 Commando Regiment when Moore had led 3rd Commando Brigade, was specifically asked to join as Commander Royal Artillery. On 14 June he witnessed the surrender document. Major David Pennefather, a Royal Marine, had the unenviable job of welding soldiers and Royal Marines signallers into an organized communications network.

On Moore's departure for the South Atlantic, Lieutenant-General

Trant took over as Military Deputy to Fieldhouse and took with him Colonel Dunphie as his Chief-of-Staff. The next problem was to ferry Headquarters Land Forces, 5th Infantry Brigade and other units down south from the warmth of an early English summer to the chill winter of the South Atlantic.

2

Waiting for Tommy

As soon as Prime Minister Thatcher announced that Great Britain was sending a Task Force, the Junta had a problem – what to do? The preferred option of raising the crisis diplomatically and forcing negotiations? Call Britain's bluff of military intervention in the hope that international mediation would prevail? Defend the Falklands?

The Junta opted for option two and, late on 2 April, orders were sent to Rear-Admiral Busser to cancel the withdrawal of the 2nd Marine Infantry Battalion. He had planned the landings but it was too late. The marines were already on their way back to Argentina with their prisoners-of-war. Also on their way back to the mainland was the 1st Amphibious Vehicle Company, which effectively denied the Argentinians a useful asset.

Army General Headquarters then sent orders for Brigadier-General Americo Daher and his 9th Infantry Brigade, which was arriving as the garrison, to be strengthened. On 6 April 8th *'General Bernardo O'Higgins'* Infantry Regiment was despatched to Fox Bay on West Falklands, where it remained until the Argentinian surrender. Later, 5th Infantry Regiment was sent to Port Howard as Task Force Reconquest. 9th Medical Company set up a small field hospital in the settlement. 25th Special Infantry Regiment defended Military Air Base, Stanley and Yorke Beaches and sent C Company to garrison Goose Green. A day later the 5th Marine Infantry Battalion battle group deployed straight on to Mount William and Mount Tumbledown to cover the southern beaches. Directly supported by the six 105mm Pack Howitzers of B Battery Marine Field Artillery Battalion, 1st Marine Amphibious Engineer Company and, later, a composite company of .50-inch M2 machine guns manned by marine infantry, it covered the south-western approaches to Stanley. H Company, 3rd Marine Infantry Battalion sent platoons to defend Naval Air Base *Calderon* at Pebble Island and the oil storage facility on Cortley Ridge.

On 3 April 1982, the day after the Falklands were taken by Argentina, Major-General Cristino Nicolaides, commander of the 1st Army Corps, examined his options for reinforcing 9th Infantry Brigade. The Argentinian Army was divided into five corps, with its tactical deployment built around twelve brigades. But Argentina had a problem. Apart from providing a strong garrison on the Falklands, she needed to keep her western and northern frontiers militarily secure, particularly with Chile.

Argentina's disagreement with Chile stretches back to 1879 when Buenos Aires took advantage of Chile's long war with Peru and Bolivia to occupy the sparsely populated area of Patagonia in southern Argentina. The Argentinian Army pushed south and seized other Chilean provinces, including territories that are now known as Santa Cruz and Chubut. Many Chileans regard these occupations as a 'stab in the back' during a period in Chilean history when her armies were involved in the north. To a certain extent, Argentina also needed to protect her northern borders with Brazil, whose army in 1982 vastly outnumbered the Argentinian Army and included two airborne infantry brigades. During the previous century the Argentinians were always able to defeat the mighty Brazilians.

Brigadier-General Julio Fernandez Torres's 4th Airborne Infantry Brigade, in Cordoba province, was the National Strategic Reserve but on standby for emergency action and internal security duties. In addition to a parachute artillery battery sent early on, it also despatched fifty para-troopers of the 2nd Airborne Infantry Regiment, commanded by First-Sergeant Carlos Villegas, who arrived in Stanley Airport on 13 June and, after a short parade for the benefit of war correspondents and the civil population, set off to reinforce 7th Infantry Regiment, singing the *Malvinas March*, and was swallowed up during the Battle of Wireless Ridge early next morning.

Of the remaining infantry formations, 11th Mechanized Infantry Brigade was deployed in the extreme south and the five Marine Infantry battalions were already on their way to defend the southern land border with Chile. To remove the 5th Mountain Infantry Brigade, which was specially trained to fight in the Tucuman Mountains, and to use the 6th and 8th Mountain Infantry Brigades, which were widely considered to be well-trained Andean mountain brigades, might have all proved a match with 3rd Commando Brigade, but they were needed to deter a Chilean threat against the oil-rich province of Santa Cruz. 3rd and 7th Mechanized Infantry Brigades were at full stretch along the Brazilian, Paraguayan and Uruguayan frontiers and any military weaknesses could have heightened tension in the north.

There was, however, one well-trained infantry brigade which was not committed to frontier defence, and this was the 10th *Lieutenant-General Nicolas Levalle* Mechanized Infantry Brigade. Commanded by Brigadier-General Oscar Jofre, it was based at Mar del

Plata and defending the 1 Corps Atlantic sector around Buenos Aires.

Brigadier-General Jofre, a big, bluff man born in Buenos Aires on 2 April 1929, would become one of Argentina's best-known generals. Throughout his boyhood and early education, he had one ambition – to be a soldier. Entering the National Army Academy at El Palomar, Buenos Aires, in 1947, he was commissioned two years later into the Infantry. In 1979 he was promoted to brigadier-general and given command of 10th Infantry Brigade in December 1980. Aged fifty-three when the Falklands War broke out, he had converted his Brigade into a useful infantry formation and was well respected by his conscripts, most of whom had European backgrounds.

Named in honour of the Argentinian general who laid siege to Montevideo in 1843, 10th Infantry Brigade was raised on 20 October 1880 and received its baptism of fire in the successful campaign of the War of the Desert (1879-1883) in the south of the country against Patagonian Indians who had been supplied with arms, ammunition and horses by the Chileans. In 1930 the brigade was involved in another campaign against the Patagonian Indians in Chaco province. Mechanized in the 1960s, most of its equipment followed United States designs or was of United States issue. Most of the night vision equipment used by its regiments was of Vietnam War vintage and issued generally only to the reconnaissance and reserve platoons. Towards the end of October 1981 Brigadier-General Jofre laid on a major exercise in which the fully armed and equipped 10th Infantry Brigade pushed its way north and west towards the General Acha training area in La Pampa province high on the lower slopes of the Andes about 1,000 kilometres from Buenos Aires. Over ninety-six hours the brigade advanced 100 kilometres along unmade roads and in the full heat of the Argentinian summer, practising night and day attacks, patrolling and defence. The climax came with a brigade mechanized infantry assault, while overhead Skyhawks, representing both friendly and enemy air support, strafed target hulks with rockets. The Argentinian Army Commander-in-Chief, Lieutenant-General Roberto Viola, paid close attention to the performance of the brigade. It tested the men. Private Alberto Carbone, a 7th Regiment conscript, remembers:

Halfway through my service there was a really big exercise involving the 10th Infantry Brigade. I don't know what the top brass had in mind at the time. Whether it was a rehearsal for the Malvinas or not – but it was big. There were at least 10,000 troops involved and I drove a vehicle with a big cannon on it. I couldn't find the exercise area at first, then I got lost trying to find the regiment and then I got lost trying to find my company. I got there in the end and they sent

me off to get a truck fitted out with a field kitchen and drive that around deliv-
ering food to the infantry. When I got to the front line all the big guns were firing
and the heat was unbelievable. They were holding this exercise in a desert. If it
was a practice for the Malvinas, they were holding it in a very strange place. The
infantry soldiers were in a very bad way. They were in a dreadful state from hunger
and thirst. They were so bad with thirst they even tried to get water from the radi-
ator of my truck. I'll never forget the dreadful state they were in.

About this time Jofre formed heliborne platoons for each of his regiments. Private Santiago Gauto, a 7th Infantry Regiment conscript of
Guarani Indian heritage, was selected to be part of the Commando
platoon for his regiment:

We had instruction at night in all weathers. It was freezing in winter. We were
taught how to make and plant booby-traps, we did lots of extra shooting and had
to strip and assemble weapons while blindfolded. They even taught us how to stop
an electric train, which was no good to us. Maybe one day I'll go to the station
and stop one!

By early 1982 10th Infantry Brigade was a much-respected part of the
Argentinian Army and a significant proportion of the conscripts were fit,
devoted and well-trained, at least by Latin American standards.
Interestingly, those conscripts of Indian parentage did not have the high
post-combat trauma rates of other groups. Maybe they were more stoical
than those of European ancestry. Jofre's brigade would lose sixty-six men
killed and 370 wounded in the Falklands.

When his brigade was placed on notice to reinforce the Falklands,
Jofre organized a series of planning conferences at Headquarters
10th Infantry Brigade. Colonel Felix Aguiar, the Chief-of-Staff, had a
reputation for being 'tough-minded and spontaneous' and was popular
with the Argentinian commandos. Lieutenant-Colonel Norberto
Villegas, the Intelligence Officer, was stout-hearted and energetic, and
would remain so. The Operations Officer, Lieutenant-Colonel Eugenio
Dalton, during the pre-dawn darkness of Monday 14 June, was seen
driving around in a jeep marshalling tired, panicky and dazed soldiers
from various units into a company and led them into Stanley's western
suburb under heavy fire. In 1989 he was appointed Central Counter-
Insurgency director.

On 7 April Brigadier-General Mario Benjamin Menendez arrived as
Military Governor and commander of Army Group Malvinas. The
Malvinas Theatre of Operations was absorbed into the South Atlantic
Theatre of Operations and brought within Argentina's sphere of military
influence. By nature conciliatory, Menendez had been selected by the

Junta because his personality would help him govern the Falklands during the difficult early negotiations with Great Britain. He remained convinced that military action was subordinate to diplomacy, even when he found himself military commander after negotiations had failed and faced by the British landing at San Carlos.

On 9 April General Headquarters mustered 100,000 reservists conscripted on and before February 1981. Brigadier-General Jofre ordered his February 1982 conscripts to be replaced by reservists, most of whom were more than willing to right a national insult to their country. Sustained by this patriotism and indignation, 10th Infantry Brigade mobilized with creditable speed. Private Patricio Perez later recalled:

Before the war I had just finished my secondary education. I wasn't working. I did a lot of sports and played music. I lived really like a student with my family. We rejoiced when the Islands were reoccupied but there was also concern. A week went by before I was called up. A letter arrived from my regiment telling me where to go, but at the barracks it turned out that I hadn't been included in the combat list. Some of us protested and said we should replace the soldiers who had just started military conscription because we were fully trained. A high degree of marksmanship was an essential in the regiment. For us it was very important because all our mates were going and we felt that we had to defend the Fatherland also. None of our superiors expected a war – we were just going to fortify the Islands. At the same time we knew there was a possibility of war; but because our friends were there, we thought that if we died we would all die together. Ever since we were kids we learned the Malvinas were part of our territory, part of Argentina, and therefore we had to defend them.

During the next week Jofre's soldiers trained at San Miguel del Monte and Ezeiza, near Buenos Aires International Airport. Private Jorge Altieri of the 7th Infantry Regiment conscript remembers weapon training:

I was issued with a FAL 7.62mm rifle. Other guys were given FAP light machine guns and others got PAM sub-machine guns. The main emphasis in shooting was making every bullet count. I was also shown how to use a bazooka, how to make and lay booby-traps, and how to navigate at night, and we went on helicopter drills, night and day attacks and ambushes.

With equipment deficiencies made up from other units, by 11 April 10th Infantry Brigade was deployed to Stanley. Although 10th Infantry Brigade was one of the best Argentinian Army formations, General Headquarters knew, as it travelled to Military Air Force Base El Palomar to link up with the aircraft taking it to the Falklands, that the optimistic soldiers were amateurs when compared to the British. Everybody hoped that they would not shame the Argentinian Army. Meanwhile

Argentinian intelligence assessments persisted with the notion that the British would land at Stanley.

Within seven days 10th Infantry Brigade was digging in around Stanley until the positions they occupied resembled a vast mining camp of bunkers, trenches and artillery gun pits. The ground on Mount Longdon, Wireless Ridge, Mount Tumbledown, Mount William and Stanley airbase was so hard that some dugouts and caves had to be blasted out with explosives. It was an exhausting task. Lorries and jeeps of the 10th Logistic Battalion rumbled through the rain and sleet on mud-rutted tracks that quickly became quagmires. Telephone lines were laid and the soldiers awaited news of the diplomatic talks and wrote letters home. Private Benitez:

We listened to the radio – the Uruguayan radio – to find out what the English were doing, how they were coming towards us, how they were mobilizing the troops, where they were going to land, how many of them and so on. In our calculations the [enemy] numbers kept growing. First there were 3,000 and then it was 6,000 then it was 10,000, and so on. Later on, when the British battleships would come closer to the shore to shell us, we would find out the names of the ships on the radio. By that time we knew most of what we had to know.

3rd Infantry Regiment covered the southern beaches. On its right flank 6th Infantry Regiment covered the approaches from the south-west and south. The regiment had acquired a fine reputation during the War of the Desert and had also fought against Russian Trotskyites when 10th Infantry Brigade was in Santa Cruz province between 1920 and 1921. Its C Company was assigned to the Reserve and replaced by A Company, 1st 'Los Patricios' Infantry Regiment, the oldest infantry regiment in the Argentinian Army and part of the Army Headquarters order of battle. In 1838, under Lieutenant-Colonel Geronimo Costa, it had inflicted heavy casualties on the French Foreign Legion on Martin Garcia Island when the Legion was part of a Franco/British force supporting Uruguayan independence. 7th 'Colonel Pedro Conde' Mechanized Infantry Regiment was placed on Mount Longdon and Wireless Ridge. Formed in 1813, in 1982 it was based in the La Plata suburb of Buenos Aires and recruited from the city. It was the first 10th Infantry Brigade regiment to train with helicopters. Major Carlos Eduardo Carrizo-Salvadores, second-in-command of the Regiment, who later defended Mount Longdon against 3 Para, recalled:

During 1981 the Regiment was selected to take part in an exercise with 601st Combat Aviation Battalion. This was a terrific opportunity for the rifle companies to work with the Army Aviation and it was excellent value. So off we went to

Magdalena forest, which is some 40 miles south of Buenos Aires, with the Army helicopters. Even our chaplain went as a rifleman.

General Galtieri visited Stanley on 22 April and during a long conference with Menendez at Moody Brook agreed that the British would probably land at or near Stanley. When Menendez asked for a regimental-sized heliborne reserve, Galtieri, believing there were insufficient troops to occupy the Falklands, which could weaken his negotiation stance, decided to beef up the garrison. Without consulting the Junta and the Chiefs-of-Staff, he sent orders for Brigadier-General Omar Parada's 3rd Mechanised Infantry Brigade, which was usually deployed along the Uruguayan border in the northern sub-tropical province of Corrientes as part of 2nd Corps, to be deployed to the Falklands. There were now elements of three infantry brigades and a marine infantry battalion landing team on the Falklands. 3rd Infantry Brigade was full of conscripts inducted only in February 1982. Named Army Group Littoral, it defended the area to the east of Mount Simon on East Falklands, leaving 10th Infantry Brigade to defend Stanley. The most inexperienced brigade was given the most difficult task.

Rich with Guarani Indians because of its proximity to Paraguay, 4th Infantry Regiment was placed on Mounts Challenger and Wall. The Guarani, Mapuche and Araucanian Indians of Argentina were as hard and mobile as the desert Indians of North America and innumerable Spanish and Argentinian soldiers lost their lives fighting them. The Guarani were particularly brave and in Paraguay's war against Argentina and Brazil in the 1860s they decimated several Argentinian and Brazilian regiments. After Paraguay's defeat, the provinces of Entre Rios, Missiones and Corrientes were absorbed into Argentina and consequently many Paraguayan Guarani Indians ended up living south of the border. Headquarters, B and C Companies were formed into Task Force *Monte Caseros* and deployed forward on Mount Wall and Mount Challenger, while A Company was assigned to the Reserve. Six machine-gun detachments sent by the largely ceremonial 1st *'General Jose de San Martin'* Horse Cavalry Regiment were initially attached to 1st *'Los Patricios'* Infantry Regiment, but later joined 4th Infantry Regiment on Mount Harriet.

C Company, 25th Special Infantry Regiment, which had been at Goose Green since early April, was strengthened by A, C and Support Company, 12th *'General Juan Arenales'* Infantry Regiment which arrived minus most of its radios, mortars, vehicles, reserve ammunition, field kitchens and other war stores which were left behind on the transport *Ciudad de Cordoba*, which had been forced to return to port after hitting a rock.

Formed into Task Force *Mercedes*, the Goose Green garrison was reinforced by two Air Force security companies from the Training Command Military Aviation School, whose primary role was to defend Military Air Base *Calderon*, the operational base of the Pucaras of 3rd Attack Squadron. Two Army 35mm Oerlikon anti-aircraft guns and an Air Force battery of 20mm Rh 202s provided air defence. 12th Infantry Regiment's missing company, B Company, which was known as Combat Team *Solari*, defended the helicopter base of 601st Combat Aviation Battalion on Mount Kent. A combined 12th/25th Infantry Regiment detachment, named Combat Team *Eagle*, was despatched to Fanning Head and Port San Carlos at San Carlos Water in mid-May.

Jofre's 10th Artillery Group, which had US 105mm guns, was replaced by 3rd Artillery Group, from 3rd Mechanized Infantry Brigade, which was equipped with eighteen Italian Oto Melara 105mm Pack Howitzers. They were considered to be more suitable for the Falklands. However, the Group had not previously worked with 10th Infantry Brigade. To replace his 3rd Artillery Group, Parada was allocated 4th Airborne Artillery Group from the National Strategic Reserve. The Argentinian artillery was assembled on Stanley Common under the command of Lieutenant-Colonel Balza at Headquarters Army Group Malvinas. In addition to 3rd Artillery Group, this consisted of 4th Parachute Artillery Group and B Battery Marine Field Artillery, all with 105mm Pack Howitzers, and a four-155mm CITEFA howitzer troop from 2nd Artillery Group, 2nd Armoured Cavalry Brigade. During the night of 12 June two 155mm of a 101st Artillery Group troop, from 1st Army Corps, were flown in and brought into action during the last night of the fighting, as the Scots Guards battled for Mount Tumbledown. Two more howitzers were flown in, but, with the airport being shelled and an air raid threatening, bringing them into action was disrupted. 10th *'Colonel Isidoro Suarez'* Armoured Recce Squadron provided armoured support for 10th Infantry Brigade. It was joined by a troop of 181 Armoured Recce Squadron of 5th Army Corps. Both units were equipped with French Panhard AML-90 armoured cars and jeeps.

With the extremely poor roads, paths and tracks, the Argentinians were heavily reliant upon the support helicopters of 601st Combat Aviation Battalion, which was part of the Infantry. The Helicopter Company had a gunship role and was equipped with nine Italian A-109 Hirundos, six Lamas and ten US Huey UH-1H Iroquois. A Helicopter Assault Company, flying eight Pumas and two Chinooks, and B Helicopter Assault Company with ten Iroquois, provided the troop-carrying capability. Additional CH-47 and Bell 212 heli-lift was also available from the Air Force 7th Counter-Insurgency Squadron and the

Coastguard. Until 1 May most of the latter were stationed at Military Air Base Condor at Goose Green. Much of its work was search and rescue of aircrew downed behind British lines.

Argentinian air defence was organized through Air Defence Command on the mainland, which extended its operational cover to include the Falkland Islands. Without high-performance fighters to protect the Falklands, Marine, Army and Air Force air defence units were integrated into a single unit working to the Air Defence Information and Control Centre. The Marine Anti-Aircraft Battery placed its thirteen Tigercat surface-to-air missiles and twelve single-barrel 30mm Hispano-Suiza guns around the airport. The Army's 601st and 602nd Air Defence Groups each brought three 35mm twin-barrelled GDF-002 Oerlikon batteries, which were connected to Skyguard fire control radar. The Air Force provided a battery of 35mm Oerlikons connected to Superfledermaus radars. Two batteries of Air Force Rheinmetall twin-barrelled 20mm Rh 202s quick-firing guns were deployed on Stanley Common. One battery was sent to Goose Green. At unit level, Blowpipe and Soviet SAM-7 Strella surface-to-air missiles were widely deployed. Early warning was controlled by the Air Force 2nd Early Warning Group, later renamed Early Warning Group Malvinas, with an AN/TPS-43F search radar and a TPS-44 surveillance radar. 601st Anti-Aircraft Group had a French Roland surface-to-air missile system, which forced British aircraft to avoid getting too close to Stanley.

Engineer Group Malvinas consisted of 9th, 10th and Amphibious Engineer Companies and 601st Combat Engineer Group from Army Headquarters. Only the amphibious engineers arrived fully equipped and consequently the army sappers undertook simple tasks such as laying mines and building bunkers. By the end of May most defences had been completed, but the bombing and shelling would ensure the need for continual repair and maintenance. It is thought that the Argentinians laid about 25,000 mines in about 119 minefields covering, in total, about twelve square miles of the Falklands. Some were laid on beaches, where their recovery was affected by shifting sands; others sank in the peat, only to rise later and threaten man and beast. Origins included Argentina, Spain, Italy, Israel and the USA. In most instances, minefields were wired off and marked by a sign 'Mina', but the wind, bombing and shelling often flattened fences. Minefields were marked on maps, but these were often lost in the chaos of retreat and withdrawal. Maps captured by the British were also lost.

9th and 10th Logistic Battalions were centralized into the Logistic Centre, each supported by unit echelons to collect and distribute supplies. There was insufficient wheeled transport to keep up with the demand, particularly by those units manning the Outer Defence Zone in the hills to the west and Army Group Littoral at Goose Green and on West Falklands. Some front-line units suffered from lack of food and fresh water and inadequate ammunition supplies, and yet the immense amount of food, ammunition, clothing and equipment found in Stanley godowns indicated a combination of inefficiency, poor routes and British air and naval interdiction on the logistic chain. The Naval Transport Service requisitioned Falklands Islands Company coasters and used its own ships to supply Goose Green and West Falklands. But when the naval transport *Isla de los Estados* was sunk, further supply runs were reduced. A heavy drop by 1st (C-130) Squadron, 1st Transport Group to Goose Green and Fox Bay on 19 May parachuted pallets containing, among other items, Wellington boots. When supplies ran low, Argentinian troops resorted to the time-honoured method of requisitioning sheep and shooting game. Many British troops were surprised by the good quality of some Argentinian rations, especially those containing a small bottle of Scotch whisky; how they would have welcomed a small tot in the freezing cold of the mountains. Both brigades brought their medical companies, and surgical teams worked at the King Edward VII Memorial Hospital in Stanley. At least one naval transport, the *Almirante Irizar,* was converted into a hospital ship during the latter stages of the defence of Stanley. Most badly wounded were flown out by transport aircraft to mainland hospitals.

Other units sent to the Falklands included the Army-level 601st Commando Company, which was Menendez' quick reaction reserve, 601st Communications Company and 602nd Electronic Warfare Company from Army Headquarters and 181st Intelligence Company, 181st Communications Company, which provided rear link and communication centre teleprinter services, and 181st Military Police, all from Headquarters 5th Army Corps. Representatives from these headquarters level units were to be found in most garrisons. The Air Force provided the Special Operations Group from 7th Air Brigade; their role was to lay out dropping zones for parachute and air-landed troops. The National Gendarmerie, a border unit, provided a small Special Forces detachment, 601st National Gendarmerie Special Forces Squadron.

Apart from the Naval Transport Service, the maritime presence on the Falklands was constricted to two modern Coastguard LLE Class 81-ton patrol boats, *Islas Malvinas* and *Rio Iguazu.* Each was equipped with a 20mm anti-aircaft cannon and two 7.62mm machine guns.

The length of the runway at Stanley Airport and its risk from attack precluded fighters being stationed on the Falklands. Close air support was thus confined to the Pucaras of 3rd Attack Squadron, which was also known as Pucara Squadron Malvinas. It had aircraft dispersed between Stanley and Military Air Base Condor at Goose Green. Twenty-four were ferried to the Falklands, all of which were shot down, damaged or captured. During the 128 sorties flown between 2 April and 13 June, two 3rd Group pilots and one 4th Group pilot were killed. The Naval Air Command 1st Attack Squadron sent six MB-339s. One, flown by Lieutenant Guillermo Crippa, was on an early morning patrol on 21 May, in response to a naval intelligence assessment that the British would land at San Carlos, and found the Amphibious Task Group. Flying through a hail of fire, he counted the ships and carried out an accurate assessment of the situation. Serviceability of the MB-339s dogged the performance of the squadron. All aircaft were destroyed, damaged or captured and two pilots were killed in action. The naval 4th Attack Squadron sent four T-34C Mentors, all of which were deployed to Naval Air Base Calderon on Pebble Island and destroyed. Otherwise the Argentinian forces on the Falklands were reliant upon fighter, bomber, transport and recce support from the mainland, which, as we shall briefly describe, was forthcoming in a number of ways.

By the end of April, the Argentinian order of battle was settled. With three brigades, two with headquarters, Menendez, as Commander Army Group Malvinas, disbanded Headquarters 9th Infantry Brigade and appointed Brigadier-General Daher as his Chief-of-Staff. Brigadier-General Jofre was appointed Commander Land Forces and concentrated his command, control and communications through his own head-quarters. He remained commander of 10th Infantry Brigade. Brigadier-General Parada with his 3rd Infantry Brigade defended the rest of the Falklands. Parada was instructed to move his headquarters to Goose Green, but was slow to comply. With the imposition of the blockade on 1 May, the Argentinian forces were isolated and could do nothing but wait for a resolution to their predicament.

3

Down South

At the end of April Cunard shipping line was warned that the 67,140-ton Royal Mail Ship (RMS) *Queen Elizabeth II*, which was then commanded by Captain P. Jackson, was to be requisitioned by the Ministry of Defence. Sent to the Vosper dockyards at Southampton, the liner was converted into a 'Landing Platform Luxury (Large)'. Chipboard was laid over carpets and floors and everything that was inflammable and breakable removed. Helicopter pads, each capable of parking a Sea King, were added at the expense of some upper deck fittings. Additional bulwarks were fitted and a standard Royal Navy communication system installed. To bring home the finality that the liner was going to war, Naval Party 1980, commanded by Captain N. James, boarded to administer naval affairs and naval signallers. Major R.G. Cockings MBE, of the Royal Corps of Transport, was the Ship's Commandant for the Embarked Force.

On the political scene, US Secretary of State Alexander Haig's triangular shuttling between Great Britain, Argentina and the United Nations had produced no tangible results. Argentina was not going to abandon the Falklands and the Dependencies. By now the British offensive was underway. On 25 April Major Guy Sheridan, the Second-in-Command 42 Commando and now commanding the military task force built around M Company, 42 Commando, was specifically tasked to recapture South Georgia. It was unfortunate that the County-class destroyer HMS *Antrim* took fright at the appearance of a World War Two vintage Argentinian submarine, which resulted in the South Georgia task force dispersing at a critical moment. Consequently all that Sheridan had was a small element of M Company, elements of D and G Squadrons, the Special Air Service, whose performance so far had cost two valuable helicopters, and a Special Boat Service section. There were suspicions that the Special Air Service was taking its operational orders direct from London anyway.

On 1 May Stanley Military Air Base was bombed, not terribly successfully, and the first Harrier raids targeted Argentinian troop positions. Special Forces patrols landed, set up observations posts and, over the next three weeks, inspected beaches. On the same day Peru and the US proposed a 72-hour truce and suggested that Britain and Argentina should withdraw its forces from the area and that the United Nations should instigate negotiations. This failed dramatically when the US Second World War 6-inch cruiser *General Belgrano* was torpedoed by the nuclear submarine HMS *Conqueror* on 3 May, which effectively meant that Great Britain won control of the seas. The air-launched Exocet attack on HMS *Sheffield* the next day hardened British public opinion but also demonstrated that Argentina could hit back.

The Peruvian plan was re-introduced on the 5th but rejected by Argentina next day. Her troops were well dug in and had sufficient supplies, the Air Force was doing well and her negotiating position was strong. On 7 May the United Nations, famous for sitting on the fence until the last moment, stepped in with a five-point plan – end hostilities, withdraw the British Task Force, open negotiations of the future of the territories, end sanctions and insert an interim United Nations administration of the Falklands. For Great Britain, these proposals had several advantages, in particular the adherence by Argentina to United Nations Resolution 502, which had been imposed on 3 April, and called for the withdrawal of Argentina from the territories she was occupying. Great Britain was already negotiating on the future of several colonies, including Belize, and to do the same with Argentina over the Falklands was not a major problem. The interim administration was more difficult, but acceptable provided the Falkland Islanders was given substantial rights of self-government. For Argentina the proposals were less acceptable. Her invasion had been a major coup for the Junta and the humiliation of a withdrawal would be worse than the relative glory of a military defeat, particularly if there were no tangible political successes.

The British kept up the pressure by bombing and bombarding Argentinian troop positions. On 9 May the Argentinian intelligence trawler *Narwal* was badly damaged by Sea Harriers and then boarded by the Special Boat Service, but later sank. By 11 May, after considerable diplomatic and political adjustments, Argentina declared that sovereignty over the Falklands was not a pre-condition to peace talks. Everyone seemed content.

On Wednesday 12 May Headquarters Land Forces, 5th Infantry Brigade, elements of 1st Signal Group and several other units assembled at Southampton to board *Queen Elizabeth II*. Two 825 Squadron Sea King helicopters, which had been converted from anti-submarine warfare to troop-carrying, were loaded. Major Lambe persuaded Headquarters Land Forces to allow Brigade Headquarters to load a small number of Land Rovers as opposed to their vehicles. The Brigade's stores and equipment split between four vessels:

□ The Whitwell, Cole & Co Roll-On/Roll-off ferry *Tor Caledonia*, which was commanded by Captain A. Scott and with Lieutenant-Commander J.G. Devine's Naval Party 2020.

□ The Stena Line roll-on/roll-off ferry *Nordic Ferry*, which was commanded by Captain R. Jenkins and supported by Lieutenant-Commnder M. St J.D.A. Thorburn's Naval Party 1850.

□ The Stena Line roll-on/roll-off ferry *Baltic Ferry*, which was commanded by Captain E. Harrison and had Lieutenant-Commander E. Webb's Naval Party 1960 in support.

□ The Cunard container ship *Atlantic Causeway*, which was commanded by Captain M.N.C. Twomey and supported by Commander R.P. Seymour RN and his Naval Party 1990. Like its sister ship, the ill-fated *Atlantic Conveyor*, it had been converted to a helicopter-carrier and had on board twenty Wessex HU5 troop-carriers from the newly-formed 847 Naval Air Squadron and eight Sea Kings. The 825 Squadron pilots spent the next weeks on intensive training for ground operations.

The convoy was named Command Task Unit 317.1.2. Although not expecting an assault landing, Brigadier Wilson insisted that his Brigade should be ready to move when it landed and thus extracted explicit and unambiguous assurances from Land Forces that there would be time at Ascension Island for the ships to be restowed. Although roll-on/roll-offs on the North Sea routes ferried troops to and from West Germany, it was always on to quays. The inability to unload military equipment direct on to beaches and into landing craft would prove a hindrance to 5th Infantry Brigade.

The same day Great Britain imposed the 200-mile Maritime Exclusion Zone around the Falklands, South Georgia and the South Sandwich Islands by threatening to intercept Argentinian warships found inside the zone. She had warned Argentina of her intentions five days earlier.

The departure of *Queen Elizabeth II* was something akin to the departure of the great troopships in their heyday – a military band in red jackets, bunting and friends, families and VIPs bidding farewell. Some wives of Royal Signallers in the Headquarters and Signal Squadron found their way to a gallery overlooking the quayside, and, together with everyone else, were waving at their menfolk. One of the ladies saw her husband, a lance-corporal. Married only a few weeks, she suddenly stripped off her blouse and bra and, according to a witness, waving the latter in the air and shouted, 'Feast your eyes while you can because you're not going to see these for a while!' Needless to say all eyes swung to the young lady, including those of an enterprising crane operator who manoeuvred the hook of his jib so that the girl could put the bra on it. He then swung the jib over to the ship where it was safely delivered to a somewhat embarrassed, but probably secretly rather proud, husband amid the cheers of those who had been watching this little cameo unfold!

At 4pm lines were thrown ashore and the liner slowly edged away from the dock and glided down Southampton Roads, accompanied by a fleet of small boats and ships' hooters, into Southampton Water. There she stopped to repair a boiler problem. Twelve hours later she sailed past the Isle of Wight, picked up speed and headed south. The boiler problem should probably have kept *Queen Elizabeth II* in port, but this was a stage-managed mid-week event that served not only to unite the nation but also send a very clear signal to Argentina that she could not win the confrontation. Britain's maritime power was supreme. The Royal Marine prisoners-of-war and the first casualties of the fighting, from HMS *Sheffield*, had arrived in England and the country was in no mood for conciliation.

Very few of those on board the *Queen Elizabeth II* had experienced ocean travel, let alone the sheer luxury of the ship. Among them was Lance-Sergeant Danny McDermid, a 26-year-old section commander in the Scots Guards. Recalled to the Battalion from the middle of a senior platoon sergeant's course at the School of Infantry at Brecon, he returned to Wales a few days later to take part on Exercise *Welsh Falcon*. Growing up near the shipbuilding yards on the River Clyde, he had watched the *Queen Elizabeth II* being built and then launched; never in his wildest dreams did he think he would one day sail on her. McDermid later described the experience as 'marvellous'. The official war artist Linda Kitson sketched and painted scenes on board including 81 Intelligence Section at work. She remained with 5th Infantry Brigade for most of the campaign. Perhaps those most astonished by what they saw were the Gurkhas. Rifleman Baliprasad Rai was a member of the Pipes and Drums and attached to B Company as a machine-gunner. He later described his feelings:

Such a ship had to be seen to be believed. It was larger that any building I'd seen at home. Never have I slept in such a big, soft bed, nor perhaps ever will. If I was to go to war, then there was no better way to go.

Once the troops had recovered from the shock of the sheer luxury of the ship, and indeed the crew become familiar with dealing with uniformed soldiers, as opposed to dinner-suited gentlemen and glamorous ladies, everyone realized this was not meant to be a holiday cruise. A rigorous training programme was soon underway with weapon training, treating battle casualties, recognition, resistance to interrogation, prisoner handling and the myriad of subjects that soldiers need to know. Headquarters and command posts carried out endless battle appreciations, but always in dry, comfortable and well-lit surroundings. Although 'tactical exercises without troops' (TEWT) had been carried out on ships before, the Gurkhas christened them 'tactical exercises without land' (TEWL)! It is not thought that this was accepted into the Manual of Staff Duties list of terminologies.

With at least a three-week voyage ahead and superb food being served by waiters in the various restaurants, maintaining fitness was going to be a problem and so physical training instructors developed running circuits and exercise areas. 9 Parachute Squadron's 4 Troop, alias the non-parachute 20 Field Squadron, soon discovered operating with the para sappers a shock to the system. It was only after Major Davies invited Captain David Foxley, who commanded 20 Field Squadron, to do ten more running circuits, after a lacklustre performance, that the conventional sappers realized that they could hold their own. Some of the Embarked Force took advantage of the small indoor swimming pool on a lower level for a game of water polo, usually without any rules. Fortunately no one drowned.

Each night the ship was blacked out with black plastic bags taped over windows and portholes and then one of the Sea Kings flew around the ship checking that it was robust. When this happened the first time, a number of soldiers had gathered on the flight deck and took photos, the flashes of which blinded the pilot. He was quite angry and a Tannoy announcement reminded everyone that the pilots needed their night vision. This alone emphasized to many of those on board the fact that the liner was a troopship bound for a combat zone.

Accommodation was tight and in every cabin someone slept on a camp bed. For instance, Lieutenants Robert Lawrence and Mark Mathewson of Right Flank, 2 Scots Guards, shared a two-berth cabin with their Company Commander, Major Simon Price, and Company Second-in-Command, Captain Ian Bryden. Guess who had the two bunks? Captain Richard Field, of the Blues and Royals, was one of six officers posted to Headquarters 5th Infantry Brigade as Operations watchkeepers:

As I and three others who shared our stateroom settled in, we tried to convince ourselves that we were, in fact, off to war and not a pleasure cruise. A glance at our well-stocked refrigerator and opulent surroundings made this difficult. As we cruised through the tropics, this sense of unreality persisted. Not really involved at that stage in the daily workings of the Headquarters, and having nobody to train but ourselves, we were left by and large to our own devices. Brigade operations procedures were read, criticized and revised. Webbing, unworn since Sandhurst, was put together and we began to run enthusiastically. Bergens were packed, were discovered to be so heavy as to be unliftable, and were constantly repacked. The miniature tape recorder was taken out and the bottle of 12-year Malt definitely left in. The unreality of life on our deck, 'Mirage' deck as it came to be known, was only checked by continuous training taking place on the lower decks, on 'Exocet' and 'Tigerfish' decks. One threaded one's way to a signal lecture through lines of blindfolded men stripping and assembling weapons, practising emergency stations and first aid. We ate excellently and the weather was kind.

Although he was told not to become involved in organizing entertainment, Father Alfred Hayes, the Roman Catholic chaplain to 5th Infantry Brigade, contacted the ship's entertainment officer to develop a radio programme, which included 'Prayer for the day' given by the various chaplains on board. Although attendance at church services and Mass was generally small, he also organized a Brigade newspaper, which included 'Thought for the day'. There were film shows most days and the various messes organized their own entertainment. Someone had also thoughtfully provided Bollywood films in Hindi for the Gurkhas. Three performances of a concert were arranged and lectures given, including one given by Captain Jackson on Cunard's transatlantic routes. There were a few weepy eyes when a BBC programme featuring the departure of the ship '*A Queen Goes to War*' was shown – families, wives, parents and girlfriends in tears on the quayside.

After about five days *Queen Elizabeth II* moored alongside a jetty at Freetown in Sierra Leone. To the disappointment of virtually everyone on board, a promised mail drop did not materialize. Several canoes and boats, no doubt expecting rich tourists, came alongside with African boatmen selling fruit and carvings. However, no one was allowed to buy anything, although a couple of Scots Guardsmen managed to acquire some coconuts. A week out, on the 19th, *Queen Elizabeth II* crossed the equator. For most of those on board, it was the first time they had done so and, as tradition demanded, King Neptune demanded homage from a chosen few.

Meanwhile the campaign moved into a new stage when during the night of 14/15 May, D Squadron of the Special Air Service destroyed several aircraft in a spectacular night raid on the Argentinian Naval Air Base at Pebble Island. Two days later a document spelling out the terms of the interim agreement was rejected by Argentina with the British clause referring the negotiations being 'initiated without prejudice to the rights, claims and positions of the parties and without prejudgement of the outcome' being crossed out. In effect, Argentina was still staking her claim to the Falklands. Negotiations were at an end. By the morning of

20 May the Amphibious Task Group was hovering undetected on the edge of the Total Exclusion Zone waiting for political confirmation to escalate the war. By the evening, when it became clear that Argentina was not going to concede, 3rd Commando Brigade was ordered to land. Covered by the Carrier Battle Group, the Amphibious Task Group slipped north past Stanley and entered San Carlos Water early on 21 May. While the Special Air Service created a diversion by raiding Goose Green and the Special Boat Service dealt with Combat Team Eagle observation post on Fanning Head, 45 Commando and 2nd Parachute Battalion landed on *Blue Beach* at San Carlos and *Red Beach* at Ajax Bay respectively. In the second wave, 3rd Parachute Battalion landed at *Green Beach* at Port San Carlos and met opposition from Combat Team Eagle, which shot down two 3rd Commando Brigade Air Squadron Gazelles, costing the lives of three aircrew and seriously wounding another. Off Port Howard, Flight-Lieutenant Jeff Glover, of 1 (Fighter) Squadron and flying a GR 3 Harrier, was shot down and was hauled, badly wounded, from the water. He spent the rest of the campaign as a prisoner-of-war in a Buenos Aires hospital. A pre-emptive strike by 1 (Fighter) Squadron on the 601st Combat Aviation Battalion forward operating base on Mount Kent during the early morning prevented any major moves against the beachhead.

The landings caught Malvinas Joint Command off balance. With its assault sections split between Stanley and Port Howard, Brigadier-General Menendez's immediate reaction force, 601st Commando Company, was unable to disrupt the British build-up and by the time it regrouped in Stanley on 26 May it was too late. Combat Team *Solari* on Mount Kent, guarding the 601st Combat Aviation Battalion helicopter base, could not help. General Headquarters, nevertheless, sought to maintain an optimistic tone as Malvinas Joint Command waited for 5th Infantry Brigade to assault Stanley by issuing a communiqué claiming that 181st Armoured Cavalry Squadron was carrying out reconnaissance and security patrols to deter landings and that commandos were harassing British activites. This was intended to ease public concern that Menendez was doing nothing about 3rd Commando Brigade when, in fact, he had no intention of sallying forth and was content to absorb a British assault and force Great Britain to the negotiating table. Over the next ten days several Argentinians were captured, including stragglers from Fanning Head, members of the School of Military Aviation manning radar beacons around San Carlos Water and Lieutenant-Commander Camaletti, a Marine Infantry officer leading a deep penetration patrol into the beachhead.

The Royal Navy was subjected to a week of punishing air raids. HMS

Ardent and *Antelope* were sunk and several others damaged on D-Day. On 25 May 5th Attack Group Skyhawks attacked the Type 42 destroyer HMS *Coventry* and Type 22 frigate HMS *Broadsword* on air defence duties off West Falklands. Nineteen sailors died when HMS *Coventry* capsized and sank. This was the second Type 42 the Argentinians had sunk. The same day the British suffered a serious logistical blow when an Exocet hit the *Atlantic Conveyor*, taking down with her a large amount of supplies and several Chinook and Wessex helicopters. Northwood had earlier told Commodore Clapp that the helicopters were not to be landed, as they were required for 5th Infantry Brigade. Not knowing Major-General Moore's plans, he did not press the idea and was content for them to be safe at sea. The loss led Lieutenant-Colonel Julian Whitehead, the Commanding Officer of 45 Commando, to remark, 'We'll have to bloody well walk.' High-level night bombing by 2nd Bomber Group Canberras was distinctly uncomfortable for the British. Throughout the raids 3rd Commando Brigade built up its strength, taking five days to unload the stores required for the land battle. This induced some impatience from Rear-Admiral Woodward who wondered what the Landing Force was doing sitting in the beachhead while the Royal Navy was taking a pounding from the South Atlantic. The answer was that Brigadier Thompson was determined to create a sound logistic base before venturing forth from behind the defences, something all sensible commanders do. But politically unless 3rd Commando Brigade did something spectacular, then at least another brigade was going to be required to defeat the Argentinians.

Always shadowed by a Soviet intelligence-gathering trawler, *Queen Elizabeth II* arrived off Ascension Island on 21 May, the day that 3rd Commando Brigade landed. Loitering below the horizon to increase security, over the next twenty-four hours she rendezvoused twice with HMS *Dumbarton Castle* to transfer personnel, mail and stores by 202 Naval Air Squadron Sea Kings and the two on board. Among those who arrived on board were Major-General Moore and the remainder of his headquarters. Critically the promised stopover at Ascension Island so that 5th Infantry Brigade could reorganize its logistic unloading did not materialise and served to encourage the idea that the Brigade was going south as a garrison. The two roll-on/roll-off ferries were already on their way south. Any notion by that they were sailing south to be the garrison was firmly dispelled when, that evening, Moore called an Orders Group for his staff and Brigadier Wilson and his key officers in which he said:

3rd Commando Brigade is now landing to secure a bridgehead on East Falkland, into which I can reinforce, and from which I can develop operations to repossess the islands . . . It is my intention to land 5 Brigade into the beachhead and then to develop operations, using both brigades to further dominate the enemy to such an extent that he cracks and gives up.

As *Queen Elizabeth II* circled the island, she was halfway along a sophisticated logistic chain developed to move men, equipment and supplies for the three Services and the civilian components to and from the South Atlantic. The 8,000 miles to the Falklands from the United Kingdom made providing 'in time' logistic support for the naval, ground and air forces harder. Pivotal to the system was Ascension Island, which became the main rear base.

With its population of about 1,000, 3,750 miles from the Falklands and 4,225 miles from the United Kingdom, Ascension was ideally placed in the middle of the Atlantic Ocean as a logistic base. One in the West Indies would have been vulnerable to interference from Argentina and other countries sympathetic to her claim. A mainland base somewhere along Africa's west coast would have required substantial armed forces to protect it. While Ascension lacked a harbour, it not only had a decent anchorage but also Wideawake airfield. It was also secure and isolated from media intrusion. Not to be forgotten in the hiatus were the residents of this tranquil island, which was converted, almost overnight, into a noisy armed camp. All those who managed to go ashore appreciated their hospitality, patience and understanding but such was the restriction on space and fresh water that anyone and anything superfluous to the operation was sent back to the United Kingdom. This happened to nine Royal Signallers, who were part of a 30th Signal Regiment satellite communication detachment.

The tranquillity of the island changed overnight on 2 April when Sergeants Maclreavy and Keeping and five Royal Signals from 1st Signal Group at Tidworth arrived with tactical satellite communications and diplomatic communications radios to provide Governor Rex Hunt at Stanley with secure communications. His surrender precluded the detachment going south, so they joined RFA *Fort Austin* and remained on board for the next eleven weeks, eventually landing at Stanley on 19 June. The Royal Naval Aircraft Servicing Unit (Naval Party 1222) arrived on 6 April and was reinforced by a team of experts from the Naval Supply and Transport Service to receive and shift all sorts of stores. Captain Robert McQueen RN commanded Navy Party 1222 and was also Commander British Support Unit. Wideawake Airport became the most stable aircraft-carrier in the world and, in mid-April, was deemed to be the busiest airport in the world. It usually handled about 250 flights annually. McQueen's organization played an important role building ranges and making arrangements for 3rd Commando Brigade to restow its equipment so that the right men and equipment were in the right place at the right time for an opposed landing, something that would be denied to 5th Infantry Brigade. While waiting for the political developments that would eventually see 3rd Commando Brigade land at San Carlos and to preserve the precious water supply, the troops remained on board their ships, apart from strictly organized training on the ranges and troop exercises.

To the Army and Royal Marines waiting to go south, Ascension Island was reckoned to be awash with Royal Air Force, which was not far off the truth. In fact, the Air Force contingent numbered about 800, compared to the 100 each from the Royal Navy and Army. Commanded by Group-Captain Jeremy Price, the Royal Air Force set up an organization to move men and equipment using nearly fifty C-130 Hercules from 24, 30, 47 (Special Duties) and 70 Squadrons, several ex-military transport Belfasts chartered from Heavy Lift Cargo Airlines and 10 Squadron VC-10 passenger and aero-medical evacuation aircraft. The Royal Air Force, in over 600 sorties, moved 5,800 personnel and 6,600 tons of stores through Ascension Island. Wideawake was also a springboard for air operations in support of the Task Force, such as the Operation 'Black Buck' Vulcan raids on Stanley Airport. It is estimated that during the campaign there were 2,500 fixed-wing flights and 10,600 helicopter rotations. As the need grew to defend Ascension Island, in early May Price was reinforced with eight GR3 Harriers from 1 (Fighter) Squadron, a Royal Air Force Regiment Wing equipped with Rapier and an early warning radar system, which was installed on Green Mountain. On 24 May the Harriers were released to join the Task Force and were replaced by 29 (Fighter) Squadron F-4 Phantoms. This unit eventually arrived on the Falklands in October when Stanley Airport was re-opened.

A most important Army contribution was the Royal Engineers, who laid a four-mile temporary aviation fuel pipeline from a storage tank farm to the airfield. Road bowsers were originally used but such was the number of aircraft using Wideawake that quantity could not keep up with demand. With their Royal Navy and Royal Air Force colleagues, 29 Transport and Movement Regiment, Royal Corps of Transport, played a significant role by installing a Movement Control Check through which men and material moved. They also provided 'movers' on ships to liaise with the ships' crews over the stowage of equipment and stores and to smooth any difficulties of soldiers on board ships. Some later saw action, such as Lieutenant Byrne of 59 Movement Squadron, who joined Headquarters 5th Infantry Brigade as the Movement Liaison Officer.

Those stationed on the island lived in three tented camps until 12 May when several twelve-man modules were hired from the United States. Each consisted of living quarters, showers and lavatories and were primarily given over to aircrew, in particular those flying south in Hercules transports, Vulcan bombers and Victor tankers. Inevitably the gathering of modules was christened 'Concertina City'.

The Royal Navy Directorate of Naval Trade and Operations co-coordinated support to the Fleet while the Defence Operations Movements moved men and material. Both departments worked closely with the Department of Industry to identify merchant ships available to support the Task Force. The Naval Supply and Transport Service operates its own fleet, the Royal Fleet Auxiliary, to move ammunition, fuel, food and other war stores for the fleet. A merchant marine service with strong naval connections and traditions, the Royal Fleet Auxiliary was formed in 1905 to provide floating coalbunkers and other support services for warships of the period. During the First and Second World Wars it saw service in every naval theatre of operations including with Arctic convoys and in the Pacific. Since 1945 it has supported the fleet at sea in conflicts and on exercises. In 1982 the Royal Fleet Auxiliary employed about 2,300 British officers and ratings and 250 Chinese ratings. Its overseas agents were responsible for making local arrangements for the refuelling of warships, either directly in port or from fleet tankers. Merchant shipping alone transferred an estimated 9,000 personnel, 100,000 tons of freight and ninety-five aircraft to the South Atlantic on 1,200 occasions, many at sea.

During the period 2 April to 14 June twenty-two vessels manned by the Royal Fleet Auxiliary and Royal Maritime Auxiliary Service and forty-three ships from thirty-three companies were taken up from trade under the Royal Prerogative. The latter ranged from the *Queen Elizabeth II* to the Wimpey Marine tug *Wimpey Seahorse*. Most had a naval party to help with communications. Of the merchant ships, twenty-one were ocean tankers supporting the eight Royal Fleet Auxiliary fleet tankers. This figure alone adequately reflects the significant characteristic of the campaign of keeping ships topped up at sea, a complicated and hazardous operation exacerbated by the dreadful weather of the South Atlantic in winter. Rear-Admiral Woodward sensibly developed a floating holding and maintenance area, known as the Tug, Repair and Logistics Area (TRALA), which was positioned east of the Total Exclusion Zone. Visited by ships damaged in the fighting or from the weather, the zone was staffed by repair ships and salvage tugs.

While 3rd Commando Brigade was inside the San Carlos beachhead, the surrounding hills and the northern part of Falkland Sound were known as the Amphibious Operations Area and was controlled by

Commodore Clapp on board HMS *Fearless*. Ships entering San Carlos Water did so in convoys under escort. Much to Woodward's disappointment, the failure of the British to achieve total air superiority meant that Clapp had to retain a heavy naval air defence presence to protect the anchorage. With the breakout of 3rd Commando Brigade on 27 May, the amphibious stage of the ground war officially finished and the Amphibious Operations Area was renamed the Transport Area and ships could now enter direct from Ascension Island. After the arrival of 5th Infantry Brigade, San Carlos was named the Force Maintenance Area and became a divisional responsibility for the central delivery and collection point of men and materials for both brigades until Stanley fell.

Helicopters were very important. The Royal Naval deployed several helicopter squadrons, two of which, the 845 and 846 Naval Air Squadrons, were equipped with troop-carrying Wessex and Sea Kings respectively. Both were thoroughly at home working with 3rd Commando Brigade. On 29 May they set up a Forward Operating Base in a gully about a mile and half north of the Ajax Bay refrigeration plant. Previously these aircraft had been flying off ships, which limited their time supporting the ground forces. In due course 825 and 848 Naval Air Squadrons joined them. Of the support helicopters five naval Sea Kings and nine Wessex, six on the *Atlantic Conveyor* and three Royal Air Force Chinook, also on the *Atlantic Conveyor,* were lost during the campaign.

For the Army and Royal Marines, organizing the collection, distribution and transportation of supplies fell to the Logistic Executive, at Andover, and Royal Army Ordnance Corps depots. Transportation was provided by regular and reserve units of the Royal Corps of Transport, which included 17 Port Regiment and its rail- and roadhead at Marchwood. Away from public gaze and free of industrial relations problems, the port proved a valuable asset supporting the ground forces. The Royal Pioneer Corps played a key role in providing labour. In the three days prior to the departure of the Landing Force Group, the military logistic organization shifted 1,250 tons of fuel and lubricants, 3,880 tons of stores and 8,260 tons of ammunition.

After the San Carlos landings, the original plan had been to keep the logistic support afloat but the ferocity of the Argentinian air attacks called for a change of plan and the disused refrigeration plant at Ajax Bay was selected as the Base Support Area and was managed by the Commando Logistic Regiment. It housed not only stores but also the field hospital and the intermediate prison camp for prisoners-of-war awaiting repatriation. A Skyhawk attacked the plant on 27 May, the day before the Battle of Goose Green, and five men were killed and twenty-seven wounded. Once ashore, the Commando Logistic Regiment organized the distribution of supplies and the lack of labour to move stores from beach-heads to helicopter collection points was solved by using anyone who was available to help, even for an hour or so. On 1 June three landing craft from HMS *Intrepid* swept the Port Salvador anchorage for mines and, when none were found, Teal Inlet was opened up as 3rd Commando Brigade's Forward Maintenance Area. Organized by Transport Squadron, supplies were then either flown forward by helicopter or taken by 1st Royal Marine Rigid Raider assault boats to the distribution point at Estancia for collection by unit echelons. The arrival of the two roll-on/roll-off ferries supporting 5th Infantry Brigade and its relatively haphazard loading added to the organizational complexities of San Carlos beachhead. Some stores were unloaded manually by gangs of soldiers before essential supplies, such as ammunition, could be reached. Much to his frustration, Lieutenant-Colonel Ivor Hellberg, command-ing officer of the Commando Logistic Regiment, incorporated 81 and 91 Ordnance Companies into his unit, but they were not familiar with amphibious operations.

To supply the operations in the South Atlantic a ' motorway' was created from Ascension Island to South Georgia and then to San Carlos along which usually unarmed and unprotected ships sailed safe, they believed, from interdiction. Traditionally the principal maritime threat could be expected to be from submarines. At the opening of hostilities, Argentina had three submarines. The Balao-class *Santa Fe* had seen service as USN *Catfish* in the Second World War and now lay crippled in South Georgia after being attacked on the surface during the recapture of the island. Nothing was known about the two post-war German Type-209 U-boats. The greatest threat actually came from two air sources. The first was Soviet Long Range Air Force Tupolev-95 maritime bombers (NATO codenamed *Bear* D) making regular transatlantic flights between Luanda in Angola and Cuba. It was strongly suspected that the Soviet Union was passing information to Argentina and, certainly, two *Bears* had taken considerable interest in the Amphibious Task Group, as indeed as had a number of Warsaw Pact auxiliary intelligence-gathering trawlers.

Argentina developed her own long-range maritime information-gathering capability. On 20 April, even though the aircraft did not have specialist reconnaissance equipment, the Boeing 707s of 2nd Squadron, 1st Transport Group, was tasked by Strategic Air Command to search for the Carrier Battle Group. The aircraft had the range and, in Wing-Commander Jorge Ricardine, an experienced pilot. Flying a triangular course, he sighted Woodward's Carrier Battle Group about 1,500 miles east of Rio de Janeiro, but was then intercepted by Sea Harriers. No action took place. Encouraged that the British only kept the Boeing under surveillance, operational control of these sorties passed to 1st Air Investigation and Reconnaissance Group, a secretive organization formed by Strategic Air Command specifically to track elements of the Task Force. Long-range missions continued to be flown until 24 April, the day before the British attacked South Georgia, when Argentina was warned, through diplomatic channels, that her Boeing 707s would, henceforth, be fired on without warning. Apart from coastal surveillance, the Boeings were withdrawn until 19 May when one was detected snooping around the Task Force. The destroyers HMS *Bristol* and *Cardiff* both fired Sea Darts, which the Boeing evaded by diving practically to sea level. Nevertheless 2nd Squadron continued to monitor ships using the 'motorway' and was probably involved in several interesting interceptions of shipping, as we shall see.

In May a disagreement developed between the Argentinian Air Force and Argentinian Naval Air Command as to who should provide maritime reconnaissance for Air Force aircraft operating over the sea. Under normal circumstances the Reconnaissance Squadron SP-2H Neptune maritime reconnaissance aircraft, all sold to Argentina by the US in 1977/78, carried out maritime tasks. One Neptune, piloted by Lieutenant-Commander Ernesto Leston, had passed the position of HMS *Sheffield* to attacking Super Etendards, which resulted in her sinking. However, by 21 May the slow Neptunes were withdrawn from operations, which left a large gap in Naval Air Command maritime surveillance. Although their crews were unfamiliar with navigation over the sea, the Air Force 1st Transport Group reluctantly accepted the task and three 1st Squadron C-130s were fitted with rudimentary radar equipment. A major problem was the inability of the aircraft to defend themselves.

On 25 May, at about 11.15am, Wing-Commander Alfredo Cano took off on a five-leg search for British ships off the Falklands, which ended in near disaster when, while stalking HMS *Coventry* for the 5th Fighter Group, he suddenly realized he was within range of the ship's Sea Dart missiles and veered away at speed. Four days later, the 25,000-ton tanker *British Wye*, skippered by Captain David Rundell, was steaming south along the 'motorway', 400 miles north of South Georgia and 1,000 miles from the South American mainland, when she was subjected to a number of low-level passes by an Argentinian C-130. Although there was a naval party on board, most were signallers. The tanker was defenceless. Fitted with Pucara bomb racks, the aircraft again passed over the ship. Fifteen minutes later, it returned at low level, and dropped eight 500lb bombs, four of which fell into the sea without exploding. Shrapnel from three caused minor damage and the eighth bounced off the foredeck without exploding. The attack was significant because that it showed the Argentinians were prepared to interdict the logistic chain from Ascension Island to South Georgia. Losses of ships could have a serious impact on the campaign. Since Woodward was reluctant to release warships to guard it, the 'motorway' was shifted further east, which increased sailing times. At about 9am on the 31st, another Argentinian C-130, intent on attacking the RFA *Fort Grange*, sheered away and made off. Two days later these maritime missions were ceased for several days when two 801 Squadron Sea Harriers, piloted by Lieutenant-Commander Ward and Lieutenant Thomas, shot down a C-130, piloted by Wing Commander Meisner, off Pebble Island. There were no survivors.

On 9 June the Ministry of Defence issued a press statement about another attack. It said that on 8 June, the day that *Sir Galahad* and *Sir Tristram* were bombed in Fitzroy Sound, a message in English had been picked up, at about midday on the distress frequency, by *Uganda* and *Hydra*, both Task Force hospital ships, from the massive 220,000-ton supertanker *Hercules*. The ship was flying the Liberian flag and had been leased by the Maritime Overseas Corporation of New York to carry ballast, i.e. was empty, from Saint Croix in the West Indies around Cape Horn to Valdez in Alaska. Too big to pass though the Panama Canal she was about 500 miles north-east of the Falklands travelling south when she broadcast the mayday. According to the Ministry of Defence, the message was:

> *Preceded by the call sign of an Argentinian radio station (we think in Ushuaia) and specifically addressed to Hercules with her call sign. This carefully identifies the vessel and means that there could have been no doubt as to the nature of the ship or her nationality. The message, which was repeated several times over 30 minutes, is as follows:*
> > *'Steer course 270 west to make Argentinian port. If cannot make port you will be attacked in 15 minutes time.'*
> *The second attack as reported by the Master of Hercules took place shortly after this message. From the description given by the Master, it was evident that a C-130 had carried out two attacks and, hardly being able to miss, had caused sufficient damage for Hercules to take on a 6 degree list and, with two unexploded bombs lodged in her empty but volatile tanks, eventually made Rio de Janeiro.*

This was the only incident throughout the entire campaign when property of a third party was attacked. The Ministry of Defence made it quite clear that *Hercules* was not involved in supplying British Forces.

Leaving Ascension *Queen Elizabeth II* sped south into such increasingly hostile seas that some fitness programmes and some military skills training on board were suspended. Events on the Falklands continued to catch the world's attention.

To the surprise of the British, Task Force *Mercedes* at Goose Green remained dug in behind their defences. It was actually of little threat. Many of the soldiers had been conscripted in February 1982 from towns and villages on Argentina's warm northern borders and thrown into the chill of the Falklands winter. Marching these inexperienced troops north across rough terrain to attack well-prepared troops protecting the San Carlos beachhead would have been near suicidal. Brigadier Thompson rejected raiding Goose Green when it became obvious that no threat was developing from the south. But politicians, in 1982 and still in these days, seem to want to run the military situation almost down to positioning trenches and Thompson was ordered to attack Goose Green, against his wiser instinct. On 26 May the 2nd Parachute Battalion battle group left their positions on Sussex Mountains, 'tabbed' to Camilla Creek House and lay up until the following night. The BBC then compromised the operation by broadcasting that a parachute battalion was about to attack Goose Green. This breach of operational security was probably a journalist deliberately being fed information by a member of Thatcher's War Cabinet to force Thompson's hand.

Shortly after breakfast on 27 May, HMS *Antrim* met the *Queen Elizabeth II* north-east of South Georgia. The destroyer had been at sea continuously for longer than any other Royal Navy surface unit since the Second World War, had led the task force to recapture South Georgia during which she had experienced a storm when huge waves sent white sheets of freezing spray breaking down the length of her hull. In the battle of San Carlos Water, she had been hit by a bomb, which bounced through accommodation below the flight deck and flopped harmlessly into the sea. Major-General Moore, keen to get up to date, selected a small Tactical Headquarters and, taking with him Brigadier Wilson and his Reconnaissance Group, transferred to HMS *Antrim*. This proved an interesting experience because the sea was choppy and the seamanship skills of the *Queen Elizabeth II* boat crews were thoroughly tested. Eventually the soldiers arrived alongside and, assisted by a burly sailor, were hauled on board. Foreman of Signals Baldwin, Headquarters 1st Signal Group, unfortunately broke his leg during the transfer and was taken back on to England on the liner.

For several days, Moore had been starved of information when the sophisticated naval secure communication system on board *Queen*

Elizabeth II failed soon after leaving Ascension. The maritime satellite communications unit was for clear speech and therefore liable to interception. An older defence secure satellite system transmitted without any voice inflection or pitch and was unsuitable for discussing strategic matters. Moore, the commander of the ground forces, was therefore left without a protected communication link to Northwood, to the Task Force and indeed to Headquarters 3rd Commando Brigade. Reliant upon BBC World Service and other international channels broadcasts but in an information vacuum, Moore was unable to issue orders because he had no idea what was happening ashore, to the immense frustration of Brigadier Wilson and his commanders. However, the time was not wasted and in the nine days it took for the liner to hammer its way through the South Atlantic to South Georgia, the headquarters on board exercised and carried out tactical appreciations for landings, including landing at Teal Inlet.

Too much of a political risk to allow direct entry into San Carlos Water, *Queen Elizabeth II* jogged into the snowy tranquillity of Grytviken Harbour at about 11am. At about the same time 2nd Parachute Battalion were squeezing themselves in the buildings and outhouses of Camilla Creek House before then attacking Goose Green. Also in the bay were *Canberra* and *Norland,* which had arrived that morning from San Carlos, to ferry 5th Infantry Brigade into the beach-head. When *Canberra* arrived home with 3rd Commando Brigade on board on 12 July, a banner rather unkindly declared 'P&O goes where Cunard fears to go!' Captain Field of the Blues and Royals had different priorities:

> *We awoke one morning to be overawed by the majestic and startling beauty of Grytviken, where during the course of the 27th of May, we were transferred to the Canberra. Reality was here at last. Not only had the Camembert run out days before and the last bottle of champagne drunk on the QE2, but also the Canberra was announced to be a dry ship.*

Conscious that the BBC World Service had broadcast the arrival of *Queen Elizabeth II* at South Georgia and believing there was a threat from the Argentinian Air Force, the Senior Naval Officer, South Georgia, Captain Nick Barker, who also commanded the polar patrol ship HMS *Endurance*, and Captain Burne, the senior naval officer on the *Canberra*, insisted that the cross-decking of the troops should begin without delay. Also waiting in the harbour were five trawlers of the 11th Counter Measures Squadron, commanded by Lieutenant-Commander David Garwood in the trawler *Pict.* The trawler crews were all Royal Navy and experienced in mine warfare. Each was commanded by a lieutenant and had the distinction of being the only ships taken up from trade entitled to fly the White Ensign. While *Pict* was hired from British United Trawlers of Hull, the other four were from Marr & Sons, also of Hull. Within the hour the Royal Maritime Auxiliary Service tug *Typhoon* and the trawlers *Pict*, *Cordella* and *Farnella* were alongside to cross-deck the two Guards battalions and other units to *Canberra* while the trawlers *Junella* and *Northella* transferred the Gurkhas to *Norland*. The RFA *Stromness* loaded stores. A small captured landing craft was also drafted in to help. Unloading took time, each man clambering down a rope ladder of one liner and up the rope ladder of another. Lance-Sergeant McDermid made the transfer in the landing craft but the worst element for him was that he did not know what was going on. The passage of information had collapsed. Throughout the next night and day, the transfers continued. Staff-Sergeant Andy Peck, of 81 Intelligence Section, later wrote:

> *The actual cross decking was very confusing; chaotic, boring and proved the old adage 'Hurry up and wait'. Corporal Ramsey and I spent nearly three hours sitting on the deck of a trawler getting very cold, as Canberra could not load troops fast enough. Once aboard, it was with real sense of urgency that we practised air attack and abandon ship drills. Sipping soup in the dining room while one's waiters cheerfully regaled you with tales of Mirages swooping in below bridge height not only gave one indigestion but also dispelled the cruise atmosphere quickly. The weather also decided to let us know what the South Atlantic could produce in the way of waves. Conscious of the fact that I had been booked that week for a cruise to Cherbourg on Gladeye, I took to my bed feeling exceptionally seasick.*

Bringing home to the new arrivals that Great Britain was at war were the survivors, including casualties, of sunken warships joining *Queen Elizabeth II* for the trip back to the United Kingdom.

Next day, the 28th, the two 825 Naval Air Squadron Sea Kings and two Wasp helicopters from HMS *Endurance* relieved the pressure on the minesweepers. The offshore patrol vessel HMS *Leeds Castle* was used as a helicopter-refuelling platform. No less than 3,000 men and 250 tons of stores were unloaded from the liner.

The same day 2nd Parachute Battalion, expecting a fourteen-hour battle, initially swept through Argentinian forward positions north of Goose Green with ease until brought to an abrupt halt below Darwin Hill, which was defended with tenacity by a platoon of C Company, 25th Special Infantry Regiment. The predicted fourteen-hours suddenly looked fragile and a forlorn attack up Darwin Hill cost the life of Lieutenant-Colonel Jones, two other officers and a corporal. Soon afterwards, the hill was captured. Major Chris Keeble, the Second-in-Command, assumed command and gave the company commanders latitude in decision-making. The momentum regained, D Company outflanked the 8th Infantry Regiment platoon at Boca House and released B Company to overrun two Air Force security companies defending the western beaches. D Company then headed south-east toward the airstrip and lost three men killed in the tragic misunderstanding of the 'white flag incident'. The press, as usual, only printed half the story. C (Patrol) and D Companies joined to attack the Schoolhouse, which was defended by another platoon from C Company 25th Special Infantry Regiment, mostly survivors of Combat Team Eagle from the Port San Carlos battle, flown in as reinforcements during the day. Low cloud prevented fighter ground support to both sides for most of the day, but, when this lifted; Aeromacchis and Pucaras attacked the paras in the area of the Schoolhouse, one dropping a small napalm bomb. A Pucara was shot down and its pilot captured. Two 35mm Oerlikons on Goose Green promontory, which had shot up C (Patrol) Company as it advanced though A Company on Darwin Hill, were put out of action by the GR3 Harrier strike. By the time night fell Task Force *Mercedes* was in serious trouble. Faced by the threat of a massive sea, artillery and air bombardment, overwhelming odds and with very little chance of relief, surrender was the only alternative.

The loss of Task Forces *Mercedes* did not really affect the Argentinian strategy of sitting tight behind their defences around Stanley. On 26 May Menendez had told Brigadier-General Jofre that he believed that 3rd Commando Brigade would advance to Stanley 'on horse'; that is overland on either side of the Wickham Heights. He believed the British would attack Longdon, Two Sisters and Mount Harriet and then would make their final push on Stanley from the south, along the main track from Goose Green, possibly on the same day. Crucially both men still believed that 5th Infantry Brigade would land on a new sector, possibly in Berkeley Sound, and attack Stanley from the north. Any doubt that there was in 5th Infantry Brigade about its role again disappeared when Argentina vowed to fight on after Goose Green. There was no question that she would climb down, evacuate the occupied territories and allow the British to garrison the dependencies.

By 9pm next day *Canberra* and *Norland* were heading into a Force Ten gale. The North Sea ferry was tossed around like a top, waves smashing into her bridge, some 74 feet above sea level. Below, most of the Gurkhas were seasick and wishing for *terra firma*. The following morning the troops woke up to seeing the Carrier Battle Group around them. Morale, which had slipped at South Georgia, improved. They were in the battle zone and the Welsh Guards deployed forty machine-gun teams on air defence duties. The ships spent the next two days waiting for permission to enter the Total Exclusion Zone and then, during the night of 31 May/1 June, this was received.

4

San Carlos – 29 May to 5 June

29 May is Argentinian Army Day, a day that would forever be remembered in Argentinian military history when 12th Infantry Regiment surrendered at Goose Green. It was also the day when snow first fell across the bleak islands. Broadcasting to the Argentinian people and referring to the catastrophe, President Galtieri told of the continuing battle on the Falklands:

> At this time of supreme sacrifice before the altar of the country, with all the humility that a man of the armed forces may have deep in his heart, I kneel before God, because only before Him do the knees of an Argentinian soldier bend. The Country's arms will continue fighting the enemy for every Argentinian portion of land, sea and sky, with growing courage and efficiency, because the soldier's bravery is nourished by the blood and sacrifice of his fallen brothers.

But among the Argentinian forces in Stanley, in armed forces frequently at odds with the government and with deep political divisions, the first seeds of discontent began to surface. The 6th Infantry Regiment chaplain, Father Domingo de Paulis, met with Lieutenant-Colonel Mohammed Seineldin, the ardent Malvinist who commanded 25th Special Infantry Regiment, and Major Aldo Rico, who commanded the newly-arrived 602 Commando Company. All were highly critical of the performance of Brigadier-Generals Menendez, Parada and Jofre so far and plotted their removal from their commands. Lieutenant-Colonel Jorge Halperin, an old friend of Seineldin, agreed to deploy his 6th Infantry Regiment to guard the various approaches into Stanley and thus free up the two Army Commando Companies to deal with officers loyal to the Junta. The 6th Regiment and commandos would then hand over to the 25th Infantry Regiment. But Seineldin changed his mind and no more dissention was raised for a few days

Meanwhile the Type 21 frigate HMS *Avenger* inserted a G Squadron patrol to watch the 5th and 8th Infantry Regiments at Port Howard and Fox Bay respectively. Ships on the Stanley gunline bombarding Stanley Common were surprised when the Argentinian 155mm gunners of D Battery, 3rd Artillery Group, learning the specialization of coastal gunnery under active service conditions, returned fire. Harrier pilots harassing Stanley found that they were now up against anti-aircraft gunners gaining in experience. During the evening a stripped-down 9th Air Transport Group Twin Otter, flying from Argentina, recovered two Air Force pilots, three Navy pilots, a seriously ill naval rating and the body of an Air Force pilot from Pebble Island.

During the early morning, about fifty miles east of the Falklands, HMS *Antrim* met with HMS *Fearless,* which had left San Carlos Water that night and was bringing Commodore Clapp to meet Major-General Moore. Brigadier Thompson was still at San Carlos on unfinished business – the surrender of Task Force *Mercedes.* Moore, Wilson and their key staff were transferred by an 845 Naval Air Squadron Wessex and were no sooner aboard when an Air Raid Warning Red was sounded for an incoming Exocet. Nothing happened, but it was enough to introduce the newcomers to the war. Screened by HMS *Active* both ships then battled their way through mountainous seas and met with HMS *Hermes* for an afternoon conference between Moore, Wilson, Clapp and Rear-Admiral Woodward. Strangely in his collaborative *One Hundred Days,* Woodward does not mention this important meeting. With Moore and Wilson now in theatre, the Task Force structure issued on 9 April had been reorganized on 12 May as follows:

❐ *Combined Task Group 317.0 was still Commodore Clapp, but now designated Commodore Inshore Naval Operations and Logistic Support as opposed to Commodore Amphibious Task Force, inferring that he was no longer expected to command amphibious operations.*

❐ *Combined Task Group 317.1 was Headquarters Land Force Falkland Islands, which was commanded by Major-General Moore as Commander Land Force Falkland Islands. Under command he had:*

  • *Combined Task Unit 317.1.1 – 3rd Commando Brigade.*

  • *Combined Task Unit 317.1.2 – 5th Infantry Brigade.*

Amphibious warfare doctrine suggests that the land force commander, in this case Major-General Moore, and the amphibious commander, in Clapp's case equivalent to a brigadier, ought to be of equal rank. With an enlarged amphibious element to the campaign Clapp suggested that to ease inter-Service command and control and enhance co-ordinated staff work, he should be appointed Chief-of-Staff (Navy) to Moore but this suggestion was rejected by Woodward, who said that he should remain as Combined Task Group 317.0 in case he needed to command ships. Technically it was Northwood's decision. As the most junior in rank of the triumvirate, Clapp was now in an invidious position and he hoped that his contribution would not be affected by his lower rank. Little did he realize just how much Northwood would interfere with decisions he was making as the man on the spot.

With more command and control assets joining the Task Force, the provision of secure communications was becoming an issue, a problem that was helpfully solved when Moore located his headquarters on HMS *Fearless*. As we have already seen, its Amphibious Operations Room was only designed to handle the equivalent of a battalion headquarters. Headquarters 3rd Commando Brigade had found it too small and the larger Headquarters Land Forces would also find it inadequate. However, it was a case of needs must.

Ashore Brigadier Thompson had another problem to resolve – the seizure of Mount Kent by the Special Air Service. A feature of uneven ridges and valleys about fourteen miles from Stanley, both sides knew that whoever held Mount Kent dominated the approaches to the town. Its occupation meant that the British would then have a formidable fortress close to Stanley. We shall examine this battle because its seizure forced 5th Infantry Brigade to make decisions when, perhaps, it was not in a position to do so.

When 12th Infantry Regiment arrived in late April, Combat Team *Solari*, which was centred on First-Lieutenant Ignacio Gorriti's B Company, was sent to defend the 601 Combat Aviation Battalion helicopter base on Mount Kent. The experienced Captain Eduardo Corsiglia commanded the force. The Argentinians did not know that for three weeks Captain Wight's Special Air Service patrol had monitored the helicopters and, during the morning of the 21 May, had guided a GR 3 Harrier raid in which several troop-carrying helicopters were destroyed. On 28 May all but Second-Lieutenant Mosterin's platoon reinforced the doomed garrison at Goose Green and was sucked into its surrender. Had Combat Team *Solari* remained on Mount Kent or another unit, such B Company, 6th Infantry Regiment, which had a 'fire fighting' role, been sent to replace it, the story about to unfold might have had a different ending.

During the night of 23/24 May D Squadron, Special Air Service, inserted a reconnaissance patrol on to Mount Kent with the promise of reinforcements. On the 25th Lieutenant-Colonel Mike Rose persuaded Lieutenant-Colonel Nick Vaux, who commanded 42 Commando, to occupy Mount Kent because he believed the feature to be lightly held and therefore vulnerable to an Argentinian *coup de main* but this was shelved because helicopters were needed to rescue survivors from HMS *Coventry*. Sergeant Peter Ratcliffe, who was serving with D Squadron, recalls that an attempt the following night was unsuccessful when poor weather and the difficult navigation led to the troops being landed in the wrong place. They were recovered, but defeating Task Force *Mercedes* meant that most helicopters were then directed to supporting 2nd Parachute Battalion. During the night of 28/29 May, while the British waited for the Goose Green garrison to surrender, more of D Squadron was successfully landed east of Mount Kent and then instructed to secure a landing zone for the fly-in of 42 Commando the following night.

The same day Brigadier-General Menendez assembled his Special Forces into a single formation under his direct command, the Special Forces Group, and issued orders to his Chief-of-Staff, Brigadier-General Daher, to establish a north-south light screen, gather intelligence on 3rd Commando Brigade's advance and capture British soldiers as a morale-boosting measure. This was known as Operation *Autoimpuesta*. Available to him he had 601 Commando Company, which was commanded by Major Mario Castagneto, Wing-Commander Alberto Cajihara's forty-strong Air Force Special Operations Group and two recently arrived units, 602 Commando Company, commanded by Major Rico, and 601 National Gendarmerie Special Forces Squadron, a border guard unit commanded by Major Spadaro.

During morning of 29 May Daher met with Castagneto, Rico, Colonel Francisco Cervo, Menendez's senior Intelligence Officer, and Colonel Isidoro Bonifacio Caceres, the Chief-of-Operations, and agreed that Mount Kent must be seized at the earliest opportunity because 'prompt and decisive action is necessary to deal with the British incursion into Stanley.' Nothing was known about British operations. Seemingly no one knew that the Second-Lieutenant Mosterin's Combat Team *Solari* platoon had been withdrawn from Mount Kent to Mount Harriet. The Special Forces Group set about planning the operation:

❐ *Mount Estancia. 601 Commando Company to establish an observation post once Mount Kent had been captured.*

❐ *Mount Simon. To be occupied by 1st Assault Section, 602 Commando Company.*

❐ *Mount Kent. Three phase operation:*
- *2nd and 3rd Assault Section, 602 Commando Company to gain a foothold on 29 May.*
- *The sixty-five-strong National Gendarmerie Special Forces Squadron to seize the summit, known as 'little Cerro Aconcagua'. This force totalled about seventy-seven men.*

- *Major Jaimet's B Company, 6th Infantry Regiment, to provide a strong defence.*

☐ *Smoko Mount. To be seized by the Special Operations Group.*

On 28 May when Lieutenant-Colonel Vaux received formal orders to seize Mount Kent, he invited his 'hacks', which included the ubiquitous Max Hastings, to the briefing and advised them there was no room for them in the helicopters. Hastings was already proving to be a bit of a nuisance. Vaux's plan was for Peter Babbington's K Company to seize the summit and then L Company, 7 Commando Battery, Mortar Troop and a Blowpipe section from the Royal Marine Air Defence Troop to follow in the second lift. The next day Vaux waited for the helicopters but when none had appeared by midday, this worried him because a heliborne assault demands considerable co-ordination. He had taken part in Great Britain's first such assault at Suez in 1956. Eventually a passing Wessex was talked down but the pilot knew nothing about the operation. The surviving Chinook from *Atlantic Conveyor, Bravo November,* then arrived followed by an 846 Squadron Sea King assault helicopter. The Chinook pilot, Squadron-Leader Dick Langworthy, clearly exhausted after the demands placed on his aircaft, offered to fly in the guns if the Sea Commando would take the troops. But the Royal Navy pilot said he could fly only two sorties, but three were needed. Vaux was understandably furious and told Major John Chester, Brigadier Thompson's Chief-of-Staff, that, like thousands of front-line officers before him and since, he had been let down by Brigade Headquarters. Tension in the command post was already electric and eventually the required helicopters appeared.

At Stanley football field, as the Argentinian commandos gathered in the bitter cold evening, the sky darkened with ominous snow-laden clouds. The fly-out, using four UH-1H Iroquois of B Assault Company, 601 Combat Aviation Battalion, was planned to be in two waves. Shortly before departure, Captains Eduardo Villarruel and Jorge Duran said they were coming out with Headquarters Section in a Puma. After a seven-minute flight, the helicopters touched down on the eastern slopes of Mount Kent. To the Special Air Service on the mountain the distinctive beat of the four Huey helicopters and a Puma approaching from the east, bringing in twenty-nine Argentinian commandos consisting of Captain Villaruel's five-strong HQ Section and Captains Fernandez' 2nd and Ferrero's 3rd Assault Sections, 602 Commando Company, both twelve-strong, was unexpected.

For the Argentinians things went wrong almost immediately. In the wintry darkness the helicopters became separated and Fernandez's section landed near Bluff Cove Peak where his arrival was detected by a Mountain and Arctic Warfare Cadre patrol. A front of rain and thick wet mist then blanketed Stanley and Lieutenant-Colonel Juan Scarpa, the senior Army helicopter pilot, had no option but cancel the remainder of the fly-out until 8am the next day. 602 Commando Company, which had only arrived a few days earlier, was on its own.

Ferrero's men advanced up the steep slopes, the thought of bumping into a British patrol or walking into an ambush keeping them alert. After about 500 metres Ferrero went forward with two men to investigate a noise. They had hardly covered 50 metres when they came under accurate machine gun and mortar fire from Air Troop, D Squadron. First-Sergeant Raimundo Viltes was badly wounded when a bullet shattered his heel. The lack of information about friendly operations led First-Lieutenant Horacio Lauria, a commando engineer, to believe that the firing came from Combat Team *Solari*, which he thought was in the area. But the weight of fire and type of weapons used, clearly British, shocked the Argentinians. Against their expectations, Mount Kent was occupied and a confused firefight broke out. Not sure of the strength of the opposition and with his section scattered, Ferrero decided to withdraw and, as another snowstorm hurtled across the bleak slopes, he, Ovieda and First-Lieutenant Francisco Maqueda scrambled downhill on their bottoms, sending noisy avalanches of stones cascading down the mountain. Oviedo became separated in the darkness. The sudden scuttling of rocks led Air Troop to believe they were in danger of being surrounded and they withdrew higher up Mount Kent, shepherding two wounded soldiers with them.

Meanwhile the insertion of 42 Commando had run into trouble. After dark K Company boarded four Sea Commandos and set off for Mount Kent in snowstorms much worse than most of the pilots had encountered, even in Norway. In 'white-out' conditions, they landed time and again to pick up visual references but it soon became obvious that the mission would have to be abandoned. In near pitch blackness, extremely poor visibility and sudden snowstorms, the pilots groped their way back to San Carlos and deposited the Royal Marines, thoroughly relieved to be back on *terra firma*, after two hours confined in a noisy metal tube.

At about 11am next day, the 30th, Captain Fernandez and his 2nd Assault Section, knowing that Ferrero had been in contact with British, emerged from their hide intending to occupy Bluff Cove Peak. With Sergeant Humberto Blas and First-Lieutenant Daniel Oneto, First Lieutenant Ruben Marquez scouting ahead, the section collided with the Special Air Service Tactical Headquarters and a firefight developed.

Marquez threw some grenades but was still killed because he was wearing gloves and was unable to use his FAL rifle. Blas also died. The ambush effectively caught Fernandez's section off balance and they withdrew into some small caves and rock runs where, while British patrols searched for them, they remained for the rest of the day. Captain Villaruel had landed on Mount Kent and, avoiding contact, withdrew to Bluff Cove Mountain to establish a field headquarters for Major Rico. He watched a five-man British patrol heading for Estancia pass below. They then contacted an Army helicopter redeploying the 4th Infantry Regiment from Mount Wall to Two Sisters and Mount Harriet and gave the pilot a map reference to pass on to Rico. Shortly afterwards two Royal Air Force Harriers screamed overhead and rocketed suspected Argentinian positions on Mount Kent identified by D Squadron. It was about 11am.

Harrier combat air patrols had delayed the fly-out of the Gendarmerie and thus it was not until shortly before 11am that their Puma took off but near Murrell Bridge it crashed, killing six and injuring eight. Mystery surrounds the crash but it may be that the helicopter was either brought down by Argentinian ground fire from soldiers on Two Sisters or Mount Longdon or, more likely, it clipped the ground avoiding rockets from the two Harriers which had passed over Villaruel's position.

Operation *Autoimpuesta* had not gone well and worse was to follow when all contact was lost with 1st Assault Section, 602 Commando Company. It had been destroyed in a short battle with the Mountain and Arctic Warfare Cadre at Top Malo House. Major Rico was appointed by Menendez to take command of Special Forces operations. Cancelling the deployment of 601 Commando Company, he instructed Major Castagneto to rescue the remnants of 602 Commando Company. With Malvinas Joint Command believing that the aircraft-carrier HMS *Invincible* had been sunk the day before and a retaliatory raid by the Special Air Service against the TPS-AN43 long-range Early Warning radar predicted, the Air Force Special Operations Group were withdrawn from the Special Forces Group to protect it.

At Headquarters 3rd Commando Brigade it seemed that D Squadron was under pressure on Mount Kent but information was scarce on enemy intentions and strength. Abandoning the feature and regrouping at Estancia were discussed but Brigadier Thompson, keen to dominate Stanley, told Lieutenant-Colonel Rose that he must hang on. Help was on its way.

The plan to insert 42 Commando improved significantly with the arrival of a Royal Navy Mobile Air Operations Team. Aviation matters also improved when 845 and 846 Naval Air Squadrons moved ashore to a forward operating base in a gully about a mile north of the Ajax bay refrigeration plant. Once again Captain Peter Babbington's K Company would lead. Taking advantage of a small window of favourable weather, shortly after dusk the three Sea Commandos hurried for Mount Kent, the pilots peering into the darkness with goggles.

At about the same time Fernandez's 2nd Assault Section, having hidden all day, emerged from their hides intending to withdraw from the area. But the Special Air Service was alert and again the Argentinians found themselves in a firefight, which was made worse when the British brought up at least one 60mm mortar. Fernandez broke contact and in the scramble down the hill Sergeant Alfredo Flores, the section radio operator, fell and was knocked out. When he came to his senses he was the prisoner of a Special Air Service clearing patrol and was later interrogated at 'Hotel Galtieri' in the farmyard at San Carlos along with the Army commandos captured at Top Malo House.

K Company were landed on the lower western slopes and, although startled by the battle, immediately headed for the summit. Flying the surviving Chinook, Squadron-Leader Langworthy then flew in the guns but, finding that the rear undercarriage tended to sink in the mud, expertly kept it at a very low hover while the twenty-two commando gunners dragged two Light Guns down the cargo ramp. The third gun was lowered from its underslung load. When Lieutenant-Colonel Vaux learnt of the fighting on Mount Kent, he halted the fly-in of the rest of his Commando but told the pilots to keep their engines running until the Chinook returned and he had a better idea of what was happening. Leaving Mount Kent at low level and a fierce snowstorm playing havoc with Langworthy's visual and technological navigation, the helicopter briefly splashed into a stream midway between Mount Kent and Teal Inlet, causing slight damage. Gunning the motors, Langworthy climbed out of trouble and on his return to San Carlos mentioned that the Special Air Service had the situation under control, which did not seem to be the case to everyone else listening to the radios.

The delay eroded the Sea Commando fuel margins and Vaux revised the schedule to a single lift to take L Company, palleted artillery ammunition and other essential personnel at the expense of rations and fuel Safety regulations cast aside. The Royal Marines and Lieutenant-Colonel Rose's headquarters piled in on top of ammunition and spare radios batteries; such is the luxury in war, of breaking the rulebook. When the Commando Regimental Sergeant Major David Chisnall had finished squeezing everyone into the helicopter, he noted that Max Hastings had also infiltrated on board claiming that he had personally been given a seat by Brigadier Thompson to accompany Rose. He could hardly claim to be essential and his reason turned out to be untrue, but such is the self-importance of journalists. Chisnall was not happy but squeezed him in. As a punishment for his dishonesty, Vaux later gave Hastings a Blowpipe missile to carry to the summit of Mount Kent. Fifteen minutes later, with the battle between Fernandez and Air Troop still being fought with Special Air Service mortars bombarding the Argentinians, the helicopters lurched on to Mount Kent landing site.

On landing, Vaux was told by Major Cedric Delves, who commanded D Squadron, that he had been operating only in the valleys around Mount Kent and it was still not known if the summit was secure. In Vaux's words, 'It seemed best not to appear surprised, although back at Brigade HQ they certainly believed the summit had been scouted.' His concern that K Company might encounter a strong enemy force turned to relief when Babbington radioed, shortly before dawn, that the Special Air Service seemed not to have scouted the area but that nevertheless he had reached the summit to find evidence of a rapid Argentinian pullout. A secondary position covering the path down to the Murrell Bridge had also been found. It will be recalled that most of Combat Team *Solari* had been sent to Goose Green as reinforcements and left nearly all their equipment behind.

With no sign of the Gendarmerie or 601 Commando Company and not knowing what was happening, Villaruel, Fernandez and Ferrero linked up and set off for Stanley at midday on 31 May in the hope that several missing men would turn up. When First-Lieutenant Daniel Oneto and Second-Lieutenant Damasco Soraides, of Ferrero's section, reached Mount Longdon, a 7th Regiment conscript on the western slopes, seeing men wearing camouflaged uniforms and believing they might be British, raised the alarm. Second-Lieutenant Juan Baldini, whose platoon covered the sector, prevented First-Sergeant Pedro Lopez's 81mm mortar detachment from opening fire and calamity was averted. It took at least a day for First-Lieutenant Lauria and Sergeant Jose Nunez to help Sergeant Viltes hobble to Estancia from where he was evacuated to Stanley. No one turned up from the 1st Assault Section. Ten years later, at The Falklands Veterans Welcome Home March in Buenos Aires on 2 April 1992, Viltes led 30,000 veterans of the war past President Carlos Menem on crutches and wearing his crisp brown uniform and his Army Commando green beret.

After a struggle of two days intermittent fighting, Mount Kent was in British hands and Brigadier Thompson now had a springboard from which to launch the assault on Stanley.

Chopped back to 5th Infantry Brigade after Goose Green, 2nd Parachute Battalion were virtually independent while they waited for it to arrive but they had not been idle. The Darwin settlement manager, Brooke Hardcastle, suggested to Major Dair Farrar-Hockley, whose A Company was still on Darwin Hill, that someone should telephone Bluff Cove, speak to Kevin Hannaway and find out what was happening in the Fitzroy and Bluff Cove area. Connecting the two settlements was Fitzroy Bridge. Its loss would mean at least a fourteen-mile cross-country detour around Fitzroy Creek to Bluff Cove, most of which was unsuitable for vehicles. Seizing both settlements would also give some protection to 3rd Commando Brigade's right flank and provide an assembly area for the 5th Infantry Brigade's attack on Stanley. Farrar-Hockley told Major Keeble of this eminently sensible suggestion. When some paras were sent to Burntside House to use the telephone, they found that the lines to the east were down and an audacious plan was drawn up to advance to the nearest settlement – Swan Inlet House. Major John Crosland, who commanded B Company and was former Special Air Service, was given the task. He allocated Lieutenant Chris Chapman's 6 Platoon, then on stand-by to raid Mount Usborne, where it was suspected the Argentinians were manning navigation outposts as a way marker to Military Air Base Stanley. Captain Greenhalgh provided his three Scout helicopters.

Next day, 30 May, in the clear wintry sun of a Falklands early morning, HMS *Fearless* glided past Fanning Head and into the calm, silent waters of San Carlos. A member of Headquarters 3rd Commando Brigade observed the arrival of Major-General Moore:

I had slept particularly well that night and was woken by someone frantically shaking me "Major-General Moore is coming ashore with his staff and the HQ 5th Infantry Brigade advance party. Stand-by to brief in the farmyard." I struggled out of my sleeping bag, grabbed my webbing and weapon and walked to the farmyard where I was relieved to find that the ever-reliable Corporal Bob Birkett had already arranged for a map to be displayed. Some chairs were collected from all over the place. We saw the LCU leave HMS Fearless and butt her way to Blue Beach. It was a glorious sunny early morning if chilly. While waiting, I learnt Tactical HQ would be moving that day.

Major-General Moore, who was wearing a Norwegian Army summer soft cap, strode up the path from San Carlos followed by a gaggle of officers, some with their trousers wet up to the knees. I had the pleasure of renewing my acquaintance with a squadron leader who I had last seen in Norway during the winter. When everyone was sat down, Major-General Moore said he would wear his cap in order not to patronize the Green Beret of the Commando Brigade and offend the Red Beret tradition of 5th Infantry Brigade. Major Chester, Thompson's Chief-of-Staff, briefed on the current situation. The Commando Brigade had split two ways with 2nd Parachute Battalion down at Goose Green and 45 Commando and 3rd Parachute Battalion marching for Douglas and Teal Inlet respectively.

40 Commando, the Commando Logistic Regiment and Brigade HQ were still confined to the beachhead. The enemy had not yet reacted to their defeat at Goose Green.

Brigadier Thompson gave his views on the situation and then handed over to Major-General Moore who concluded by ordering the two Brigade HQs to meet and plan the defeat of the enemy on the basis that 3rd Commando Brigade was to continue its northerly axis while 5th Infantry Brigade took the southerly route. For us who had been ashore for the seven days, talk of the approach to Port Stanley was exciting and we looked forward to leaving San Carlos.

I noticed a scruffy unkempt individual, whom I recognized to be the journalist Robert Fox, pushing himself forward to speak to Brigadier Thompson. He had been at Goose Green and I recognized the nervousness of a man recently exposed to unusual danger. I edged forward and listened as he described the battle emphasizing that at one stage the group he was with had been pinned down for five hours. He analysed the Argentinian surrender to be a matter of honour, which did not seem to add up considering the tactical situation. He expressed some concern for the civilians at Port Stanley who could be held hostage; they were anyway.

Fox was then introduced to Major-General Moore, who seemed a little impatient with him. Moore said he had landed to take the political pressure off Brigadier Thompson and allow him to advance on Port Stanley. This statement was a relief, for the political pressures imposed on our Commander had begun to seep through to some members of the HQ Staff. Every time we saw him going on board HMS Fearless to use the satellite communication link, we sympathized – another reprimand from someone 8,000 miles away with very little concept of our difficulties.

Returning to the Intelligence Section, I was delighted to find that Colour-Sergeant Neil Smith had brought the remainder of the team ashore all of whom were thoroughly relieved to be off HMS Fearless. Neil told me he had been ferried ashore in the same LCU as Major-General Moore. When it reached the beach, the ramp splashed down and all the officers looked at the widening expanse of cold water between it and the beach. 'Troops Out!' This explained the wet trousers. The coxswain then told Neil to remain where he was and took the landing craft alongside the jetty and our Royal Marines landed dry shod.

Thompson and Clapp had both agreed that opening up a flank to the south of Wickham Heights along the Darwin to Stanley track was unnecessary and open to considerable risk. The coast was low-lying and full on inlets in which patrol craft could lurk and, since it was not well charted, a navigational nightmare, particularly at night. Thompson favoured the idea of using 5th Infantry Brigade to secure San Carlos Water and Darwin Peninsula to block an Argentinian counter-attack from the south. Clapp relayed this view to Rear-Admiral Woodward. In the event that an opportunity to capture Stanley arose before 5th Infantry Brigade arrived, Thompson had planned that 3rd Commando Brigade should:

❏ Occupy the arc of high ground from Long Island Mount through Mount Kent to Mount Challenger in preparation for a night assault on Stanley.

- 45 Commando to take Two Sisters.
- 42 Commando to tackle Mount Harriet.
- 3rd Parachute Battalion to seize Mount Longdon.

❏ If resistance was light and there was still sufficient darkness and casualties did not decrease combat effectiveness, the Brigade was to continue the advance with:

- 3rd Parachute Battalion taking Wireless Ridge.
- 45 Commando assaulting Mount Tumbledown and Mount William.
- 42 Commando on immediate reserve.
- 40 Commando and 2nd Parachute Battalion to be Brigade reserve.

❏ The Brigade would then seize Sapper Hill on a one battalion frontage and break out on to the flatter ground of Stanley Common with the units leapfrogging into a thoroughly demoralized Argentinian army.

Moore was aware that Woodward's ships were taking a pounding from the South Atlantic and it would be only a matter of time before they and their crews became non-operational. He was therefore keen to attack Stanley as soon as practical. His plan was for 3rd Commando Brigade to left-hook from the north while 5th Infantry Brigade opened up the southern flank and right-hooked from the south, its objectives being Tumbledown and Mount William. 3rd Commando Brigade would seize Wireless Ridge. Although there was an opportunity to reform both brigades by sending 3rd Parachute Battalion back to 5th Infantry Brigade, Moore left it with 3rd Commando Brigade. 2nd Parachute Battalion remained under command of 5th Infantry Brigade. While Thompson kept the Mountain and Arctic Warfare Cadre, the Special Air Service and Special Boat Service were to be tasked by Headquarters Land Forces, principally for operations on West Falklands. To defend San Carlos, Moore initially preferred one of the Guards battalions, but eventually opted for 40 Commando, much to the frustration of its Commanding Officer, Lieutenant-Colonel Malcolm Hunt. The Royal Marines were better equipped and trained in amphibious and helicopter work to deal with any Argentinian interdiction from West Falklands than the Guards, whose expertise was mechanized infantry warfare. The Gurkhas were also to remain at Goose Green and deal with any Argentinians who had escaped to Lafonia.

Following the briefing, Brigadier Wilson flew to 2nd Parachute Battalion at Goose Green to outline his plan to advance to the Port Pleasant sector. Expected to open up the southern flank, he was already under pressure but his Brigade had been rushed south, had not landed and yet was being committed to an advance to contact, but minus half its stores and with little tactical preparation. Things did not go well from the start. During Exercise *Green Lanyard* in February 2nd Parachute Battalion had lost confidence in Wilson's general tactical ability and methods of handling parachute troops, at least that was their opinion. Their confidence was further reduced when he arrived wearing a red beret and green hunter Wellington boots, a dress code that offended Parachute Regiment airborne sensitivities and undermined his authority as leader – again their view. Others thought Wilson's dress code sensible and his Light Infantry dark green beret represented a far longer and more glorious history.

Wilson rejected Keeble's Swan Inlet House plan and, using a large map covered in symbols so loved by Staff College instructors of the period, explained that he intended to march to Port Pleasant with 2nd Parachute Battalion securing his left flank by picketing Mount Usborne and Wickham Heights, which, by this time, were covered in snow. Since there were no decent beaches, everything would have to be carried or flown. Military etiquette cast aside, his proposal drew the memorable response from one of the company commanders 'Brigadier, are you fucking pissed?' Although the officer was not aware of the pressures Wilson was under, he had a point.

Between 1945 and the late 1980s British military doctrine on command and control centred on Restrictive Control in which commanders issued detailed orders. These sometimes failed to take into account enemy reactions and unforeseen eventualities. Wilson, and others before and after him, was taught this throughout his career from the time he entered Sandhurst until he took command of 5th Infantry Brigade. It was a necessary strategy because of the multi-national command structure of NATO and a political policy forced on the British in its internal security campaigns since 1945. The closer to home, the more stringent the restraints, in particular in Northern Ireland where some military activities appear to be criminal offences, at least according to the police. There was little room for imaginative strategy by senior commanders.

The alternative was Directive Control, which had been widely practised by German armies for at least two centuries. This strategy accepts that battle is chaotic but can be exploited by flexible, imaginative and quick-thinking command and control at all levels. However, its weakness is that opportunities taken by commanders may not comply with the general strategy and therefore success is at risk. The problem was that the history and culture of the Parachute Regiment demands Directive Control. The few times its battalions had operated with armoured and mechanized infantry in a NATO setting were not exactly successful.

Both military doctrines had been displayed at Goose Green. Lieutenant-Colonel Jones' detailed orders were unable to deal with a crisis at Darwin Hill without his direct intervention, at least that appears to have been his belief. On Jones' death, Major Keeble's flexible command style allowed the company commanders to fight their battles. But in the British Army of 1982, there was little acceptance of those who played 'fast and loose' by practising Directive Control, no matter how successful. It was usually career limiting.

Common to both stratagems was for the plan to be made known to every man in the unit, a requirement that takes time as the commanding officer briefs his company commanders who then develop the plan and briefs their platoon commanders until the most junior soldier knows his part in the plan. If a unit is spread over a wide area, the communication can take time.

The naval equivalent is Mission Command. By its very nature, sea warfare requires flexibility and historically naval commanders have greater flexibility in command and control. 'Here is your problem. Here are the resources. You are the man on the spot. Solve it and let me know when you have finished. By the way, try not lose your ship or else you will be court-martialled' Unfortunately, mistakes often end up in court-martial but more than one successful admiral had previously been court-martialled! The man on the spot makes the decisions; at least that is the theory. Communication is much easier. A flotilla commander briefs his commanding officers and they brief their men using the ship's tannoy and therefore changes in the plan are much easier to achieve. There is no doubt that some naval officers did not appreciate the difficulties of the ground forces. It is also a fact that in ground forces engagements, the action of a small unit can lose a battle or one man can win it by closing with the enemy.

Wilson's strategy was thus typical of the Cold War military doctrine of positional warfare that prevailed at the time. 2nd Parachute Battalion was essentially a light infantry battalion, which traditionally provided advance guards, rearguards and flank protection but committing them to the Wickham Heights without sustained support was risky. 45 Commando had already found that its 'yomp' to Douglas, with each man initially carrying an average 120lbs, was a sobering experience. The Blues and Royals had collected stragglers from the 3rd Parachute Battalion 'tab' to Teal Inlet. So far as marching to Fitzroy is concerned, the track from Burntside House to Stanley in winter was unsuitable for mass movement of men and vehicles.

When the briefing broke up, Wilson was angry at 2nd Parachute Battalion's response to his plan. He was, after all, the Brigade Commander. But the Battalion was full of imaginative officers and NCOs who had just won a highly-publicized battle. The Argentinians had not reacted to their defeat at Goose Green and remained sealed behind their walls in Stanley. This was now a time to reject the structured strategy of Restrictive Command for positional warfare and exploit Directive Command of 'get on with winning the battle within these loose parameters'.

On 1 June *Atlantic Causeway* arrived in San Carlos Water and landed 63 Squadron, Royal Air Force Regiment, its ninety vehicles and eight Rapiers, with their all-weather 'Blindfire' radar, to take over the air defence of the anchorage. The twenty Wessexes of 847 and four Sea Kings of 825 Naval Air Squadrons were flown ashore, the latter immediately deploying to help move the Goose Green prisoners while the Wessexes moved north to support 3rd Commando Brigade. Crews soon found ground operations were far less comfortable and wetter than on ships.

Next day there was general relief, ashore and on board, when *Canberra* and *Norland* nosed through the fog and drizzle of a grey dawn into San Carlos Water and anchored south of Fanning Island. Argentinian air raids were unlikely, but so anxious was Captain Burne, the senior naval officer on board, about the vulnerability of the ship that within thirteen minutes a landing craft was alongside to ferry the troops ashore. Four ship's boats were also lowered to help in the disembarkation. It was hoped to unload the 3,000 men by the end of the day, which seemed vastly optimistic by any imagination. It had taken over twenty-four hours to cross-deck the Brigade at Grytviken.

As far as 5th Infantry Brigade, and everyone else, was concerned, three weeks to the day since leaving Southampton in such a hurry, this was not an assault landing but an administrative landing. An administrative landing is one in which troops are landed on secure beaches. One of the first units ashore was Lieutenant Ash's 407 Troop, Royal Corps of Transport, to set up the Brigade Maintenance Area and over the next fortnight, his men worked ceaselessly to land men, stores and equipment. Communications were a problem and, at one stage, Ash had detachments at Fitzroy and San Carlos and on the *Nordic Ferry* and HMS *Dumbarton Castle*. BV 202s loaned from the Commando Logistic Regiment and requisitioned tractors were invaluable for moving supplies from beaches through muddy moorland to dumps.

Disembarkation was hazardous. Most helicopters were committed to supplying 3rd Commando Brigade and so 5th Infantry Brigade was reliant on water transport. Using the ship's tannoy, units were called forward to the Pilot's door where a rope ladder was draped into a landing craft. Festooned with their battle order webbing, personal and support weapons, radios and ammunition belts, the troops, one at a time, scrambled, jumped or fell into the landing craft. The 2nd Parachute Battalion had experienced exactly the same problems disembarking from *Norland* on 21 May and, as a consequence, 3rd Commando Brigade's landing schedule was slipped by an hour. It took twenty-four hours of continuous ship-to-shore shuttling before the two passenger ships were empty and could return to the safety of deep water. The ever-willing ship's crew on *Canberra* formed a chain gang to move bergens and heavy equipment. According to Clapp, Burne commented harshly on the perceived lack of urgency of the Army and Clapp himself was tetchy. Both were concerned about Argentinian air raids, but the weather was poor and cloud base low, almost perfect weather for an efficient disembarkation. Burne could have been helped by arranging for a gangway to be lowered so that the heavily laden soldiers could have stepped into a landing craft.

An added complication was that while some of the Brigade's vehicles and stores were being unloaded from the *Baltic Ferry*, *Nordic Ferry* was not scheduled to arrive for another day and it would take four days before she was empty. The fourth ship carrying Brigade stores, the *Tor Caledonia*, did not arrive until after the Argentinian surrender on 14 June. The Headquarters and Signal Squadron managed to land a few Land Rovers fitted with radios. Some vital stores never reached their units. The gun sights of 97 Battery took days to arrive and the gunners were reliant upon quadrants and prismatic compasses. The Battery never received field cookers or cooking equipment.

The units landed with no firmer orders than they were to move into defensive positions. 1st Welsh Guards dug in around the general area of Old Horse Paddock, which is about three miles south of San Carlos. Near Battalion Headquarters, 81mm mortar ammunition and rations dumped by 2nd Parachute Battalion were appropriated by Mortar Platoon. The Scots Guards took over positions around San Carlos. The 1/7th Gurkhas scurried ashore 'like heat-seeking ferrets' thoroughly thankful to be off *Norland* and ashore in an environment which they understood. The Chinook then flew them to Goose Green, which released J Company to rejoin 42 Commando. Major Mike Kefford's D Company deployed to 2nd Parachute Battalion's draughty positions on Sussex Mountain. As 3rd Commando Brigade had discovered, digging was a nightmare of water-filled trenches and so peat sangars became the order of the day. Father Alfred Hayes, the 5th Infantry Brigade Roman Catholic chaplain:

> *Once ashore, the order came from RSM Bill Hunt 'Gentlemen, dig in or else you will die'. This spurred us into digging shell scrapes above Blue Beach. I cooked some soup, then went over to the place that I though it best to be, the Field Ambulance. There I encountered difficulties with the CO, who told me that he didn't want a Chaplain since, in his experience, the sight of a priest at a dying man's side made the man give up. I said that in my four years as hospital chaplain in a large general hospital before joining the Army, I never had that experience, and had usually found that patients got genuine comfort from the priest.*

It was an extraordinary statement for the medical unit commanding officer to make. Taken aback, Hayes patched up the disagreement and managed to get himself billeted in the Field Ambulance Command Post, which was located in the house of Paddy Short, the San Carlos settlement manager. The Field Ambulance had already upset the 3rd Commando Brigade rear echelon by demanding that 'Hotel Galtieri', the small stable complex being used to process Goose Green prisoners, be handed over, a suggestion which was rejected with two-word soldierly robustness. The echelon also despaired of the Field Ambulance's near total lack of tactical appreciation.

Next day Father Hayes flew down to Goose Green where he helped bury the Argentinian dead and said Mass over their graves. Among the mounds of kit littering the battlefield, he picked up several letters and photos from Argentinian families. One was from a boy who prayed not only for his countrymen but also for 'the English, who are not our enemies, but our brothers and for the peace of the world'. It was a poignant statement in a pointless war.

Still under pressure to advance quickly, but with his Brigade still sorting itself out, it seemed to Wilson and his headquarters that everything was conspiring against a simple move but determined to contribute to the defeat of the Argentinian, he re-examined the 2nd Parachute Battalion plan.

1. Brigadier Tony Wilson, Commander 5th Infantry Brigade. *(Soldier Magazine)*

2. General Galtieri and Brigadier-General Menendez on Stanley Common, 21 April, 1982.

3. Exercise *Welsh Falcon*. RAF Pumas and Army Gazelles. *(Barrie Lovell)*

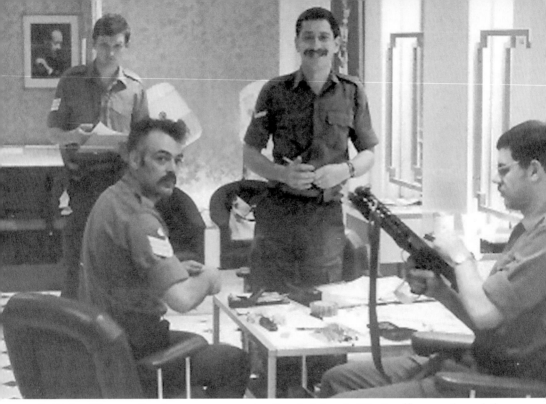

4. 81 Intelligence Section en route to the South Atlantic. Their offices on board the *QE2* and the *Canberra* were the hairdressing salons. *Left to right:* Sergeant Steve Massey, Staff-Sergeant Andy Peck, Lance-Corporal Barrie Lovell and Corporal Rich Ramsey cleaning his Sterling. *(Paul Wayne)*

5. Two Sea Harrier aircraft on the flight deck of HMS *Hermes*. *(Will Fowler)*

6. HMS *Canberra* off Grytviken, 28 May.   (*Barrie Lovell*)

7. The tug *Yorkshireman* alongside the *QE2* at Grytviken.   (*Will Townsend*)

8. An Eager Beaver of the Commando Logistic Regiment unloads a 17 Port Regiment RCT Mexeflote alongside an HMS *Fearless* Landing Craft Utility at Ajax Bay. In the background is an HMS *Fearless* Landing Craft Vehicle and Personnel.

9. The Scots Guards land at San Carlos with, in the foreground, one of their .50 Brownings used in the air defence role.

10. Gurkhas apply camouflage before going on patrol. *(Will Fowler)*

11. Steve Nicholls stands in front of Fitzroy Bridge during a visit to the Falklands. He was a member of the Mountain and Arctic Warfare Team which was watching the bridge from Mount Smoko. *(Steve Nicholls)*

12. This photograph shows the cramped conditions in which the Scots Guards were taken to Bluff Cove in an HMS *Intrepid* Landing Craft. *(Soldier Magazine)*

13. Elements of 5th Infantry Brigade at Bluff Cove, 12 June.

14. The 5th Infantry Brigade Maintenance Area, Fitzroy. In the foreground life rafts
    used to abandon *Sir Galahad*; in the background the LSL.   *(Will Townend)*

15. *Sir Tristram* in the foreground with *Sir Galahad* in the background, off Fitzroy.
                                                              (Lt. Cdr Alex Manning)

16. A Harrier lands on the flight deck of HMS *Fearless*.

17. 2nd Lieutenant Valdez who commanded 4 Platoon of 5th Marine Infantry
Battalion on Mount Tumbledown.

18. 5th Marine Infantry Battalion on Mount Tumbledown.

19. Marine Infantry queue for food on Mount Tumbledown.

20. Marine Infantry collect breakfast. The one holding the dixie is wearing a combat waistcoat.

21. Commander Perez's trailer-borne Exocet in Stanley after the surrender. It caused much anxiety to the Royal Navy after it launched the missile which hit HMS *Glamorgan*.   *(Lt. Cdr. Alex Manning)*

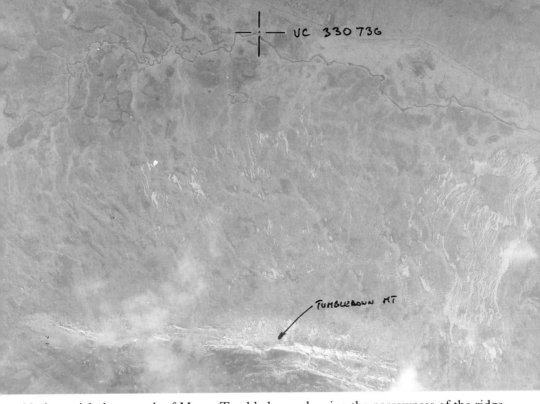

UC 330 736

TUMBLEDOWN MT

22. An aerial photograph of Mount Tumbledown, showing the narrowness of the ridge.

23. A Sea King from 845 Naval Air Squadron collects an underslung load.

24. Lieutenant Mark Coreth's troop of the Blues and Royals near Sapper Hill
(Royal Marines Museum).

25. A rare photograph of Argentine troops retreating into Stanley.

26. View from HQ Company 2nd Scots Guards, Mount Tumbledown on 14 June, shortly before the Argentine surrender. *(Paul Haley)*

27. Argentine soldiers, still carrying their rifles, await repatriation at Stanley Airport, 16 June. *(Will Fowler)*

28. A group of Scots Guards celebrate the Argentine surrender. *(Paul Haley)*

29. Lieutenant-Colonel David Morgan who commanded 1/7th Gurkha Rifles. *(David Morgan)*

30. Lieutenant-Colonel Johnny Rickett watches the Duke of Edinburgh pin the South Atlantic Medal on the tunic of Major Peel-Yates (HQ Coy). On his right are Major Bremner (3 Coy), Major Drewry (2 Coy) and Major Sayle (Prince of Wales Coy). *(Brigadier J. Rickett)*

31. 17 June. Argentinian prisoners being searched by 160 Provost Company, Royal Military Police, on the public jetty at Port Stanley before repatriation.

32. Resupply convoy seen from the stern of HMS *Dumbarton Castle*, 19 June.

33. Gurkhas gather round a captured RH 202 twin-barrelled anti-aircraft gun.

34. A day out at the Palace. *Left to right:* Sergeant Roman Wrega MM, Corporal John Foran MM, Major Chris Davies MBE, all of 9 Parachute Squadron, RE. *(Chris Davies)*

A Bold Move – 2 to 7 June

During the morning of 2 June forty Argentinian Army sappers from 2nd Section, 601 Combat Engineer Company, arrived at Fitzroy Bridge by truck and prepared it for demolition. The 150-foot timber bridge fed the Darwin to Stanley track over Fitzroy Inlet and was marked on a Royal Engineer Briefing Map as 'difficult to bypass'. Blowing it up would slow down any advance on Stanley. An Army helicopter piloted by Lieutenant Anaya, who was the son of Admiral Anaya, the naval representative of the Junta, flew in other equipment. Soon after midday, when the decision was made to blow it, an army engineer officer, Lieutenant Horacio Blanco, not convinced that the marines had laid sufficient explosive, added 80 kilos of Trotyl explosive. When the smoke cleared, about forty per cent of the bridge had collapsed into the cold waters of the inlet. Mines were then sewn in the wreckage but, with night drawing in and the need to be clear of the area, the sappers did not have time to booby trap them, although some were prepared in an attempt to make the finder anxious.

At about midday Brigadier Wilson reappeared at 2nd Parachute Battalion and, referring to the seizure of Swan Inlet House, told Major Keeble, 'Do it'. With the Gurkhas now deployed to the Darwin Peninsula and with no sign of a counter-attack from West Falkland, he had a unit spare. In spite of the setback of the first briefing, 2nd Parachute Battalion had continued planning the Swan Inlet House operation and within three hours not only were Bluff Cove and Fitzroy seized but it had a new Commanding Officer, Lieutenant-Colonel David Chaundler.

As Brigadier Thompson had shown with the seizure of Mount Kent, the nature of the Falklands campaign gave commanders some rare tactical latitude. The Fitzroy operation was ideally suited for parachute troops – the seizure of an important feature to be held until relieved. Not exactly a bridge too far but more akin to the seizure of Pegasus Bridge on D-Day 1944. Key issues would be good communications, air defence and formidable reinforcements.

David Chaundler was in a staff appointment at the Ministry of Defence when he was appointed by Headquarters Parachute Regiment to take command of 2nd Parachute Battalion after the death of Jones at Goose

Green. He was the natural choice anyway, having been earmarked to succeed Jones, although the appointment had yet to be formally ratified. Given hardly any time to prepare and after a long flight from the United Kingdom via Ascension Island, during the afternoon of 1 June he parachuted from a C-130 into the sea near the Carrier Battle Group and was picked up by the Leander Class frigate HMS *Penelope*. By this time the leading elements of 2nd Parachute Battalion had seized Fitzroy and Bluff Cove. Chaundler arrived on HMS *Fearless* at 2am on 2 June and gained the impression that his presence was not required; after all, Major Keeble had competently commanded 2nd Parachute Battalion at Goose Green. Having served with Brigadier Wilson at the Ministry of Defence, Chaundler had hoped for his support and told Wilson that he was now the Commanding Officer of the Battalion and any question regarding his authority was his own problem. Two hours later Chaundler found himself a bunk, no mean feat in a ship, in the belief that Wilson would take him to Goose Green. But the next morning he discovered that Wilson had already departed; nevertheless, he scrounged a seat in a Sea King going to Darwin and then walked to Goose Green. Only Major Keeble knew of his intended arrival and therefore it was something of a shock when the Battalion found it had a new Commanding Officer, all the way from the United Kingdom. After being briefed by Keeble on the plan to seize Fitzroy and Bluff Cove, Chaundler judged it unwise to interfere at this late stage and told him to execute it. He would take full command next morning.

6 Platoon was still detailed for the Swan Inlet House task and would be accompanied by Colour-Sergeant Alan Morris, from the Battalion Intelligence Section, and Major Crosland. Captain Greenhalgh provided five 656 Squadron Scouts, two fitted with SS-11 missiles, from its forward operating base with 3rd Commando Brigade Air Squadron at Clam Valley. The French SS-11 is an air-to-surface, wire-guided anti-tank missile and is manoeuvred using a simple line-of-sight optical sight unit. Scouts usually had two missiles mounted on pylons fixed on both sides of the rear door. The co-pilot in the left-hand seat is the gunner.

Leaving the three troop-carrying helicopters, each with a section of four paras, about 800 metres to the west of Swan Inlet House, the two SS-11 Scouts softened up the settlement. Corporal Lord, Greenhalgh's gunner, scored direct hits on two buildings, but two other missiles misfired and disappeared. Covered by two paras armed with Sterling submachine guns in the SS-11 helicopters, the assault helicopters then landed. Fanning into a triangular formation, the paras cleared the settlement and found it deserted. A stone was hurled through a window of a building and Morris and Crosland entered. Finding a telephone, Morris cranked it and was answered by twelve-year-old Michelle Binnie, daughter of Ron Binnie, the Fitzroy settlement manager. Asked if there were any Argentinians at Bluff Cove or Fitzroy, her father replied, 'No,' to which Major Crosland replied, 'We'll be seeing you shortly'. The news was radioed to Keeble that 'Fleet' (Fitzroy) and 'Balham' (Bluff Cove), places of significance to Crosland, were clear of enemy. Keeble advised Brigadier Wilson, who abandoned his plan of marching to Fitzroy in preference for a heliborne *coup de grace*.

By this time the British dependence on support helicopters for troop movement was extremely limited, not only by the small number available after the sinking of the *Atlantic Conveyor* but also the tasks expected of them. One consequence was that they were sometimes hijacked, which then upset formal tasking and maintenance. 'Hijackings' were part of the 'can do, must do' culture on which the military thrives.

With darkness approaching and the possibility that the Argentinians might become aware of the telephone conversation, the Chinook was hijacked at Goose Green by 2nd Parachute Battalion. The pilot, Flight-Lieutenant Grose, said that he would only be able to take two 'sticks'; a 'stick' in a Chinook being forty men. When the helicopter's loadmaster complained about this, he was apparently hoisted off the tailgate by a para company sergeant major with the words, 'That's one less!' The Royal Air Force has a history of tending to abide by the rule book until the reality of the situation is explained. Headquarters A Company and two platoons, Headquarters B Company, a Mortar section and an Anti-Tank section then crammed into the Chinook. Greenhalgh's helicopters were already taking two Reconnaissance Platoon patrols to mark out landing sites. Grose took off into the gathering gloom and low cloud base of a Falklands late winter afternoon and, flying over ground technically not cleared of enemy, dropped the paras on Fitzroy Ridge and returned to Goose Green. Unfortunately no one had advised Headquarters 3rd Commando Brigade, or indeed Headquarters Land Forces, of the operation.

Lance-Corporal Steve Nicoll was with Lieutenant Murray's Mountain and Arctic Warfare Cadre patrol on Wickham Heights. Fresh from the battle at Top Malo House, they knew that the Argentinians had Chinooks. These were with 7th Counter-Insurgency Squadron. Nicoll:

Our team was due to be tasked again and we were ready and impatient to be deployed, this time watching the area of Fitzroy. The outline tasking was deliberately vague: 'Watch the road/track for any evidence of troop movement and activity.' In particular a large wooden bridge which would be vital to any flanking movement by friendly forces if they were to advance towards Stanley.

77

On arrival we positioned ourselves on Smoko Mount in a fairly bleak, windswept position but it was the only possible vantage point that offered cover from view and an escape route. Near us was a flagpole, complete with slapping halyards, which helped to confirm where we were in the low and poor visibility on the walk-in. It was also used to elevate the radio antenna.

Our main focus of attention was the wooden bridge and the immediate area either side of it. Whenever the mist cleared, we could see the Argentinians scrambling over the struts. It had all the hallmarks of being prepared for demolition and this we reported. By now our routine was much smoother and we continued to work radio schedules, reporting at fixed times but always with the ability to report in if needed. Visibility proved difficult with a wet, clinging mist frequently enveloping the position for several hours at a time, obscuring the bridge and approaches. We could hear vehicles and voices but it was all routine. As at Teal Inlet the Argentinians were not alert, no sign of sentries being posted or any attempts to position a fire team on high ground. They did not have the appearance of being particularly well disciplined or tactically aware, nor were they bivvying in the immediate area. Our pattern of life in the OP was dull, damp and uneventful.

The sound of helicopters on 2nd June was unusual, as none had been previously sighted. Mist and low cloud cover prevented us from seeing anything. It then became apparent that there were several helicopters, including the distinctive deep 'swish, swish' of the twin rotors of a Chinook. Our intelligence suggested that only one had survived the loss of the Atlantic Conveyor. The activity below us suggested a fairly large troop deployment but without a clear view, we could only guess at their identity. Occasionally the mist lifted for a few seconds and we were able to identify heavily laden troops moving around but never long enough for a positive identification.

Calculating co-ordinates for a fire mission on the troops, who were bunched and in the open, I opened up communications in clear, seeking confirmation of friendly forces movement to prevent any loss of reporting time. Cadre HQ at Teal Inlet, who were co-located with HQ 3rd Commando Brigade, confirmed there should be no friendly troops to our front. After several questions and answers to confirm details, the fire mission was accepted. We originally planned for a small-scale fire mission but, as the size of the target grew, we requested that more guns to be made available. The cloud cover continued to mask most of the area to our front, but the helicopter activity continued and increasing numbers of troops could be seen out in the open. We received confirmation that the guns were prepared.

In his headquarters on Mount Kent Lieutenant-Colonel Vaux listened as 29 Commando Regiment, at Teal Inlet, accepted Murray's report of troops in the area of Fitzroy Bridge to be enemy and relay the information to 7 (Sphinx) Commando Battery, just eight miles to the north of the target. In his command post, the Battery Commander, Major David Brown, was completing his fire orders and soon everything was ready – guns loaded, range and bearing calculated and Number Ones standing by waiting to give the order 'Fire!' Confirmation of the fire mission was then sought from Brigade Headquarters. Nicoll continues:

> *We were waiting for the executive order of 'Three rounds fire for effect,' which would initiate a salvo of three rounds from each gun to target the area. These were zeroing rounds that would be adjusted by us to hit the target. Once the guns were 'on' they would commence the full fire mission. The gap between final confirmation and opening fire is usually very short one. Our checks and controls were complete and delays could allow the target to escape. Precisely at this point the cloud cover opened a 'window' and we saw the easily recognized figure of a Scout helicopter with British markings. We knew the Argentinians were not equipped with them. It all unfolded in a few very brief seconds, the radio handset was already poised and the command 'Check, check, check, confirmed sighting of a Scout helicopter'. This was repeated back from the gun lines and the net went instantly silent.*
>
> *It still wasn't clear if all the activity could be attributed to the British but it was apparent that we had been very close to bringing down fire on our own side.*

The incident was a near disaster. A fundamental principle of warfare, particularly at night and in poor weather, is to keep neighbouring units informed of strategies that may affect them. On this occasion Headquarters 3rd Commando Brigade had no idea what was happening and a potentially very damaging military and political 'blue on blue' had been avoided by a fortunate break in the clouds. Nevertheless 5th Infantry Brigade had gained important territory. Now that Fitzroy Bridge was under British control, Murray's patrol was extracted within two hours by a Wessex. This was essentially the end of Nicoll's war. He later joined 45 Commando as a section commander and returned to the Cadre in 1984 to complete the senior Mountain Leader course at the same time as the BBC was filming the unit in *Behind the Lines*.

Dropped, he believed, near Fitzroy, Lieutenant Chris Connor, the 2nd Parachute Battalion Reconnaissance Platoon commander, ordered the strobe light to be switched on to guide Grose, bringing in the second stick of Lieutenant-Colonel Chaundler and Major Keeble, Tactical Headquarters and B Company. This Chinook was equally full of troops – eighty-four squeezed like sardines in a can. Chaundler remembers that the loadmaster drew a huge laugh when he invited everyone to sit down, tongue in cheek. The helicopter dropped the troops on Fitzroy Ridge and about a mile short of Fitzroy, a settlement of white houses, wool warehouses, a bridge and a jetty jutting into a natural harbour. Just in case there were Argentinians in the settlement, Connor was instructed check it out. Chaundler used the pause to be briefed by Keeble on 2nd Parachute Battalion's campaign so far, in particular what had happened at Goose Green.

Leaving his patrol in cover, Connor and his radio operator entered the settlement and found Ron Binnie's house, which was on the northern point of the settlement. All was clear and Keeble brought Tactical Headquarters and B Company forward and, as Chaundler puts it, 'We walked forward and had tea with Ron Binnie'. With Mrs Linda Binnie soon producing cakes and tea, her husband confirmed that there were no Argentinians in the area but that Fitzroy Bridge was damaged. Connor gathered a patrol and, arriving at the bridge in a civilian Land Rover, found the damage could be repaired. This information was passed to Major Chris Davies at 9 Parachute Squadron.

As night was falling Squadron-Leader Langworthy strolled into the Amphibious Operations Room on HMS *Fearless* with the news that 2nd Parachute Battalion had seized Fitzroy and Bluff Cove. Although good news, it was entirely unexpected and was initially received with disbelief by Moore's staff, unaware that Brigadier Wilson was planning such a *coup de main*. As far as they were concerned the Chinook helicopter was heavily involved in transporting prisoners to San Carlos and flying 5th Infantry Brigade stores and equipment to Darwin. Little else was known about the helicopter's specific activities because its radio was broken.

Prior to the seizure, Michael Nicholson, the Independent Television News reporter, was one of several journalists who filed tapes which referred to Brigadier Wilson being with an infantry company and making the telephone call at Swan Inlet House. By this time the press were complaining of being manipulated. In an article on 30 May *The Observer* commented that the Ministry of Defence was discreetly using a variety of mechanisms to mislead the press, and indirectly Argentina, with disinformation about British operations, i.e. the deliberate spreading of inaccurate information. The article cited that, although the nuclear submarine HMS *Superb* was reported to be in the South Atlantic in early April, she was in fact in the United Kingdom; that South Georgia had been liberated on 23 April when this did not happen for several days and that on 21 May raiding parties had landed on East Falkland when in fact it was D-Day.

Next morning the remainder of 2nd Parachute Battalion, now commanded by Lieutenant-Colonel Chaundler, was flown in and confusing it proved to be. C (Patrol) Company was delivered to Fitzroy instead of Bluff Cove and D Company was flown to their position on the eastern shores of Bluff Cove Inlet in full view of the enemy-held Mount Harriet and two miles from their intended position. Eventually the Battalion sorted themselves out with A Company on high ground near Bluff Cove and C (Patrol) Company covering the approaches from the north-east. D Company remained east of Bluff Cove Inlet to deal with any approaches directly from Stanley and was already under intermittent artillery fire. B Company remained in depth on Fitzroy Ridge. Battalion Headquarters and the Regimental Aid Post were at Fitzroy. Tactical Headquarters was at Bluff Cove. Perched on a windy mountainside was Corporal Bank's vital radio relay link to A Echelon at Goose Green. His men were actually seen by a Gurkha Reconnaissance Platoon patrol searching for Argentinian-manned radar beacons. Deciding they were enemy, a Harrier strike was arranged until the error was realized.

Since 2nd Parachute Battalion wanted to get as many men forward as possible, only light battle order was taken and their bergens were left at Goose Green, which meant that the soldiers would be without sleeping bags and rations for the next four days. The appalling weather also precluded ammunition being moved to Fitzroy. In short, the Battalion was not really fit for battle and it was fortunate that the 'bold move' had not been opposed.

The Kilmartins of Bluff Cove did much to rejuvenate the soldiers with mutton, hot meals, somewhere to dry socks and transport to help move men and equipment. Nine Polish seamen, who had defected from their ship in February and had made their way to Fitzroy, were conscripted as labourers. The kindness of the civilians in the 'camp' is often overlooked when the story of the war is told. Those who came into contact with them are unlikely to forget their generosity in raising spirits and maintaining morale. It had started with the Millers at Port San Carlos and the Shorts at San Carlos opening up their houses and farm buildings on the morning of 21 May, and carried right through Goose Green, Teal Inlet, Fitzroy, Bluff Cove and several other settlements to the end in Stanley. Their contribution to the campaign was significant.

A day later, acting on information received from a 'kelper', Lieutenant Peter Kennedy, Second-in-Command of C Company captured three Argentinians coming from Island Harbour and apparently intent on setting up an observation post. Under the limited questioning available to the Battalion, they divulged the location of another post, which was later captured by the Gurkhas. In its post-operation report 2nd Parachute Battalion later complained about the poor passage of Intelligence. Not for the first time, they failed to help themselves. These important prisoners had been in Stanley but were not sent as high priority to the San Carlos interrogation centre, any more than four prisoners captured the day before the Battle of Goose Green were notified to Headquarters 3rd Commando Brigade.

So far there had been no reaction from the Argentinians to the seizure of Fitzroy, probably because the dreadful weather precluded their observation posts on Wickham Heights from seeing what was happening. 10th Infantry Brigade had considerable counter-attack forces, including armoured cars, but this was also not a good time for the Argentinians. The Special Forces Group had just been defeated on Mount Kent and was regrouping. Army Group Malvinas was still expecting 5th Infantry Brigade to land at or near Stanley and still had no idea that it was landing at San Carlos. Thus three full-strength infantry regiments and two armoured car units were waiting for something that would not happen.

The speed of 2nd Parachute Battalion's move caught virtually everyone by surprise, particularly Headquarters Land Forces, which had no idea other than Wilson had taken a huge risk and had pulled off a bold move worthy of far greater credit than was given to him. As Wilson later said on television, 'I've grabbed my land in this great jump forward. Now I want to consolidate it,' ready to support the divisional attack. Nevertheless, Moore should have been kept informed. The move caused huge logistic problems for Headquarters Land Forces because isolated, exposed and without a logistic tail, 2nd Parachute Battalion was vulnerable. The best way to move large numbers of troops and their equipment was by sea and the Royal Navy now had the experience and organization to execute a sea move. By this time 3rd Commando Brigade were settling into their positions in the mountains to the north and the first patrols were probing the Argentinian defences. But supporting them was now at risk as helicopters, in particular, were diverted to support 5th Infantry Brigade. The consequence was that the Brigade suddenly found itself short of warm clothing, shelter, regular rations and fresh water. Some of the troops would be without their bergens for nearly five days in temperatures that dropped to −11 degrees. The sickness rate from exposure, hypothermia and illness began to creep up, even among those familiar with the cold of Norway, which therefore reduced combat effectiveness.

By about midday on 3 June most of 5th Infantry Brigade had disembarked from *Canberra* and were moving into positions around San Carlos. The *Baltic Ferry* had been unloaded and the *Nordic Ferry* was due in at midday, but it would not be until next day that Tactical Brigade Headquarters was set up with a skeleton radio fit. Major-General Moore wanted to attack the Stanley defences as soon as possible and the date being worked on by 3rd Commando Brigade was 7 June. If it was to be a divisional attack, then there was an urgent need for 5th Infantry Brigade to be in position, with its artillery and other assets, at least by 6 June. But the new arrivals were still marrying equipment landed from the ships. Northwood, 8,000 miles to the north and with very little local knowledge about conditions, looked at the maps and decided that the troops should march, fully laden, in an advance to contact, to Fitzroy across ground not cleared of the enemy. Brigadier Wilson was placed under intense pressure to advance almost from the minute he landed but his Brigade needed to walk, fully supported, before it could run. Unlike 3rd Commando Brigade, 5th Infantry Brigade had been given weeks to prepare its campaign, but did not know its role until shortly before it landed.

29 (Corunna) Battery had supported 2nd Parachute Battalion during the Battle of Goose Green and on 3 June the Chinook collected the command post, seventy gunners and a Light Gun from their position at Head of the Bay House and flew them to gun positions near A Company. The helicopter was then diverted to another task, which left the gun without any ammunition, a situation that lasted for two days. The command post received several fire missions about which it could do absolutely nothing. Unfortunately the gunners managed to select a hollow for the gun position and after torrential rain next day this turned into a watercourse. In its post-operation report, the Battery blamed Brigade Headquarters for this state of affairs. When A Company ran short of food, the gunners shared their rations. On 5 June the remaining five guns and ammunition arrived and the gunners were soon registering targets identified by D Company. A Naval Gunfire Support team, commanded by Captain Kevin Arnold of 148th (Meiktila) Commando Forward Observation Battery, also arrived at Fitzroy with communications to the gunline off Stanley.

Meanwhile Major Chris Davies had been ordered by Brigadier Wilson to repair Fitzroy Bridge. Even if passable only by men on foot, its repair would save hours of cross-country marching. Hitching a lift in a Sea King, he arrived a few hours after 2nd Parachute Battalion had seized Bluff Cove and was guided to the bridge by Tim Dobyn of Bluff Cove. With three of his Signals Section, he inspected the damage and found that about 66 feet of the 150-foot bridge had collapsed at the eastern end and wooden decking was missing. Of the load-bearing supports, one had been completely demolished, another was damaged and the third had been pitted by the explosion, but otherwise the bridge was undamaged, if precarious. Davies noted that explosive charges had been planted on the wooden piles and a detonation cable ring led to a firing point on the northern shore, or at least so he believed. When the campaign was over, Davies met Lieutenant Blanco, who had laid the explosive, and learnt that there were no booby traps. Prodding the ground with his bayonet and finding some mines, he dragged them out with cord but there were no explosions. The group then found the camp abandoned by 601 Combat Engineer Company to be littered with boxed explosive, mines and loose ammunition. To his surprise, there were no booby traps and so he decided the make the bridge as safe as possible. With the help of 2nd Parachute Battalion's Assault Engineer Platoon and some local civilians, Davies and his signallers dismantled the explosives and erected a wobbly footbridge across the gap. Davies sent details of material that would be needed to repair it to Headquarters 5th Infantry Brigade by radio, letter and note. The requirements were then passed to Major Taffy Morgan, commanding 61 Field Support Squadron at San Carlos, who despatched sappers to beg, borrow and scavenge ships and supply dumps for welding gear, bags of nails, timber and rolled steel joints.

By this time the general intelligence assessment was that Argentina had accepted that the military defence of the Falklands was inevitable and that Great Britain must be dragged to the negotiating table by staging a high-profile incident, for instance targeting HMS *Hermes* or *Invincible*. But the Argentinian Navy had lost the maritime battle. Strengthening its military presence on West Falkland to threaten San Carlos and sandwich the British between Stanley and West Falkland with the airborne Strategic Reserve was another option. The Air Force had sufficient transport with its C-47s Dakotas, F-27 Fellowships and C-130 Hercules for a mass drop. The Navy could help with its three L-188 Electras, as could the Army with its three G-222 transports. But the Air Force could not guarantee a lengthy period of air superiority unless the two British aircraft carriers were neutralized, either by the weather or attack.

Soon after the start of British attacks on 1 May the Argentine Navy evaluated the possibility of installing an Exocet surface-to-surface system at Stanley to deter the Royal Navy from bombarding military positions. Transporting a shipboard system would take at least forty-four days and when a simple system needed to be devised, an engineering officer, Commander Julio Perez, and two civilians were tasked to come up with a solution, which they did within ten days. Christened the 'Do-It-Yourself Firing Installation', Perez's development consisted of a generator, supporting hardware and two ramps for the Exocet box launchers all mounted on two trailers. The launchers themselves were cannibalized from two of Argentina's A-69 corvettes. Perez's team designed a firing sequence from a box with four telephone switchboard switches; these were manual to save time. Each had to be thrown in specific order timed by a stopwatch. This land-based system was ready in mid-May, but an attempt to fly it and Perez to Stanley on 24 May was thwarted by British air activity. Eventually, in early June, the system was landed, but by this time very wet weather had set in and since there was a danger of the Firing Installation trailer becoming bogged down in the mud, a short stretch of the tarmac road between the town and airport was selected as the firing point. Each night at 6pm the system was dragged from beneath camouflage netting and placed behind a 16-foot high bunker. It had to be ready by 8.30pm when British ships tended to begin their bombardments. The Air Force Westinghouse radars with the 2nd Air Surveillance and Control Group swept a 60-degree arc to the south of Stanley Common for long-range search. The Army provided fire control with its AN-TPS 43 Early Warning radar. Three Exocet missiles were sent. The first one proved to be defective, the second was wasted when a connection to the transformer was incorrectly fitted and veered to the right, as opposed to the left. The third was more successful.

On the night of 27/28 May a large projectile hurtled across the flight deck of HMS *Avenger* while she was on the gun line south of Port Harriet and out of range of conventional artillery. It was then correctly assessed that Argentina might well have installed an Exocet system on the Falklands and to minimize the risk, Rear-Admiral Woodward created a 25-mile sanitized circumference from the suspected launch pad that no ship was to enter. It is significant that Exocet is a sea-skimming missile and therefore it is suggested that the Argentinians would have some difficulty hitting anything to the west because of the landmass. The problem for the Royal Navy was that Exocet was a weapon widely used by NATO and consequently a counter-measure had not been developed. The sinking of HMS *Sheffield* and the *Atlantic Conveyor* led to some Royal Navy commanders becoming pre-occupied with it almost to the exclusion of risk-taking.

Four more missiles arrived by C-130 during the night of 5 June, but it was not until about 2.35am on the night of 12 June that a target presented itself. At 2.15am HMS *Avenger* and the County-class destroyer HMS *Glamorgan* had both completed the night's mission of providing naval gunfire support to 3rd Commando Brigade attacking Mount Longdon, Two Sisters and Mount Harriet and left to return to the Carrier Battle Group. Unfortunately for her Commanding Officer of HMS *Glamorgan*, Captain Michael Barrow, his destroyer clipped the sanitized area and when her radar footprint was detected by the Exocet launch team, a missile launched. Originally mistaking it for a 155mm shell, HMS *Avenger* recognized the radar configuration to be an Exocet and the target to be HMS *Glamorgan*. Barrow held his fire and then, when the missile was within a mile and half, he opened up with a Seacat but missed. However, the incoming missile was deflected sufficiently upward to miss the hull of the destroyer, but it slithered across the pitching deck into the hangar and exploded. Burning fuel from a wrecked Wessex helicopter spilled down a hole in the deck into the galley area, causing a major fire, and a fireball ripped into the gas turbine gear room. An officer, six air maintenance crew, four chefs, a steward and a marine engineer, totalling thirteen men, were killed and fourteen injured. Very many of those ashore witnessed the glow of the missile and the tiny explosion on the horizon as the Exocet exploded. Although HMS *Glamorgan* had an 8-degree list from the weight of water needed to fight the fires, she maintained a steady 18 knots and remained fully operational in spite of the damage.

The opposing air forces were operating from different distances, the British restricted by the number of aircraft limited to the two carriers, the Argentinians by the distance from the mainland and the inability of their jets to use Military Air Base Stanley because of the unsuitability and vulnerability of the runway. While the Argentinians had C-130K tankers to keep their aircraft in the air longer, the British Sea Harriers and GR3 Harriers had a limited time over the battlefield and had to return to the carriers to refuel, maybe 100 miles out to sea. Whoever responded to air interdiction first would win the air war. The Harriers, with their short take-off and landing capability and AIM-9 *Sidewinder* missiles, held the key.

In his post-Operation *Corporate* report, Lieutenant-Colonel Geoff Field MBE RE, Commander Royal Engineers at Headquarters Land Forces, reported that one of the first tasks of 59 Independent Commando Squadron was to find somewhere for the Harrier forward operating base to enable aircraft to be on call for close air support at very short notice. A site close to *Green Beach* at Port San Carlos was selected because it had a natural ski jump and the ground was firm. It initially became known as 'West Wittering' and then, by the Royal Air Force, irreverently if fondly, as 'Sid's Strip', named after Squadron Leader Brian 'Sid' Morris AFC, 'West Wittering's' Commanding Officer. The Fleet Air Arm christened it HMS *Sheathbill*, after a seabird, as with all naval air shore bases.

On 23 May 1 Troop, 59 Independent Commando Squadron, erected the Emergency Fuel Handling Equipment for the delivery of aviation fuel for helicopters and, eventually, the Harriers, but the frequent air raids and a faulty design of two pumps meant that the transfer of fuel was painfully slow. Next day 11 Field Squadron, Royal Engineers, a specialist airfield construction unit commanded by Major Bruce Hawken, landed from *Sir Bedivere* to build the strip, but it had no equipment, not even a shovel. 500 tons of equipment destined for 'West Wittering', plant, vehicles and war stores, was on the *Atlantic Conveyor* at the bottom of the South Atlantic. This loss was compounded by the inability of 59 Independent Commando Squadron to unload their stores and vehicles from *Sir Lancelot,* which had been hit by two bombs, both of which failed to explode but were still thought to be dangerous.

Fortuitously loaded on board the Royal Fleet Auxiliary *Stromness* before she departed from the United Kingdom were strips of Prefabricated Surfacing Airfield, which were originally intended for 59 Independent Commando Squadron to repair bomb damage and for a vertical take-off and landing pad. Some of these heavy 10 x 2-feet aluminium panels were landed in bundles by helicopters and landing craft near *Green Beach* and then hauled to the operating base using vehicles loaned by the settlement manager, Alan Miller. By 2 June 11 Field Squadron, working on unprepared ground and without any heavy equipment, had slotted together by hand over eighty strips to build an 850-foot runway, a pad for vertical take-off and landings and dispersal areas for four aircraft. Originally ten dispersal areas had been planned. The sappers used their ingenuity and redesigned the fuel-handling system into one capable of pumping ashore 40,000 gallons of aviation fuel.

But no sooner had the sappers laid down their tools, a job well done, than the rotor down-draught of the Chinook, which landed close to the runway, lifted several panels and buckled them. Since no spares were available, the Royal Engineers, no doubt cursing the ancestry of the pilot, stripped most of the runway and re-laid it. This would not be the only time that aircraft damaged the precious runway, as we shall see. Poor weather then prevented flying and it was not until 5 June that Squadron-Leader Bob Iveson led a pair of GR 3s to 'Sid's Strip' from HMS *Hermes*. Iveson had been shot down over Goose Green the day before the battle and evaded capture until 30 May. Ejecting had injured his back and he was soon sent back to the United Kingdom as a battle casualty, arriving on 24 June. Thereafter two GR3s and two Sea Harriers arrived from the Carrier Battle Group at first light and remained for the day. Apart from a short period, 'Sid's Strip' proved a most valuable asset, with over 150 operational sorties being flown during the period 5 to 14 June, and helped the British to win and maintain air superiority. The Royal Engineers managed 'Sid's Strip' until it was finally taken over by Royal Air Force ground crews in August.

During the morning of 3 June Lieutenant-Colonel Chaundler advised Brigadier Wilson that the Argentinians had not threatened Bluff Cove or Fitzroy and recommended that, since there was no immediate need for fighting troops, air defence and logistics should be moved before more infantry battalions. Air defence assets included the Blowpipes of 43 Air Defence Battery and the Royal Marine Air Defence Troop and the Rapiers of T (Shah Shujah's Troop) Air Defence Battery and 63 Squadron of the Royal Air Force Regiment.

Formed in October 1838, T Battery took its name from the support it gave Shah Shujah el Mook and his 6,000-strong force that helped the British Army invade Afghanistan. Fortunately it did not take part in the disastrous retreat from Kabul in 1841. During the 1857 Indian Mutiny

Lieutenant G.A. Rennie was awarded the Victoria Cross for gallantry at the siege of Delhi. The Battery saw service in the Second Boer War, First and Second World Wars, Palestine and Northern Ireland, where its gunners were deployed as infantry. In 1982 the battery was commanded by Major Graham Smith and consisted of G, H and I Troops, each of four Fire Units commanded by a lieutenant. It was attached to 29 Commando Regiment, Royal Artillery. The Rapiers were early versions and consisted of three units – the launcher of four missiles, an optical tracker and a generator. Seven gunners can bring the weapon into action within fifteen minutes and can reload in two and a half minutes. Each Firing Unit has a radar range of ten miles to a height of 10,000-feet with optimum target acquisition of six seconds. As often as necessary, certainly after a move and once daily, the detachment carry out tests and adjustments, the so-called 'T and As', to ensure the Rapier is calibrated correctly and working properly. It is exactly comparable to the rifleman zeroing his weapon to ensure his sights are calibrated to the barrel and the tank gunner aligning his guns to his and the commander's sights. It is a critical procedure.

Although landed at Ascension Island, T Battery did not have the opportunity for live firing and thus when its fire units were landed on 21 May, according to one of the gunners, several frustrating minor equipment failures emerged, particularly with the sensitive tracker units, as a direct consequence of being 'humped and bumped down innumerable companionways from the hold to the tank deck on the long sea voyage south, and less than gentle landings when being flown ashore'. The gunners also experienced depression difficulties locking on to Argentinian aircraft hurtling at low level through the U-shaped valley of San Carlos Water, but they developed techniques for the missiles to chase aircraft. There was a great fear that the expectations of Rapier were to be dashed until Sergeant 'Taffy' Morgan's firing unit contributed to the downing of a Skyhawk

On 3 June Wilson issued orders to consolidate around Fitzroy and Bluff Cove and decided that it was more important to move his infantry forward so that it would be ready to move through 3rd Commando Brigade in the attack on Stanley:

❑ *Half the Welsh Guards to take over from 2nd Parachute Battalion at north of Bluff Cove.*

❑ *The Scots Guards to take over from 2nd Parachute Battalion east of Bluff Cove Inlet.*

❑ *2nd Parachute Battalion to pull back to Fitzroy as Brigade Reserve.*

Not surprisingly, Lieutenant-Colonel Rickett was not prepared to split his Battalion and gained Wilson's agreement to march his Battalion the twenty miles to High Hill, which is about five miles north of Darwin and at the head of the track to Bluff Cove, by first light on the 4th.

Although not invited to any of Brigadier Wilson's daily morning Orders Group on HMS *Fearless,* Commodore Clapp watched with increasing anxiety as the southern flank was opened up. He and Brigadier Thompson had previously disregarded the concept as impractical but now the Army presumably expected support from the Royal Navy. Major-General Moore knew he could rely upon Clapp to manage inshore operations and on 3 June Colonel Ian Baxter, his commando-trained senior logistics officer, had no alternative but to ask him to examine moving 5th Infantry Brigade by sea to Fitzroy. Clapp, although anxious to help, never really liked the idea of a sea move and hoped that it could be avoided. Critical of subsequent events off Fitzroy, he acknowledges that, while warfare 'requires dash and initiative', combined amphibious operations are unable to accept unplanned and uncoordinated moves along a sea flank, and he is right. Throughout the planning, he regarded the move as an administrative sea landing, not an amphibious operation. In 1982 the NATO amphibious doctrine defined an amphibious operation as 'An operation launched from the sea by naval and landing forces against a hostile or potentially hostile shore'. Technically the only amphibious operations so far were the Argentinian landings at South Georgia and the Falklands and the British at San Carlos Water because they were from the sea on hostile shores. Special Forces landings, such as the British recapture of South Georgia, were known as Advanced Forces operations.

Clapp would later admit that he did not appreciate the lack of understanding of joint amphibious operations by 5th Infantry Brigade. While being frank, as an experienced naval officer and now heading operational amphibious warfare, he and his staff, which included two Royal Corps of Transport officers with maritime experience, should have realized that this was an Army brigade with no such experience. Nevertheless, to their great credit, Clapp's staff quickly set about solving the problem.

Sitting in his Forward Operating Base at *Blue Beach Two* near the San Carlos jetty and with not much to do was Major Ewen Southby-Tailyour, a Royal Marine who was commanding landing craft operations. Between 1977 and 1979, while commanding Naval Party 8901, he had carried out a detailed survey of the Falkland Islands coastline for a yachtsman's guide, but was unable to find a publisher until after the war. This knowledge, which was in a school exercise book he had classified as Secret, had already been invaluable during the 21 May landings. Hearing that plans were being developed to move 5th Infantry Brigade, Southby-Tailyour suggested to Clapp's staff that, to save time, he could ferry it by landing craft from San Carlos to Brenton Loch, which is an inlet that reaches in from Falkland Sound and laps on to Cantera Beach on the western side of Darwin Peninsula. From there the troops would then march across the Goose Green battlefield to Darwin and pick up the main track to Stanley, which passed through Fitzroy. In a day move air cover would be required.

During the evening Commodore Clapp, as the Inshore Operations Combined Task Group commander, signalled Rear-Admiral Woodward advising him of his intentions:

> ❑ At first light on 6 June to land the Scots Guards and half the Welsh Guards from HMS Intrepid in the Bluff Cove area using four Landing Craft Utility and two Landing Craft Vehicle and Personnel. The ship had to be back in San Carlos by first light on the 7th.

> ❑ The Landing Ship Logistic Sir Tristram to ferry the remainder of the Welsh Guards, a Rapier detachment, the Brigade War Maintenance Reserve and a Mexeflote for the Forward (5th) Brigade Maintenance Area to Fitzroy. She would return when she was empty.

But a fly in the ointment was that the route to be taken by the ships, south down Falkland Sound, east around Lafonia and then to Port Pleasant, had yet to be cleared of the enemy. It was known that there were regimental-sized garrisons at Fox Bay and Port Howard on West Falkland, but nothing was known about the area between Swan House Inlet and Fitzroy. Clapp therefore asked Woodward for two escorts, naval gunfire support and a permanent combat air patrol to protect the move. He also wanted to take advantage of the wet and foggy low cloud base that was prevailing at the time. The beachhead at Fitzroy and Bluff Cove had not been attacked, although Argentinian observation posts suspected to be in the general area of Mount Usborne, to the north, were being hunted by the 1/7th Gurkha Rifles Reconnaissance Platoon. With all these factors in mind, it is more accurate to describe the operations to reinforce the beachhead as maritime supporting operations because, as described in the British Maritime Doctrine, 'Once the focus of attention moves ashore, the emphasis [of naval forces] will shift from enabling to being supportive.... Additional tasks are likely to be protection and logistic support – protection of units using the sea lines of communication, of the maritime flank; and of logistic support to forces ashore and afloat; and sustainment of sealift'. Any combined and specialized operation – an all-arms battle, parachute drop, amphibious landing – is complex and requires close co-ordination. To use Winston Churchill's description of an amphibious landing, it has 'to fit together like a jewelled bracelet'.

But in this most amphibious of wars since 1945, some Royal Navy officers seemed to have forgotten that, once they have seized the initiative, their traditional role is to create an environment from which the ground forces can destroy or force the surrender of the opposing seat of government. Safe in the cabin of his aircraft carrier, but now relegated to a support role, Rear-Admiral Woodward was finding the inactivity ashore as 'irksome'. By the beginning of June his warships had won total control of the sea, but were now relegated to an enabling role to support the ground forces. On the other hand, the less glamorous Royal Fleet Auxiliary ships and associated merchantmen were continuing to provide a significant support role and the naval units under Clapp's command were bombarding Argentinian shore targets. As Major-General Moore would later tell Rear-Admiral Woodward, 'Only the land forces could win the war, but the Navy could always lose it.' The air war was still in the balance, although favouring the Royal Air Force and Fleet Air Arm.

In preparation for the move, Clapp instructed a beach reconnaissance team consisting of a Special Boat Service section and 1 Fleet Clearing Diving Team to check the proposed beaches at Fitzroy and Bluff Cove for mines and other underwater obstacles. Lieutenant Richard Willet, who commanded 1 Troop, 9 Parachute Squadron, accompanied this reconnaissance, as did Lieutenant-Commander Chris Meatyard, Clapp's Mine Countermeasure and Intelligence Officer. The team was flown to Fitzroy during the night of 4/5th June and until it reported, Clapp could not advise the ship's commanding officers where to anchor.

To reach High Hill by daybreak next day Rickett decided to follow the track over Sussex Mountains and then pick up the route pioneered by 2nd Parachute Battalion on 26 May. His men would have to carry all their personal equipment. Rickett:

We were all extremely frustrated being in San Carlos. I remember meeting Tony Wilson, our Brigade Commander, with Mike Scott and one or two members of the Bde HQ staff the morning after we had landed. There were no available 'assets' to be given to the Brigade as the Commando Bde were on their positions in the mountains and were preparing for the build-up for the next phase – the taking of the Mount Harriet/Two Sisters line. The only way we could get anything was by 'pirating' the odd passing helicopter to give us a lift.

I suggested to Tony Wilson that the best way for us to get out of San Carlos was by walking and I volunteered to get things going by leading off with my battalion towards Darwin where Brigade HQ Tactical now was; thence we would march on from there towards Bluff Cove or 'to the front' wherever we were required. Tony Wilson agreed instantly and I asked if my Recce Platoon could be

91

lifted forward ahead of us to be my eyes and ears; this was also agreed and heli-copters would lift them forward but short of Darwin/Goose Green at last light. He also said that he would do his best to get us some Snocats, which was all he had at his disposal, to take our mortars, Browning machine guns, ammunition and bergens. Notwithstanding this, I tasked my 2ic to beg, borrow or steal some sort of tractor lift from the settlement at San Carlos, as I was not sanguine that we would get any Snocat lift.

At last light our Scout helicopters arrived and took off with Recce Platoon. We waited, in vain, for the promised Snocat and then set off with our 81mm mortars, Milans and ammo loaded on a light tractor and farm trailer. We carried our heavy Browning machine guns. About an hour after our departure the Snocats appeared from the direction of Darwin, empty of fuel and unclear of what they were meant to be doing. It was immediately apparent that these vehicles would 'bulk out' in any case – there simply wasn't space for our equipment. So I decided to press on. Morale was high and, providing the tractor kept going, I was confident we could get across the Sussex Mountains and marry up with the Recce Platoon. The tractor, which was a small wheel-based one, immediately bogged down piling the mortars and ammo into the mud. We dug it out once, twice, three times, but by this time I realized that to carry on in this way was hopeless. We waited in vain for the sound of any returning Snocats but to no avail. I had two choices – either we could continue on light scales, but bearing in mind we were to march to the Bluff Cove area, not just to Darwin, or we could return to San Carlos and wait for some other means to get us forward. I wasn't prepared to fight a war without my mortars and other heavy weapons and with the chaos reigning around us I wasn't prepared to be separated from our equipment. After all it had been my idea to move under our own steam self-contained, now it was the turn of somebody else to give us the support we required to get us forward.

So, extremely tired with morale now on the low side, we returned to our foul area in San Carlos ready to start again the next day, but this time with proper support. At first light somehow I managed to 'pirate' a helicopter to take me to Brigade HQ at Darwin where I reported our position and demanded some means of support to get the battalion into line. After a while I was told that the battalion would be taken round by ship.

By this time I was getting extremely anxious about my Recce Platoon as we had heard nothing from them and I asked for a helicopter to search for them and make contact. Sharing a helicopter with Captain Tim Spicer, Operations Officer of the Scots Guards, who wanted to go forward to recce Bluff Cove as 2nd Parachute Battalion had made their great leap forward by then, we set off. We searched in vain for the Recce Platoon but had to go on to Bluff Cove, as fuel was getting tight, which was highly frustrating for me as I was extremely worried about them. Eventually returning to San Carlos, I learnt with great relief that the Recce Platoon had made contact with Brigade HQ and was safe. I also learnt that 2 Scots Guards were to be shipped round to San Carlos that night; in fact they were on their way by then. We were to be shipped round the following night on Fearless.

According to a gunner officer attached to the Battalion, the long heavily laden columns set off at 11pm local time, but within two hours the march was discontinued when the track, already carved up by the tracks of BV 202s and boots of soldiers, proved impassable to the tractors and their trailers.

Since he had no communications to Headquarters 5th Infantry Brigade, Commodore Clapp was unaware of this march and continued planning the sea move of both battalions to Bluff Cove. He later considered the march not to be such a 'tall order', but had not appreciated the difficulties such a march would impose on a heavily laden battalion expected to take everything it possessed, without wheeled transport, along rutted tracks at night. The Commando Brigade had also experienced problems marching to Douglas and Teal Inlet.

Next morning, 4 June, Clapp summoned his staff to finalize the detail of sending HMS *Intrepid* and *Sir Tristram* to the Bluff Cove area and Fitzroy respectively. He was keeping Admiral Fieldhouse informed of his intentions, as he was also doing in his daily communication with Woodward, and had the impression that they were committed to the proposals.

During the morning Southby-Tailyour joined Clapp's planning team. He recommended that beaching two logistic ships full of troops at Fitzroy was a non-starter because there were no suitable beaches. Unloading them with Landing Craft Vehicle and Personnel and Mexeflotes would be slow. One alternative was to ferry a battalion and a half by assault ship to Bluff Cove, but no more, in case it alerted the enemy, but since it had to be in San Carlos by daybreak, time would be a constraint. The remaining troops could be landed at Fitzroy and then march to Bluff Cove via Fitzroy Bridge. Southby-Tailyour recommended against this because of the shallowness of the water and natural underwater obstacles in Port Pleasant and Fitzroy Sound and the inability to conceal a large ship off Bluff Cove. Colonel Baxter believed that only one logistic ship was needed to take the Brigade's stores. He had been told by Brigadier Wilson over a lunch that, if a ship tucked itself close inshore under a cliff at Fitzroy, it could not be seen by Argentinian observation posts.

Clapp reconsidered the options and cancelled his warning order of the previous day. Knowing that Fitzroy Bridge had been blown and a Fitzroy landing would commit troops to marching across the difficult country to Bluff Cove, he was prepared to put a single battalion ashore at Bluff Cove. The rest could make their way from Fitzroy. This, then, formed the substance of his planning. Clapp issued orders to Captain Robin Green, captain of the logistic ship *Sir Tristram*, to load a Rapier troop, 16 Field Ambulance, which was to set up in Fitzroy in preparation for

93

the offensive, and Sergeant Derrick Boultby's Mexeflote. The landing ship's aviation fuel tanks were topped up.

As the day wore on Clapp began to receive suggestions from Northwood and Woodward, which often bore striking similarities. At 10.15am Clapp received a surprising signal from Woodward suggesting that a 'more robust plan might be to move the troops forward by foot/helo and provide logistic support by one/two relatively inconspicuous LSLs at Teal.' In effect, 5th Infantry Brigade would have to advance to Fitzroy across ground not yet cleared of enemy troops and risk being cut off from the proposed logistic centre at Teal by low cloud over Wickham Heights. It would also take at least two days for the advance on foot to be completed. In any event, Clapp, as 'the man on the spot', rather kindly later puts the suggestion down to a communication problem between colleagues separated by miles of turbulent ocean. Others might not have been so reasonable. At about 3.15pm a signal arrived from Admiral Fieldhouse, co-incidental to Woodward's idea, that the Bluff Cove option should be abandoned in favour of putting the two Guards battalions ashore at Teal Inlet. Fieldhouse believed the risks from the Argentinian 155mm artillery, the air threat and sea-mines outweighed the likelihood of success. So far as the naval and military planners in San Carlos were concerned, while it may have brought the leading elements of 5th Infantry Brigade into a good position to follow through 3rd Commando Brigade, it did not solve the isolation of 2nd Parachute Battalion. Fitzroy and Bluff Cove had not been attacked and were out of range of the 155mm howitzers anyway.

Woodward wrote in his diary of his concerns that Moore was proposing a mini D-Day at Bluff Cove and that such a move 'could blow the success of the operation' and proposed that the troops should march to Fitzroy. He wanted the San Carlos anchorage emptied, but didn't explain how the two brigades should be supplied. Fortunately Clapp rejected the suggestions, but agreed that as the conventional forces closed in on Stanley, the Special Forces should target the Port Howard and Fox Bay garrisons on West Falkland to watch for movement against San Carlos. The problem was that discussing the move of 5th Infantry Brigade with Northwood was really of limited direct concern to Woodward, as the Carrier Battle Group commander, nevertheless his views inevitably filtered to Moore and Clapp as suggestions by Northwood. The views only served to confuse a difficult situation, particularly as both then came under pressure from Admiral Fieldhouse 'to get on with it' when they were necessarily not in a position to do so or it was strategically unwise. Neither was aware that some ministers of Prime Minister Thatcher's government were suggesting that the

Argentinians should be besieged. None of those who made the suggestion had ever experienced the Falklands in winter.

When the Welsh Guards aborted their march Woodward suggested they must try again. It shows just how isolated those on ships can become from the reality ashore. As opposed to the needs and comfort of the sailor contained inside a hull, the soldier carries his personal and fighting needs on his back and is reliant on efficient logistics for resupply. The motives of Woodward are entirely understandable. His men and ships had been at sea for nearly two months and he was concerned about their health after the constant and fearful battering of the unforgiving South Atlantic. He lobbied for a second Harrier forward operating base at Goose Green so that he could withdraw the Carrier Battle Group further to the east and out of reach of air-launched Exocet. Indeed on 3 June, when he received unconfirmed intelligence of the land-based Exocet at Stanley, he had pulled his ships from the gunline earlier than normal. If 5th Infantry Brigade were 'tardy', as apparently he suggested, it was three days before Clapp and Headquarters Land Forces had everything in place for the first ship to leave San Carlos for Fitzroy. Half the problem was that the Armed Forces were inexperienced in amphibious warfare, a far cry from the Second World War. That the country's amphibious capability in 1982 centred on sixteen landing craft and some helicopters, operating from two assault ships each designed to take a tank regiment, illustrates just how weak it was.

Woodward later accused the Army battalions of being 'ceremonious duffers' with no room for initiative and imagination. Like his illustrious predecessor, Lord Nelson, he fails to acknowledge that fighting a land battle with minimum casualties takes great skill and flair. He appeared not to appreciate just how slow land warfare is – the need to plan, build up supplies, move troops, issue orders down the channels of command to the most junior soldier so that he knows what he must do and then attack with minimum casualties. Once in contact with the enemy, the battle can last for weeks. The commanding officer of a warship can respond to a simple signal and brief his men over a tannoy. Those 'ceremonious duffers' had considerably more combat experience since 1945 than most naval officers, most recently in Northern Ireland. A major factor faced by the 'ceremonious duffers' was that settling into a watery disposal yard on the bottom of the South Atlantic was the *Atlantic Conveyor* with several thousand tons of much-needed supplies, including helicopters, all condemned by the Royal Navy's failure to protect a defenceless ship. The six Wessex and three Chinook could have lifted half a battalion at a time and thus it is no wonder the ground forces were slow. While Woodward would later write that he could not afford to lose an aircraft carrier, equally the ground forces could not afford to lose supplies and equipment and, arguably, the war. Sixty years previously warships and armed merchantmen sacrificed themselves to protect convoys. But, to be fair, Woodward is later gracious enough to seek Major-General Moore's understanding of his problems.

Southby-Tailyour returned to his operating base late that afternoon of 4 June. Clapp's staff continued to examine the move, but each time came to the same conclusion – landing craft were needed and therefore an assault ship was critical to the move. During the evening Moore and Clapp signalled Northwood that the only sensible plan was to ferry both Guards battalions in HMS *Intrepid* at dusk the next day, 5 June, and land them in two waves at Fitzroy, from where they would then march to Bluff Cove. This would ensure the ship could be back in San Carlos Water by daybreak. While their staffs set about finalizing the plan, Colonel Baxter issued orders for the two Guards battalions to embark, along with 3 Troop, 9 Parachute Squadron, and a forward observation party from 49th Field Regiment, who were attached to 4th Field Regiment. Major Smith was instructed by Headquarters Land Forces to send a Troop of four Rapiers to Fitzroy, but he had a problem – too few Rapiers. Embarkation began during the morning.

San Carlos was the beachhead for ground operations and therefore required substantial air defence. On clear days the Argentinian Air and Naval Air Forces invariably attacked. Four Rapiers were already protecting the 3rd Commando Brigade Forward Maintenance Area at Teal Inlet and now he was being asked to send four to Fitzroy, which would leave him just four to protect the San Carlos anchorage. On the other hand, 63 Squadron of the Royal Air Force Regiment were still setting up. Smith selected Lieutenant Adrian Waddell, who commanded H Troop, to lead a composite Troop whose loss could be afforded. Of the four Firing Units selected, Bombardier Stewart McMartin's Rapier on a hill above Port San Carlos had experienced a misfire when a missile fired at a Pucara bounced off a building. It turned out the fault was with its command transmitter. This is the nerve centre of the Rapier into which the operator feeds the variables of weather conditions and environment so that the missile can be aligned. Without a functioning command transmitter, the Rapier cannot be fired.

Meanwhile the Special Boat Section patrol commander of the beach reconnaissance team had met Brigadier Wilson and told him that Bluff Cove was suitable for the establishment of the Brigade Maintenance Area. But Major Davies, of 9 Parachute Squadron, had the impression that the Royal Marine had little idea of the requirements for a brigade maintenance area and suggested that the idea was ridiculous. It took a spirited discussion to persuade the patrol commander that the settlement was too small, had no decent-sized godowns, was in insufficient cover from Argentinian positions on Mount Harriet and the water supply was meagre. Since he had a direct interest in the analysis, for it would be his Squadron that would provide the sapper support to find water, build roads and help dig in units, Davies suggested that since Fitzroy was screened from Argentinian surveillance, had large godowns that could shelter troops from the appalling weather and a larger anchorage, it should be used by Brigade Headquarters and the Brigade Maintenance Area. Bluff Cove was selected as a better, but not ideal, place for the Distribution Point. Wilson agreed.

The unexpected appearance of Lieutenant Willet with the reconnaissance team was a godsend to Major Davies. For a couple of days he had been asking for 1 Troop to be sent forward to repair the Fitzroy Bridge but his messages had not been getting through. Willet was a diver and always looking for something exciting to do, but now he was needed as Troop Commander and was therefore a bit 'miffed' when Davies refused to let him stay with the Special Boat Section and insisted that he reconnoitre the bridge and draw up a plan for its repair.

During the afternoon the beach reconnaissance team arrived back on HMS *Fearless* and reported to Commodore Clapp that they had found no mines or beach obstacles at Fitzroy or Bluff Cove, but that the beaches were useless at high tide and the exits were bad. In spite of this report and his own reservations, Clapp saw no reason why he should not give the go-ahead for the operation.

Everything seemed set and then at about 3pm a signal arrived from Fieldhouse addressed to Woodward, Moore and Clapp instructing that the two assault ships were not to be risked out of San Carlos in daylight, in case their loss, as capital ships, would force the Government to negotiate for a cease-fire. The cynic might suggest that, since efforts to persuade Clapp to discard the Fitzroy operation had failed, the only way to persuade him to do so was formally to declare that the two assault ships to be politically sensitive. They certainly had not been capital ships at San Carlos or in the approach to the Falklands, but all of a sudden they now had political value. All the recipients were nonplussed. If ministers were responsible for such a statement, it seems that the War Cabinet were again meddling in military affairs, just as they had done before the Battle of Goose Green, but someone, either in Cabinet or at Northwood, was remarkably defeatist. The British had just won a victory at Goose Green, 3rd Commando Brigade were beginning to get the upper hand, 5th Infantry Brigade were itching to get to grips with the Argentinians and, most importantly, it looked as though Galtieri had thrown in the towel. The political and military initiative lay with Great Britain. The Argentinians had not submitted when the *General Belgrano* was sunk, but it now seemed the Government's resolve in defeating them was to be tested by risking an assault ship in a move by sea.

Shocked by the signal, at 4.45pm Clapp replied that the only alternative was to send two landing ships, to which Fieldhouse replied that this was politically more acceptable, but 'the man on the spot must decide'. This was precisely what Clapp had been doing for the last three days, but he had always feared, as the junior in the command triumvirate, his opinion would be challenged and so it had been. But he had the strength of character not be bludgeoned by his fellow Combined Task Unit commanders. It was not easy for him and he remained determined to help the Army and now proposed:

❑ *Land the Scots Guards during the night 6/7 June at Bluff Cove by landing craft from HMS Intrepid.*

❑ *Leave the Landing Craft Utility at a tactical forward operating base at Bluff Cove.*

❑ *The Rapiers and other essential stores and equipment to be delivered to Fitzroy in Sir Tristram and unload, even if this meant in daylight.*

❑ *The landing craft to meet an assault ship during the night 7/8 June and land the Welsh Guards at Fitzroy*

Brigadier Wilson agreed and re-issued his orders accordingly. Naval strategies were at last beginning to affect military operations. Major Iain Mackay-Dick, the Scots Guards Second-in-Command, commanded the Embarked Force. Orders were then sent to HMS *Intrepid's* Commanding Officer, Captain Peter Dingemans, not to load the Welsh Guards, who were at the San Carlos jetty waiting to embark. For Lieutenant-Colonel Rickett and his men it was order, counter-order, disorder! They returned to their soggy trenches. Dingemans was an experienced assault ship commanding officer who had spent the last two years on HMS *Intrepid*.

While sending a logistic ship was judged to be an acceptable risk, a warship was not part of the plan because, some believed, sending a frigate might draw attention to Fitzroy and Bluff Cove and provoke an Argentinian counter-attack. The reality is that Port Pleasant is too shallow for warship operations and, although the Type 21s and Leander class frigates both had automatic radar-controlled guns, their radar was geared to deep sea operations against the Soviet threat and therefore was susceptible to coastal clutter. The Airguard radar was equally unreliable close inshore and the look-out was proving as good as the technology. Stationing a warship a couple of miles out to sea, where she would have been more valuable for air defence and naval gunfire support, was also out of the question because Bluff Cove and Fitzroy were both inside Woodward's Exocet sanitized area and therefore in range of the suspected launcher in Stanley. The only air defence would be small arms, Blowpipes and the Rapier Troop. It would turn out to be a serious miscalculation, considering the aggressive nature of the Argentinian Air Force and that the two settlements were in view of Argentinian ground forces on Mount Harriet. To some of Wilson's men, inexperienced in naval warfare as they were, it did seem that, while San Carlos Water had been heavily protected since 21 May, the same naval protection was not being made available to 5th Infantry Brigade.

Even while the final preparations were being resolved and having been assured that he, as 'the man on the spot', must decide, Clapp continued to receive signals from Woodward. In one he suggested that all six logistic ships with the Task Force be loaded with troops, sail into Port William and land in Stanley Harbour. The problem was that this signal had been sent on a low classification and, when its content filtered down to the logistic ships' companies', morale wavered. It was an unrealistic suggestion and again illustrates just how isolated a seaborne commander can become of ground operations and only served to confuse the situation.

The afternoon drew into evening and, still twiddling his thumbs on *Blue Beach Two,* Major Southby-Tailyour was anxious to be involved in the move. He believed the use of landing craft to speed up the advance eastwards 'would be a bonus' and so when Captain Chris Baxter, who commanded the Rigid Raider assault boats of 1st Raiding Squadron, Royal Marines, told him that he was required on board HMS *Fearless,* he was taxied to the ship at speed. While still favouring Brenton Loch, he was interrupted by Clapp who said that Major-General Moore wanted both Guards battalions to relieve 2nd Parachute Battalion and be ready to advance as soon as possible. Southby-Tailyour said it would not be possible to get to Bluff Cove and back in one night and proposed that the landing force should get close enough to be lifted ashore by landing craft. Another option was to sail from San Carlos in landing craft and shelter in creeks on the way. Clapp thanked Southby-Tailyour, who then returned to *Blue Beach Two.*

Having drawn up a plan and with the military units embarking, Clapp faced another frustration when, while briefing Captain Dingemans, he was informed by him that he believed his ship carried the same political weight as an aircraft-carrier and should not be risked outside San Carlos Water during the day. Although it can be argued that assault ships are expected to land troops on hostile shores, they do not have the same strategic value as aircraft carriers, which can fly weapons deep into enemy territory. Dingemans' view was also that since no one knew how long the war was going to last, the loss of one of the two assault ships could have serious operational consequences not only in reducing the ability to carry troops but also providing an alternative platform for Headquarters Land Forces. Clapp acknowledged Dingemans' concerns, but so far as he was concerned the risks to the success of the operation were from the surviving Argentinian patrol craft, mines and the weather. Nevertheless, applying the traditional naval principle of 'the man on the spot must decide', he told Dingemans that, as commander of the operation, he should release the landing craft as close as he dared to Bluff Cove, but that Northwood would be less than pleased if the land battle was indecisive and a political stalemate developed as a direct consequence of the Royal Navy not helping.

War is full of risk and the Royal Navy has never minded losing ships provided that the cause is justified. The threat assessment was low risk. The operation was to take place at night, which restricted air activity. The submarine threat did not exist. Of the two Argentinian patrol craft known to be in the Falklands, one, the *Rio Iguazu*, was beached in Button Bay after its aborted attempt to transport two 105mm Pack Howitzers to Goose Green. Mines were an unknown factor. The threat from the land-based Exocets at Stanley was minimal, provided Dingemans remained outside the sanitized zone. If HMS *Intrepid* was hit, the British had sufficient control of the sea to organize a safe tow. Clapp, who had previously been in HMS *Norfolk* trialling Exocet, was not particularly concerned about the threat.

Within ten minutes of arriving back at *Blue Beach Two* Southby-Tailyour, still under the impression that he would be taking the Welsh Guards by landing craft from San Carlos to Cantera Beach for their march to Fitzroy, was summoned to HMS *Fearless* where he was briefed by a member of Clapp's amphibious warfare staff that he was to transfer to HMS *Intrepid* and, using her four Landing Craft Utility, was to:

❒ *Travel in HMS Intrepid to the vicinity of Elephant Island.*

❒ *Then ferry the Scots Guards by landing craft to Bluff Cove.*

❒ *Rendezvous with HMS Fearless the following night and take the Welsh Guards to Fitzroy (from where they would march to Bluff Cove).*

Southby-Tailyour then met with Clapp, who told him he was keen to keep the soldiers in a landing craft for no more than four hours and that two routes had been discussed:

❑ *West of Lively Island and into Choiseul Sound and then along the coast.*

❑ *Dropped at Middle Island, which is in the mouth of Choiseul Sound, or possibly Elephant Island, but no closer, and ferry them at Bluff Cove. This was a voyage of about four hours at six knots or two and half hours at full speed.*

Clapp said he favoured the second option. Southby-Tailyour assured him that he knew the navigational hazards of the planned route. Dingemans was anxious to leave and time was short, so short that Southby-Tailyour was unable to return to his headquarters and collect his navigation notes and charts then lying in his trench. Clapp then briefed Woodward and warned him that his ships would be passing through an operational area controlled by the Carrier Battle Group. Woodward continued to express his opinion that the Army should march to Fitzroy.

Woodward was expecting 3rd Commando Brigade operations during the night and assigned the Type 42 destroyer HMS *Cardiff*, commanded by Captain Michael Harris, the Type 12 frigate HMS *Yarmouth* and two Type 21 frigates, HMS *Active* and *Arrow*, to support them. Then, when it became clear that 5th Infantry Brigade would not be ready to assist, Major-General Moore postponed operations at 4.15pm, but it does seem that Woodward did not receive this transmission and at 7.40pm signalled HMS *Fearless* asking if his ships were still required. Several minutes later the 4.15pm signal was received by the Carrier Battle Group and so Woodward recalled the two frigates and left the other ships to ambush aircraft blockade-runners using the Wickham Heights as a navigation mark to Stanley. The box was essentially an ambush of a route across Wickham Heights used by Argentinian aircraft flying to and from the military air base at Stanley. Woodward, as the senior officer, was expected to monitor operational activities between his Carrier Battle Group and Clapp's inshore forces and circulate procedures as to where command should be exchanged in order to avoid friendly 'blue on blue' engagements. However, it does seem that Commodore Amphibious Warfare was not briefed about the ambush.

The Type 42 destroyer HMS *Exeter* was already on air defence duties near Swan Island in the middle of Falkland Sound, ready to intercept Argentinian aircraft. Woodward assured Clapp that he would not have any ships in the area where HMS *Intrepid* would be operating. Captain

Dingemans had HMS *Penelope* as his close escort and its commanding officer, Commander Peter Rickard, commanded the defence of the task force. Captain Hugo White of HMS *Avenger* was the advance guard with orders to divert the attention of the Fox Bay garrison and then investigate the steep-sided and narrow Albemarle Harbour as a suitable bolthole for any ship caught in the open. This caused a minor eruption with Woodward, who sent a signal this was not to happen. Clapp, whose Combined Task Group controlled inshore operations, ignored it. HMS *Arrow* was on guard at the north end of Falkland Sound. In a final conversation with Woodward, Clapp was startled to be informed that the Admiral intended to withdraw HMS *Hermes* about forty miles to the east to clean her boilers after 20,000 miles. It meant that air operations would be further limited except for the Harriers using 'Sid's Strip'. This does seems a strange decision considering that an important sea move was imminent.

At 8.30pm, on radio silence, the small task force built around HMS *Intrepid* weighed anchor and crept out of Fanning Head in a night of good visibility and relatively calm seas. Captain Dingemans then received a confirmatory signal from Commodore Amphibious Warfare, copied to Rear-Admiral Woodward, that at last light he was to leave San Carlos Water with his escorts and conduct a fast passage to Lively Island where he was to unload his four landing craft and return to San Carlos before first light. With HMS *Penelope* about two miles ahead, this would be the first time that a ship of HMS *Intrepid's* size would sail south through Falkland Sound on a course that would take her past ground not yet cleared of the enemy. As a precautionary measure, ahead of him Captain Greenhalgh, in his Scout, flew over some of the many islands searching for the enemy, but without success. A Gurkha reconnaissance patrol checked Lively Island and found no enemy. With trails of thick kelp marked on charts, dark islands, no lights and the ever-present threat of the enemy, navigation was not easy, but Dingemans was fortunate to have a highly experienced navigator, Lieutenant-Commander Bruce Webb, who periodically called out the positions of islands and navigational features for those on the darkened bridge to identify, so that he was able to keep to an average speed of 18 knots. The next gamble of Wilson's bold move was underway.

6

The Move to Port Pleasant – 5 to 8 June

As the darkened ships steamed south at action stations, the only evidence was the grey-green fluorescence thrown aside as they ploughed through the water. Major Southby-Tailyour joined Captain Dingemans on the bridge of HMS *Intrepid* as part of his planning team, together with Lieutenant-Commander Webb.

During the course of their discussions, Dingemans told Major Southby-Tailyour that HMS *Intrepid* was not going east of Lively Island because the political risk to the ship was too great. Some controversy surrounds this announcement because Southby-Tailyour, who was not then aware of the political implications of the assault ships, had understood from his briefings on HMS *Fearless* that he would have a four-hour hop voyage to Bluff Cove, but he was now faced with an eight-hour sea voyage in craft designed for inshore work. On board the assault ship, he had been briefed first by Clapp's staff that he would be dropped near Elephant Island and then by Commodore Clapp that it was either to be off Middle Island or possibly Elephant Island. Elephant Island was inside the Stanley-based Exocet window, whereas Lively Island was outside it. In spite of the different briefings, Southby-Tailyour had not expected to be dropped off Lively Island. On the other hand, Captain Dingemans had been signalled to release the landing craft off Lively Island, but, as Commanding Officer and 'the man on the spot', the decision was ultimately his. It seems both men had different orders and expectations.

Southby-Tailyour was unable to persuade the adamant Dingemans that he should drop the landing craft east of Elephant Island, but there was no way that he could seek clarification of the orders. He believed that to do the trip once without charts was bad enough, but twice was tempting fate, because the Argentinians would be alerted. He also asked for a frigate escort for the landing craft as far as East Island, where, on board HMS *Fearless,* he had also been told that he might be dropped. This request had previously been rejected by Clapp, who wished to retain an element of surprise. He tried to persuade Dingemans that the loss of 600 soldiers at this point in the war was far more significant than the loss of an assault ship. The atmosphere on the bridge was amicable, if tense, but Dingemans had the last word. Churchill's jewelled bracelet of amphibious warfare was a touch tarnished.

As it travelled south only a few miles off the east coast of West Falkland, the task force experienced a few frights. Vehicle lights were seen south of Port Howard at 9.20pm and HMS *Intrepid* went to Air Raid Red when three radar scans were picked up to the north-west, but these turned out to be spurious. HMS *Avenger* intercepted radio traffic and radar scanning from the Argentinian naval transport *Bahia Paraiso*, which was flying hospital ship colours, although there was good Intelligence that she had also been involved in operational activities. Approaching the southern exit to Falkland Sound at about 10pm, as HMS *Avenger* left to bombard a suspected radar site on Sea Lion Island, a Marine Infantry Tigercat air defence missile locked on to HMS *Intrepid*, but nothing happened. When a C-130 Hercules radar reflection was picked up flying along Wickham Heights to Stanley soon afterwards, Dingemans ordered weapons tight. A returning C-130, probably the same aircraft, was picked up about an hour later.

At about the same time the Argentinian Joint Operations Centre intelligence warned Major-General Garcia that 3rd Commando Brigade was about to launch an all-out heliborne assault on the Stanley Outer Defence Zone. Brigadier-General Menendez placed his forces on immediate alert and instructed Brigadier-General Jofre to send Special Forces fighting patrols to disrupt 3rd Commando Brigade operations. Quite how the Argentinian Intelligence staff came to this conclusion is a mystery. It is likely the source was intercepted radio traffic, but was certainly misinterpreted. True, Major-General Moore had planned for 3rd Commando Brigade to assault the Stanley defences as soon as possible but it may be that the departure of the HMS *Intrepid* task force was somehow predicted to be a prelude to an assault. The radio messages surrounding the loading of the two Guards battalions were interpreted to be preparations for a helicopter assault. But all but one of the Chinook heavy-lift helicopters were sitting at the bottom of the ocean, an event well-publicized by the world's media. True, more Sea Kings had arrived in theatre and conceivably this prompted the Argentinians to give the British a troop-lift capability they did not have. In any event there were insufficient helicopters to carry out a three-battalion assault on well-defended positions.

At about the same time as the troops were filing into the landing craft, communications between Corporal Daughtrey and Brigade Headquarters failed. Major Lambe instructed the Headquarters and Signal Squadron A Troop Staff Sergeant, Joe Baker, to fly to Pleasant

Peak and fix the problem. When Staff-Sergeant Christopher Griffin arrived for the task, Lambe was delighted because he knew Griffin to be a good pilot who had demonstrated his abilities in Wales. Major Forge then unexpectedly appeared and insisted on accompanying Baker. The night was fine and the flight plan was in friendly territory, at least as far as Brigade Headquaters was concerned, and therefore there was no need to inform anyone else. But Brigade Headquarters was not aware of Rear-Admiral Woodward's Wickham Heights 'shoot-to-kill' box. It also seems that Commodore Clapp was unaware of the box. As the instigator, Woodward should have made his colleague Task Group commanders aware of anything that might have affected inshore operations.

As HMS *Intrepid* passed Sea Lion Island, Captain Dingemans planned unloading the landing craft. He wanted to place them as close to Bluff Cove as he could but he had to take into consideration the current and predicted sea state, tactical situation and Exocet threat against the guaranteed unloading of troops. As his ship came south around Lively Island it experienced a marked increase in the height and motion of the swell. Although the night was still clear, worsening weather was predicted. Whatever happened, the dock gate had to be lowered in order to flood the tank deck and allow the landing craft to leave. To achieve this, the ship was flooded with 7,000 tons of seawater, which pitches her aft down from 23 feet to 30 feet and drops her speed to about four knots. HMS *Intrepid* could be a ponderous old lady butting into the incoming sea and at risk from the Exocet at Stanley. Launching the landing craft in open sea with a deepening swell also risks severe damage to the landing craft and injury to those on the tank deck because, every time the ship pitches and yaws with every crest and trough, this is magnified in the narrow confines of the tank deck where the water rushes in and then, as it ebbs, it meets incoming seawater. Landing craft crash into each other with screeching and thumping and the men risk injury. Dingemans had two choices – carry on to the east of Lively Island and unload the landing craft in exposed sea conditions with no cover or retire to the leeward side of Lively Island and calmer waters. As the Commanding Officer of the ship with responsibility for the 540 sailors and 650 soldiers on board, he chose the latter, but it was not an easy judgement for he knew the soldiers were now committed to a long sea voyage in open landing craft.

Controversy surrounds this decision. Dingemans knew the Royal Navy had never previously minded losing ships, provided the overall aim was achieved. He knew that four very lightly armoured and armed landing craft, full of soldiers, were about to enter an area in which any ship encountered was expected to be Argentinian along a coast not yet cleared of the enemy with worsening weather predicted. Balanced against this

105

were his orders to be back at San Carlos Water by daybreak. Dingemans had worked with Major Southby-Tailyour on several NATO exercises and knew him well. He had total confidence that if there was one man who could execute the final stage to Bluff Cove it was Southby-Tailyour.

At about 2.30am on 6 June HMS *Intrepid* hove-to two miles west of Lively Island, opened the dock gate and flooded the tank deck. A haze lying on the surface disrupted good visibility. Dingemans told Southby-Tailyour that the only ships he would see would be enemy. It seems that the need for the landing craft to be provided with the Carrier Battle Group recognition signal was not discussed. The four landing craft with the Scots Guards, 3 Troop, 9 Parachute Squadron, and some other troops on board retracted into the swaying sea. According to Lance-Sergeant McDermid, the 150 men in each landing craft were briefed that the voyage would not last long. Although each man was equipped with a life jacket, none had a survival suit. HMS *Intrepid* then left the scene at 4.30am, leaving the four landing craft bobbing around on the ocean. It seems that Southby-Tailyour was not given a fix and, leading in *Tango One*, he headed for Lively Island to get one. When Dingemans checked his radar as he left, the landing craft were moving line ahead in the general direction of Bluff Cove. Phase One had been completed.

While the troops were filing into the landing craft, at about 4am, as Staff-Sergeant Griffin was approaching Pleasant Peak from San Carlos, a radar operator informed Captain Harris on HMS *Cardiff* that there was an unidentified air contact moving west to east across Wickham Heights in the same general area that Argentinian Air Force C-130s were using to navigate to Stanley, but he thought it to be a helicopter. Since it was inside the 'shoot-to-kill' box and no one on his ship had any knowledge of friendly aircraft in the area, Harris ordered Sea Darts to be fired at the target. The second missile connected at a range of eleven miles near Pleasant Peak and the blip on the screen disappeared. HMS *Cardiff* was now keyed up with a 'kill'.

At about 4.15am Corporal Daughtrey, who had moved higher up Pleasant Peak to improve communications and for better defence, heard Griffin searching for them and showed a light. It seems this was not seen and the next thing that Daughtrey and his men knew was a violent orange light, large explosion and shockwaves shuddering across the mountain. When communication was lost with the helicopter the rebroadcast team were asked by Brigade Headquarters to search for it, but after an hour and with the weather closing in, Daughtrey's men returned to their hide.

East of Lively Island *Tango One's* fragile radar packed up, possibly because Southby-Tailyour was flicking it off and on to get fixes without giving away his position or vessel type. Midway along the coast, high explosive suddenly fountained in the sea and, although its origins are not known, they could have been two spent Exocets thought to have been fired by the land-based system that night, in which case Dingemans' concerns about this threat seem justified. In any event, the incident remains a mystery, but was enough to highlight the vulnerability of the landing craft. While Southby-Tailyour was rafted alongside *Tango Three* to check his position with Colour-Sergeant Garwood's radar, a fast aircraft seemed to pass by at high speed and disappear. This turned out to be an anomaly of Garwood's radar, but of more concern were two more fast contacts that had developed about four miles astern. Since he had been briefed by Dingemans that there were no friendly ships in the area, Southby-Tailyour assumed them to be hostile and to disguise his destination altered course toward the dark and craggy shelter of Dangerous Point, which is on the north-east coast of Lively Island. This seemed a pointless gesture and a few minutes later he decided to head for Choiseul Sound to take advantage of the shoals and shallow entrance in case the landing craft had to be abandoned. By now the wind was rising and short, icy breakers were slamming against the steep angular sides of the landing craft and hurling solid waves into the packed well deck. The weight of the load also meant that the scupper ports, which were designed to let water out, were frequently below the surface and consequently the sea poured in, quickly soaking the soldiers. As anyone who has travelled in a landing craft in rough seas will testify, without shelter it is an unpleasant and demoralizing experience to be exposed in the well deck. The next few hours for the unprotected soldiers could only get worse. There was nowhere to sit and making a brew was out of the question. They were also unaware of the drama. Agreeing with Major Mackay-Dick that the speed of the landing craft, about nine knots, was no match for the approaching ships and that they had few options, Southby-Tailyour set course for East Island on his original heading. It seemed to him that on this night when the Royal Navy was most wanted, as his tiny flotilla sailed along a coast technically not cleared of the enemy, they were conspicuous by their absence.

Carving at speed through the rising seas behind them, HMS *Cardiff* and *Yarmouth*, on their way to the Stanley gun line, had picked up four surface contacts soon after launching the Sea Dart. Having been briefed by Rear-Admiral Woodward's staff that there were no British inshore operations planned for the night, Harris assumed they were Argentinians, possibly fast patrol boats. According to Southby-Tailyour and others several years later, it seems that Harris and his gunnery officer flipped a coin to decide whether to load his 4.5-inch main armament with high explosive or illumination.

Southby-Tailyour and his command team were really concerned. Through their binoculars they could see the bow wave of a fast warship evidently pursuing 600 men in four slow blunt-nosed landing craft thrashing into unsettled seas. Since Dingemans had told Southby-Tailyour that there were no British warships in the area, the two contacts had to be Argentinian. Suddenly six star shells burst in quick succession over the landing craft. In the sodden well deck of his landing craft, Lance-Sergeant McDermid had no idea of what was happening and when the star shells burst into the inky darkness there was mayhem on board as soldiers reached for weapons and fitted magazines. In the darkness of the night he never saw the ships.

In the inky darkness a tiny signal light flickered in Morse code, 'Heave to'. Southby-Tailyour ordered his flotilla to stop. At least the message was in English, which was good sign. The next signal sparkled, 'Friend'. Southby-Tailyour replied, 'To which side?' No reply and then the mysterious ships, whining turbines racing, disappeared into the darkness of the south-east. Southby-Tailyour was furious. No counter-identification from the ships, his presence compromised and no offer of assistance – nothing.

Although Woodward knew about the Fitzroy operation, having had several discussions with Commodore Clapp, it seems that Captain Harris and Commander Morton, of HMS *Cardiff* and *Yarmouth* respectively, were not aware. He would later claim, when his book was reviewed, that the landing craft were late and in the wrong position. Absolutely correct, the landing craft should not have been in the area. The consequences of a 'Navy blue on Army blue' would have been politically disastrous and thus it was fortunate that Captain Harris, already anxious about the validity of the air contact, had fired star shell. Next morning Harris expressed concern to Woodward that his air contact might be the missing Army Gazelle. He must have been distraught that he nearly had a second 'blue-on-blue', potentially a major disaster.

Fright over and still several hours to go, Southby-Tailyour resumed the course for East Island. With an error of ten degrees on the radar and aware of a magnetic anomaly south of Port Pleasant, which was marked on his chart left in the bottom of a trench at San Carlos, he led the landing craft into the 'Exocet Box' and was fortunate to identify Direction Island before it disappeared into the radar clutter of an increasing northerly gale. It was not the weather for landing craft. Creeping along the coast, the flotilla reached 'Z Bend' just as light began to crack the eastern horizon. There was now a decision to be made – either motor straight through a maelstrom of its currents or go east around East Island and into Fitzroy Sound. With 600 soaked soldiers on board, Southby-

Tailyour chose the latter, admittedly longer and wetter but safer. Motoring through the choppy waters of Port Fitzroy, at about 8am the landing craft nosed through the narrow neck of Bluff Cove Inlet and the few houses of the settlement were sighted, to the immense relief to those on board.

Ashore, Bombardier Marsh, of 29 Battery, had just woken up and, looking out of his shelter, saw the four landing craft about 100 metres to his front and shouted, 'There are enemy landing craft in the bay!' Sergeant Morgan, the Number One on Gun A, brought his gun to bear over open sights. Two other guns stood to. A frantic radio conversation with the Battery Commander, Major Rice, established that the landing craft were bringing the Scots Guards. But communications between Darwin and Bluff Cove were still intermittent. The 2nd Parachute Battalion group was unaware of the landings.

The four landing craft came alongside the jetty and the cold, stiff, soaking soldiers clambered out. It is a credit to their discipline that there were only three cases of exposure and a damaged knee. The weather was atrocious – heavy rain, a battering wind and dropping temperatures. Since Lieutenant-Colonel Scott yet had to arrive, there appeared to be some indecision among his officers of what was expected of them. A few soldiers found shelter in a warehouse, but most remained outside waiting for orders. The few weather casualties suffered during the night rose alarmingly and two parachute regimental medical assistants were soon working hard to keep the more severe exposure and hypothermia cases alive. Major Mackay-Dick and Captain Tim Spicer, the Operations Officer, visited the 2nd Parachute Battalion Tactical Headquarters and were told by Lieutenant-Colonel Chaundler that they should move north and dig in. Spicer later retired from the Army, founded the company Sandline International and supplied 'military consultants' to several countries. A little later Chaundler went outside to find hundreds of Scots Guardsmen still standing in the lee of the warehouses with rain pouring off their helmets. He was not amused and when he found two senior officers in some shelter, advised them that if they didn't get their men sorted out the Battalion would be written off as an effective unit. One of them replied that nothing could be done until the Commanding Officer arrived.

After leaving her landing craft off Lively Island HMS *Intrepid* had steamed at near full speed to be under the San Carlos defensive umbrella by daybreak. She was about an hour short and off Great Island when Commander (Engineering) Brian Rutherford informed Captain Dingemans that the collar around the bearings of her main engine was defective. Dingemans had two options – slow down to about 10 knots and guarantee returning to San Carlos but risk air attack or continue steaming at full speed and risk permanent damage to his engines. Midway between the two Argentinian garrisons and with the enemy coast not far off his port quarter, Dingemans opted for the second choice and dropped anchor in San Carlos Water at 10.27am. While his engineers began repairs, he visited Commodore Clapp on HMS *Fearless* and briefed him on the night's events, maintaining that sending the assault ships was a considerable risk. Clapp explained that the ground forces were about to attack Stanley and Major-General Moore needed everything in place for success. In the event HMS *Intrepid* was to make six trips to Lively Island and transfer supplies, equipment and ammunition to landing craft from Fitzroy.

Phase One of the 5th Infantry Brigade move to Fitzroy and Bluff Cove was complete and early that morning Brigadier Wilson flew to Fitzroy, taking with him his Tactical Headquarters, Lieutenant-Colonel Holt and Major Barney Rolfe-Smith, a Parachute Regiment officer posted to Brigade Headquarters as a senior Air Operations Officer, and set up in the sheep-shearing shed. Lieutenant-Colonel Scott arrived at Bluff Cove where, after meeting Chaundler, the Scots Guards took over from 2nd Parachute Battalion, which prepared to fall back to Fitzroy as planned. In order to assemble his Battalion, Southby-Tailyour agreed with Chaundler's request that the landing craft be used to ferry the men across Bluff Cove Inlet. Chaundler felt that his Battalion would soon be required and needed to sort itself out. Brigadier Wilson agreed, but by the time a runner arrived at the jetty, the landing craft had gone and they could not be raised on the radio. Southby-Tailyour had given orders to his four coxswains to remain in the general area of Bluff Cove until he returned. But the 5th Infantry Brigade's communications were still experiencing considerable problems and so he persuaded a Sea King crew to fly him to San Carlos to confirm orders for the next night, where, on HMS *Fearless*, he briefed Major-General Moore's and Commodore Clapp's staff on the events on the night before

On Pleasant Peak at first light a small party sent out by Corporal Daughtrey found the wreckage of Griffin's helicopter and confirmed that there were no survivors. As far as Brigadier Wilson was concerned, his intelligence assessment was that the Gazelle had been shot down by an Argentinian patrol believed to be operating on Wickham Heights. He therefore instructed Lieutenant-Colonel Morgan, whose Gurkhas were looking for suspected Argentinian positions on Mount Usborne, to destroy them. Issuing orders to Lieutenant (Queen's Gurkha Officer) Rai Belbahadur to fly to the scene, secure it and then find the Argentinians responsible, Morgan told him 'to take out anyone up there'. Belbahadur's thirty-man patrol from C Company was flown to Pleasant Peak that morning, but the higher the Gurkhas climbed the mistier it became. Finding nothing, they were about to search the lower slopes when a scout heard voices above them. Belbahadur decided to surprise whoever it was by creeping up on them and opening fire, then discovered that the voices belonged to Daughtrey and his signals team.

The bodies of four British were later flown to Ajax Bay where post mortems at Ajax Bay confirmed beyond doubt that their fatal injuries – extensive lower body and limb injuries – were conducive to a large explosion beneath them. When air crash investigators examined the site, they later reported in a confidential document that there was no evidence that the Gazelle had been shot down by a Sea Dart. Griffin left behind a seriously ill baby in Great Ormond Street Hospital for Sick Children and had gone south because he felt it was his duty to do so. But the families, in particular that of Griffin's aircrew, Lance-Corporal Simon Cockton, were not convinced and forced the Ministry of Defence to hold another inquiry. On this occasion, findings by a forensic team confirmed that the wreckage included parts of a Sea Dart. The Ministry of Defence were forced to conclude that the shooting down of the Gazelle had been a 'blue on blue', most probably by HMS *Cardiff*.

Meanwhile Lieutenant Oates and his 1/7th Gurkha Rifles Reconnaissance Platoon were searching the vast soggy mass of Lafonia for Argentinian patrols thought to be targeting helicopter routes and also rounding up Argentinian stragglers who had escaped the defeat at Goose Green. Carried in 656 Squadron Scouts, patrols systematically cleared settlements and houses. At about 1pm on 6 June a patrol reported enemy at Egg Harbour House and asked for helicopter support. Sergeant Ian Roy flew from Darwin and, skipping over a ridge, saw four Argentinians evacuate a building and take cover in a gully, but then lost them. He requested support and Captain Philip Piper flew forward in a Gazelle and took over from Roy, who returned to Goose Green to refuel. Piper and his co-pilot, Lance-Corporal Les Beresford, circled the gully to keep the enemy pinned down. Roy then returned, bringing with him Captain Sam Drennan in his Scout. At Goose Green Gurkha reinforcements were loaded into an 825 Naval Air Squadron Sea King. The pilots of the three light helicopters agreed to winkle out the Argentinians from the gully. Roy approached the gully and his co-pilot, Corporal Johns, loosed a SS-11 missile, which exploded on what was reported to be an enemy position but turned out to be a crop of rocks! As Drennan flew over another part of the gully, eight Argentinian soldiers ran into the open and raised their hands in surrender. Drennan landed and, when his co-pilot, Lance-Corporal John Gammon, jumped out to take the Argentinians prisoner, his belt buckle broke and he was forced to marshal them holding his sub machine-gun in one hand and his trousers with the other. The Gurkhas then arrived, but none were fluent in English and none of the Argentinians spoke English, let alone Nepalese. The Army Air Corps aircrew only spoke English. And so it was all a little muddled. The Argentinian officer in the group refused to lie down, as instructed, because it was undignified and also wet, but was persuaded to do so when a Gurkha NCO drew his kukri. Among the captured weapons was a Soviet SA-7 *Strella* ground-to-air missile, one of 130 delivered from Peru on 24 May. The kukri was later auctioned to raise funds for the Soldiers', Sailors' and Airmen's Families Association and raised £1,300.

Commodore Amphibious Warfare set about organizing Phase Two of the 5th Infantry Brigade move:

❐ *Load and despatch Sir Tristram with sufficient ammunition and other stores that can be unloaded in one day, in line with Commodore Clapp's policy.*

❐ *Move the Welsh Guards, 4 Field Troop, 9 Parachute Squadron, 16 Field Ambulance and others to Fitzroy in either HMS Fearless or HMS Intrepid.*

But 16 Field Ambulance was still not ready for loading. With HMS *Intrepid* still experiencing engine problems, Commodore Clapp accepted an offer from Captain Jeremy Larken, the commanding officer of HMS *Fearless*. Clapp:

It would have been stupid to send Intrepid in again. He (Dingemans) clearly thought we knew his problem but I don't think it was clear to us exactly what was implied. There was also an uncomfortable rivalry between the two ships which meant that I and Div staff, who were on Fearless, were sometimes, I suspect, given a biased view of Intrepid.

The plan was now to:

❐ *Rendezvous with Major Southby-Tailyour and the four HMS Intrepid Landing Craft Utility, coming from Bluff Cove, south of Elephant Island.*

❐ *Cross-deck the troops into two of them and two Fearless landing craft, Foxtrots One and Four, for the return trip to Fitzroy.*

❐ *Bring two remaining HMS Intrepid landing craft back to help with the unloading of ships in the Transport Area in San Carlos Water.*

Now fully briefed, Southby-Tailyour returned by helicopter to Bluff Cove to prepare for the night's operation. Rain-laden, storm-force wind had whipped up the sea and blasted across the moorland, but at least a window of moderate weather was expected that night, which would ease ferrying the troops to Fitzroy. Intending to assemble the *Tango* landing craft, he found one sheltering under White Point but of the other three there was no sign. Thankful to be told by the helicopter loadmaster that it was too dangerous to be winched down, Southby-Tailyour gave the pilot a handwritten message to be delivered to Clapp that the weather at Bluff Cove was bad but expected to moderate. He did not mention the missing landing craft and had no reason to do so. Dropped at Bluff Cove settlement and sheltering with the Scots Guards, he was confident that the landing craft would re-assemble once the weather moderated. As the hours passed, Southby-Tailyour was forced to concede that, with three landing craft still missing, he would not make the rendezvous. True to style, he described it as an 'embarrassment'.

At 7.30pm HMS *Fearless*, accompanied by *HMS Penelope* and *Avenger,* left the sanctuary of San Carlos Water and steamed south through Falkland Sound. HMS *Avenger* sped ahead to drop a Special Boat Squadron patrol to search Sea Lion Island for the suspected radar station. Two hours later *Sir Tristram* left San Carlos. Southby-Tailyour radioed HMS *Fearless* that the weather was still bad at Bluff Cove and the operation might have to be cancelled, but they caused some puzzlement because, at sea, conditions were much better.

By about 2.00am on 7 June Captain Larken was hove-to south of Elephant Island, but there was no sign of Southby-Tailyour and the landing craft. Risking compromise, he launched his Lynx helicopter to search for them, without success. Faced with a quandary, Larken had Major Guy Yeoman, a Royal Corps of Transport officer and one of Clapp's Operations staff officers, wake Major Tony Todd, also of the Royal Corps of Transport with maritime experience and an additional Operations Officer also on Clapp's staff, with instructions that he was to lead the landing craft operation. Yeoman briefed Todd that the four *Intrepid* landing craft had missed the rendezvous and he was to take half the Welsh Guards and the parachute engineer squadron in the two *Fearless* landing craft to Bluff Cove. In fact, Clapp's Phase Two plan was that the troops should be landed at Fitzroy.

On the tank deck Lieutenant-Colonel Rickett was faced with having to split his Battalion, something he had striven not to do since landing. Seeking out Major-General Moore, he said he was not happy about the proposal, particularly as his orders from Brigadier Wilson were to dig in north-east of Bluff Cove astride the track from Stanley. Moore assured him that the rest of the Battalion would be landed the following night. Rickett, more confident, ordered his Land Rover-borne Battalion

Headquarters and Reconnaissance Platoon into *Foxtrot One,* while Number 2 Company, Anti Tank Platoon, Machine Gun Platoon and Tactical Headquarters filed on to *Foxtrot Four.* 1 Troop, 9 Parachute Squadron, who had been sent for by Major Davies to repair Fitzroy Bridge, was also embarked, as was Major Jordan, the Battery Commander of 97 Battery, which was supporting the Welsh Guards. This left the Prince of Wales Company, commanded by Major Guy Sayle, and 3 Company, commanded by Major Charles Bremner, Captain Foxley's 4 Field Troop, 9 Parachute Squadron and several small units, including a 3rd Commando Brigade Royal Signals rear link detachment, unable to land.

At about 4.14pm under clear skies, *Foxtrots One* and *Four* retracted into slightly bumpy seas and, escorted for the first part of the nineteen-mile voyage by HMS *Avenger,* set off. HMS *Fearless* returned to San Carlos. In a fine example of seamanship in unfamiliar craft in strange waters and aided by a satellite communication system, Todd guided the landing craft and at 8am came alongside the Bluff Cove jetty. The first that Southby-Tailyour knew of their arrival was the appearance of two Welsh Guards Provost Staff on motorcycles. It was still raining heavily and Rickett's soaked and cold men plodded through the settlement and, led by Lieutenant Symes's Reconnaissance Platoon, took over the positions of A Company, 2nd Parachute Battalion. Rickett established his command post in some caravans abandoned before the Argentinian invasion by workers constructing the new road to Stanley. Symes's patrols fanned out and within hours were in contact with Argentinian activity south-east of Mount Harriet. *Sir Tristram* then anchored in Port Pleasant off Fitzroy and began to unload.

1 Troop, 9 Parachute Squadron, was ferried immediately by landing craft to Fitzroy Bridge with the equipment that had been unloaded from *Sir Tristram* during the morning. Working in appalling conditions for two days, 15 feet above the decidedly uninviting water, they rebuilt the abutment and manufactured a new pier. Sheltering beneath his poncho, Lance-Corporal Singer welded four rolled steel joints together to bridge the 66-feet gap. By the time the repair was finished it was suitable for loads up to 10 tons, although originally built for 4-ton farm vehicles. However, Major Davies reckoned the weight of overloaded Scorpions would have been too much and, on his advice, they were sent around via Ridge Camp, at the head of the creek, when the time came for them to move forward to Bluff Cove and beyond. Davies later reflected that the bridge was completed with methods 'that Alexander the Great would have recognized. In all, I was quite proud of our efforts there.'

During the building Sapper Everrett developed an ear infection and was shipped back to 2nd Parachute Battalion's medical centre where Captain Steve Hughes, the Medical Officer, had sent him to the Fitzroy Community Centre to keep him out of the wind and let his ear heal. He was still at the centre when casualties from the bombing of the two ships began to arrive. When it was all over, Everrett had disappeared. Davies sent his Chief Clerk around all the ships and hospital ships to find Everrett but this one was 'lost'. A few weeks later Davies saw a newspaper and there, on the front page, in Cambridge Military Hospital in Aldershot was Everrett drinking a bottle of that famous Task Force brew that only the privileged few tasted. The medical system had swept him up, shipped him on to the *Uganda* and then to England as a wounded hero with earache. But there was no record of him moving between Fitzroy and Aldershot.

So far fortune had favoured the British. Over two nights they had managed to land the Scots Guards and half the Welsh Guards at Bluff Cove without any interference with 2nd Parachute Battalion regrouping at Fitzroy. The unloading of *Sir Tristram* was underway using landing craft and Sergeant Boultby's Mexeflote. But the cost had been high – a 656 Squadron Gazelle, its crew and two Royal Signals confirmed killed, and three HMS *Intrepid* landing craft and their crews missing. Important issues also needed to be addressed, in particular ferrying the troops left on board HMS *Fearless* to Fitzroy in time for the attack on the Stanley defences.

Dawn brought a window of moderate weather. Still concerned at not finding his three missing *Intrepid* landing craft, Major Southby-Tailyour, in preparation for the swift unloading of the *Sir Tristram*, led the two HMS *Fearless* and one HMS *Intrepid* landing craft through the now more tranquil 'Z' Bend and secured on the Fitzroy jetty. Throughout the voyage, the crews were watching for signs of the predatory Pucara ground-attack aircraft. To his relief, Southby-Tailyour saw the three missing landing craft and called for a report from the coxswains as to why they had missed the rendezvous the previous night. Their account did nothing for his humour.

It will be recalled that, when he had delivered the Scots Guards to Bluff Cove, Southby-Tailyour had agreed to Lieutenant-Colonel Chaundler's suggestion that 2nd Parachute Battalion should be ferried across Bluff Cove Inlet by the landing craft, but by the time a runner had been sent to find them the boats had disappeared into the mist to find shelter. According to General Frost, in his book *2 Para Falklands,* 2nd Parachute Battalion believed that the four landing craft were sheltering from high winds, low cloud and driving rain at the mouth of Bluff Cove Inlet. Borrowing Brigadier Wilson's helicopter, Major Keeble was despatched by Chaundler to find the landing craft and located them sheltering from the appalling weather. Flying alongside them, according to Frost, Keeble was–

a past master at such negotiations. His style of bluff and rhetoric, matched by the occasional wave of a pistol in the direction of the coxswain, soon left no doubt as to the urgency of the need.

While Keeble, an honourable and humane man, had negotiated the surrender of Task Force *Mercedes* at Goose Green, he did so under the control of Headquarters 3rd Commando Brigade. Accounts that he poked his pistol in the stomach of a Royal Marine coxswain are incorrect. In any event, during the late afternoon three very reluctant coxswains felt they had no alternative but disobey Southby-Tailyour's instructions not to move until he contacted them, collected the parachute companies from their various locations and entered Port Fitzroy. Without charts, hindered by poor visibility, faulty radar and needing to avoid the lengthy tentacles of the kelp, navigation was very difficult and within two hours the landing craft were back in Bluff Cove Inlet. Frost records that Chaundler was somewhat irritated and accused a young Marine of getting lost after being told that the radar was intermittent. As a peace-time yachtsman, Chaundler found it incomprehensible that the landing craft should end up in the same place from which they had departed. The appearance of hot soup for the sodden paras was taken to be an apology instead of a humanitarian gesture. The landing craft set off again, this time in pitch darkness, with Chaundler apparently taking a much keener interest in events, and, as calm dawn broke, they tied up at the Fitzroy jetty where they were met by 2nd Parachute Battalion's Technical Quartermaster, Captain Banks Middleton, with a line of hayboxes of steaming stew and tea. But a weather front then steamed in and the landing craft became stormbound and were unable to return to Bluff Cove and wait for Southby-Tailyour. Thus, they missed the rendezvous.

In claiming that the production of the pistol had been necessary, however extreme, Frost did himself, as a courageous man, and his advisers little credit. However, it was an act symptomatic of the 'must do' culture. The inescapable fact that the Royal Marine coxswains had been instructed to remain at Bluff Cove, as part of a wider plan, seems to have been irrelevant to 2nd Parachute Battalion. The inability of the three landing craft to return to Bluff Cove was a catalyst that would contribute to 5th Infantry Brigade taking casualties without firing a shot. Chaundler's criticism of the coxswains is a little unfair. They were not only colour-sergeants but fully qualified and experienced Landing

Craftsmen Class 1s trained in detail on coastal and offshore navigation and with a working knowledge of ocean seamanship. Their final exams included offshore passages to France. All were perfectly capable of taking a landing craft from Bluff Cove to Fitzroy, if they had charts, which they did not have, but without them it would have been foolhardy even in peacetime to do so, let alone in wartime along a coastline not cleared of the enemy and toward Stanley. The voyage the previous night had been their first trip to Bluff Cove and they had no idea of navigation markers, islets, kelp range, shallows, shoals, strength and direction of the current and weather predicted. As anyone who has navigated at sea can testify, one does not always have the benefit of three-dimensional observation and it can be difficult to identify landmarks and features without a decent compass and chart or maps. Foul weather had reduced visibility and the forces of wind, current and tide while navigating in unknown waters close to the enemy added to the coxswains' difficulties. As we have seen a radar was faulty and could only be calibrated in dock, so it was only by the sheer seamanship and experience of Major Southby-Tailyour that the landing craft reached Bluff Cove.

Commodore Clapp's Phase Two was still incomplete and, despite his reservations about more sea moves, was vigorously persuaded by Colonel Baxter to plan a third trip to Fitzroy so that 5th Infantry Brigade would be at full strength for the offensive. The complication of the embargo on HMS *Fearless* and *Intrepid* being unable to leave San Carlos during the day remained and all but one landing ship were on other tasks. The only ship available was the *Sir Galahad,* which was commanded by Captain Philip Roberts and had just arrived from Teal Inlet, fortuitously empty. Against his instincts but keen to support Moore, Clapp placed Roberts on immediate notice to take troops to Fitzroy.

Like her sister ships, the *Sir Galahad* displaced 4,473 tons and had a top speed of 17 knots. She could carry 400 fully equipped troops, 340 tons of war stores, two Mexeflotes and could handle three light helicopters or two support helicopters on her two flight decks. Unlike the other landing ships, except *Sir Percivale*, she was equipped with one 40mm anti-aircraft gun instead of two. So far *Sir Galahad* had led a charmed existence. Entering San Carlos Water at 9am on 21 May, she had escaped damage, but two Gazelle helicopters from the 3rd Commando Brigade Air Squadron operating from her were shot down off Port San Carlos while covering a Sea King moving T (Air Defence) Battery ashore. On 24 May a 100lb bomb hit her on the port side when she was packed with 300 men of the Commando Logistic Regiment. Fortunately it failed to explode but caused some fires. Captain Roberts' concerns at having troops on board in daylight were ignored and so he assumed the risk had been accepted. Another raid came in and Daggers strafed the landing ship. On fire, the *Sir Galahad* was beached and a bomb disposal team from Fleet Clearing Diving Team 3 found the bomb in a smashed battery store. It was carried on to the upper deck where Driver Mark Brough, of the ship's Port Operating Detachment, craned it into an inflatable boat full of corn-flake packets to cushion it. Brough was Mentioned in Despatches. The day before the BBC World Service had broadcast that Argentinian bombs were not exploding and, not for the only time during the war, did the BBC broadcast operational military information. The corporation has never been publicly held to account for these breaches in national security and the risks to the Service personnel fighting a real enemy as opposed to media ratings, any more than have the media managers in the Cabinet Office and/or the Ministry of Defence, who must have supplied the information. Refloated with the bomb heaved over the side, *Sir Galahad* joined other logistic ships in Woodward's loitering area on 25 May. During the night of 2/3 June, accompanied by *Sir Bedivere* and escorted by warships, she sailed to Teal Inlet with supplies for 3rd Commando Brigade. She repeated the supply run the next night independently and on the 5/6th acted as helicopter refuelling base for the Sea Kings and Wessex flying war stores forward before returning, empty, to San Carlos Water.

Clapp had another problem. The naval logistic organization in San Carlos Water was near collapse because he lacked landing craft to speed up unloading ships, some of which were now sailing direct into San Carlos from Ascension Island. The anchorage was becoming crowded and thus, with better weather predicted, was at risk from air raids. Two HMS *Fearless* landing craft were at Teal Inlet. The remaining six landing craft, *Foxtrots One* and *Four* and the four from HMS *Intrepid*, were at Fitzroy. Clapp desperately needed them and issued orders to Captain Larken to collect his two from Teal Inlet and Dingemans to recover his four from Fitzroy. This left the two *Fearless* landing craft at Port Pleasant unloading *Sir Tristram*. Clapp was not prepared to assign any landing craft to Wilson because, quite naturally, he felt that 5th Infantry Brigade lacked amphibious experience and would not use them 'sensibly'. He was never asked by Headquarters Land Forces to provide a naval liaison team to the Brigade because he presumed their Royal Marine liaison officer, Major Andy Keeling, was coping. He, however, had injured his back and spent some time in the HMS *Fearless* sick bay.

Meanwhile Commodore Clapp's and Major-General Moore's staff struggled with getting the remainder of 5th Infantry Brigade to Bluff Cove. One scheme was to beach *Sir Galahad* at Fitzroy, another to cross-deck the troops to two landing craft south of Elephant Island and ferry them to Bluff Cove and another for the ship to transfer the troops into two landing craft at Fitzroy and be taken around to Bluff Cove. Much depended on the weather, which, after days of foul wind, rain and snow, promised near clear skies. The trouble was that Clapp did not know about the window because he was not receiving satellite forecasts, although it does seem that Northwood and Woodward thought that he was, and no one was telling him from Fitzroy, in spite of requests.

Under pressure, and seemingly assured by Moore that his brigade would have logistic parity with 3rd Commando Brigade, Wilson had lobbied hard for equity but without much success. For instance, 3rd Commando Brigade had brought its Swedish BV 202E 'Snocats', which were used for its winter operations in Northern Norway and were now being put to good use transporting the heavy equipment. Brigade Headquarters was entirely BV-mounted. Wilson's headquarters never had that luxury and his request for some 3rd Commando Brigade BVs was rejected. Throughout the campaign his headquarters was either manpacked or relied upon the Royal Navy or helicopters to move its Land Rovers. The command post tentage eventually arrived when it was at Fitzroy. These difficulties reinforced the perception that 3rd Commando Brigade was the favoured son when it came to resource allocation, when, in fact, it actually needed all its resources to complete its deployments. The need for its men to be in the best possible condition to attack Stanley meant that it could not afford to wait for Wilson to catch up.

During 7 June the balance of the Welsh Guards, 16 Field Ambulance, 4 Troop, 9 Parachute Squadron, a 825 Naval Air Squadron Sea King to help land the Rapiers and troops from several other units, totalling 470 Embarked Force, transferred from HMS *Fearless* to *Sir Galahad*. Major Davies urgently needed his men to support the forward Brigade Maintenance Area – latrines to be dug, tracks to be repaired and water points to be erected. It had been intended that *Sir Galahad* would leave with HMS *Intrepid* at 5.50pm but cross-decking was slow. The assault ship was on her way to Low Bay, Lafonia, to collect her landing craft after another long, unprotected voyage from Fitzroy. The two Welsh Guards companies embarked in the belief that they would be taken direct to Bluff Cove to join the rest of the Battalion, as had been instructed by Lieutenant-Colonel Rickett before he left HMS *Fearless* the previous night.

When Major Smith and Lieutenant Waddell, of T (Air Defence) Battery, set about identifying the composite Rapier troop needed at Fitzroy, they found that Bombardier McMartin's Rapier still had a fault with its command transmitter and Sergeant Bob Pearson's unit was developing a problem. Even when reinforced by the Rapiers of 63 Squadron, Royal Air Force Regiment, the two officers therefore had a tactical dilemma – send four operational Rapiers to Fitzroy and leave San Carlos exposed or send two fully operational and two malfunctioning weapons in the hope that the latter could be repaired and thereby ensure that the beachhead was fully defended. Since the protection of San Carlos was a higher priority, Smith and Waddell selected the second option and detailed a Royal Electrical and Mechanical Engineers electronic technician to accompany the faulty Rapiers. The decision cannot really be faulted; after all, the entire Fitzroy sector was much smaller and less important than San Carlos. When the tired and dirty gunners arrived on *Sir Galahad* in the early afternoon they made themselves comfortable near a Combat Engineer Tractor. Fortunately some Welsh Guards took pity on their bedraggled state and gave up their cabins so that the gunners could shower, clean up and sleep in some comfort. This was in sharp contrast to the rifling of personal property and equipment left behind on the ships and on mess decks used by the troops. On one occasion this led to a commanding officer threatening that looters would be shot on sight.

While all this was happening, the Argentinian 1st Air Photographic Group reconnoitred San Carlos Water in support of plans being developed to attack the anchorage. 1st Air Photographic Group was part of 2nd Air Brigade and based at Paraná in Entre Rios province. In 1978 six Learjet-35As supplemented its six Guarani-11s. One Learjet had already caused an international stir on 19 March 1982 when it in-explicably landed at Stanley Airport. The Learjets flew 129 sorties during the campaign, all undertaken with considerable skill and associated good luck. Several HS-125 commercial aircraft were conscripted, with other commercial aircraft and helicopters, into the shadowy Phoenix Squadron. The HS-125s, which possessed more sophisticated avionics than fighters, were sometimes employed as lead aircraft for attacking formations. Commercial Learjets were also employed on search-and-rescue and escort duties. Some are thought to have tempted British combat air patrols by decoy and 'spoof' missions.

At about 12pm on 7 June, in near blue skies, four Learjets led by Wing-Commander Rodolfo de la Colina, the squadron commander, were over San Carlos, line abreast covering several miles, at 40,000 feet in the belief they were safe from interdiction. HMS *Exeter*, which was in Falkland Sound, identified the flight as Canberra bombers and fired two Sea Darts. Those who witnessed the incident are unlikely to forget the missile spearing upwards, and upwards and impacting on de la Colina's aircraft in a small blinding flash and a faint thump, which blew off the tail but left the pressurized cabin intact. Nose down, the spinning Learjet left a white streamer and, for two minutes, slowly spun and cartwheeled to earth, the doomed crew coherent but unable to bale out, before it smashed on to Pebble Island. In 1995 relatives were permitted to visit de la Colina's crash site. He was the most senior Argentinian officer to die in the campaign.

In 2002 the *Daily Telegraph* journalist Patrick Bishop described the most sorrowful sight on the Falklands to be the Argentinian cemetery near Darwin: *The brown eyes of the Diegos and Marios stare out from under clumps of rosary beads and taffeta flowers in the undying wind. There they will stay, left behind as markers of a futile dispute until Argentina's strange covetousness fades.* During visits by Argentinian relatives, the Falkland Islanders have shown sympathy and understanding of their needs. In 1991 the first large visit of about 300 Argentinian relatives visited Darwin under the auspices of the International Red Cross. In 1997 monthly summer overnight visits by groups of Argentinians up to fifteen strong with a priest visited the Darwin cemetery and other graves. Then, under the Argentinian/British Joint Statement agreed on 14 July 1999, a major reconciliation breakthrough was achieved when Argentinian passport holders could enter the islands on the same basis as visitors from other countries. Generally groups of about twenty relatives fly on scheduled flights from Rio Gallegos to Stanley.

At about 8.30pm on 7 June Captain Roberts, reporting that *Sir Galahad* was ready to sail, appealed for a twenty-four-hour delay so that he could sail to and from Fitzroy at night. Commodore Clapp was catching up on much-needed sleep and, on being woken, rejected this on the grounds that covering 130 miles to Fitzroy, unloading in one day and returning the next night was sufficient. *Sir Galahad* then slipped out of San Carlos Water and headed south. Since the port side accommodation had been wrecked by bomb and fire damage, most of the troops were accommodated in the cavernous tank deck. South-west of Lafonia she passed HMS *Intrepid*, which was on her way back to San Carlos after collecting her landing craft from Low Bay.

On alert in San Carlos Water for air raids during the day and with the ship's Executive Officer, Commander Bryan Telfer, on other duties to ensure the smooth running of the ship, Captain Dingemans and Lieutenant-Commander Webb were unable to hand over to him and had to endure the problem of fatigue. Telfer's concern was that the Commanding Officer and navigator should not be asleep at the same time during these passages to Lively Island. Later, on her way to meet with landing craft coming from Fitzroy collecting supplies and equipment, HMS *Intrepid* had just reached open water south of East Falkland when her radar picked up an incoming raid at a range of 134 miles. It was two 2nd Bomber Group Canberras and two 8th Fighter Group Mirages tasked to attack British positions on Mount Kent, which included Headquarters 3rd Commando Brigade. The raid continued on a steady bearing but was deflected by a scrambled 800 Squadron Sea Harrier combat air patrol from HMS *Hermes* and passed the ship three miles astern. Within a few minutes the two Mirages appeared on the radar and so Dingemans closed the coast until he found a snowstorm in which he circled until the aircraft disappeared. In Falkland Sound HMS *Cardiff* and *Exeter* had been alerted and launched a salvo of Sea Dart missiles at the four aircraft, one of which connected with the Canberra crewed by Captains Roberto Pastran and Fernando Casado and damaged the front fuselage. Pastran ordered Casado to eject, but he could not – his seat had refused to fire. With the aircraft spinning earthwards, Pastran ejected and landed in the sea near Fitzroy. Blown ashore, he landed and walked to a hiding place overlooking Port Pleasant and watched British operations around the settlement before activating his search-and-rescue beacon and was picked up by a British helicopter. At the time the British were not aware that they had shot down a Canberra. About the same time, ten miles to the east, HMS *Glamorgan* was hit by an Exocet fired from Perez's launcher on Stanley Common.

During a visit to the 5th Infantry Brigade Tactical Headquarters at Fitzroy, Major Southby-Tailyour had considered a request from Major Rolfe-Smith to send a landing craft to Goose Green to collect Land Rovers fitted with radios for Brigade Headquarters. He was doubtful of the prospect. Quite apart from needing both landing craft to unload *Sir Tristram*, there was no means of advising the Gurkhas, who were guarding the approaches up the Choiseul Sound, of its arrival. They had orders to shoot at anything that moved on the water. Convinced by Colour-Sergeant Brian Johnston, coxswain of *Foxtrot Four*, and taking everything into consideration that the risk was not worth it, Southby-Tailyour rejected the request.

It is a credit to the Scots Guards that within a day of their soaking voyage from Lively Island they had sorted themselves and were actively patrolling, although most never quite got rid of the salty residue. Working on information from 81 Intelligence Section and the Special Air Service that there were two 105mm Pack Howitzer gun positions somewhere around Port Harriet and radar on Seal Point, Captain Spicer briefed Captain Scott, the Reconnaissance Platoon commander, to find and destroy them. So began Operation *Impunity*. Leaving Sergeant Colin Coull's section behind, the remainder of the platoon with Captain Miller, a Forward Observation Officer, and a 9 Parachute Squadron engineer reconnaissance section commanded by Corporal Ford, left Bluff Cove at last light and marched the twelve miles to Port Harriet House. At first it was thought the building was occupied but this turned out not to be the case and Sergeant Michael Allum's section moved in. Allum was the Reconnaissance Platoon Sergeant. Scott then took the remaining sections to find the guns but failed to do so. In fact, they never existed.

The following day a G Squadron, Special Air Service, patrol commanded by Sergeant Noble turned up at Battalion Headquarters. Earmarked to identify Argentinian guns on Stanley Common and watch for Exocet launches from an observation post on Seal Point, they had some spare time and agreed to join Reconnaisance Platoon and help locate the radar. With Major Bethel, who commanded Headquarters Company, and Spicer, Noble's patrol set off in two Land Rovers driven by Tim Dobbyn and Mike Mackay. Both lived at Bluff Cove. With only about 600 yards to go before they reached Port Harriet House, Dobbyn's vehicle hit a mine and shredded a tyre. An examination of the area led the group to conclude they were in the middle of a minefield. Extraction was difficult with everyone gingerly following the wheel tracks. Both vehicles were then carefully reversed. The tyre was changed and the group returned to Bluff Cove.

Reconnaisance Platoon continued gathering useful intelligence, in particular that it was evident that the Argentinians were well prepared to meet any attack along the Stanley-Darwin track. This provided collateral information from an earlier Scots Guards patrol, again with Dobbyn and his Land Rover, which had run into a minefield near Pony Pass. Corporal Caswell of 9 Parachute Squadron led this patrol out of trouble. A Welsh Guards patrol, again accompanied by sappers, found the whole area littered with mines.

Meanwhile 1/7th Gurkha Rifles, less C Company, which was on rear security duties at Goose Green, and D Company, were flown to Little Wether Ground, a bleak area north of Fitzroy Ridge. Lieutenant-Colonel Morgan recalls that Battalion Headquarters arrived just before dark but he was not sure what was required of him or his Battalion. Deposited on a misty featureless landscape and not knowing where he was, he sent a four-points-of-the-compass patrol to find some navigation points. One reported that they had found some identifiable rocks and these he used as Battalion Headquarters. Next day it emerged that the rocks were not far from the 29 Battery gun line and he moved to a safer, and less noisy, area.

On 5 June Brigadier Wilson had selected D Company to be his Brigade Patrol Company and instructed the Company Commander, Major Mike

Kefford, to install his company in the general area south of Mount Wall and seek out Argentinian positions, in particular the artillery and radar units thought to be somewhere in the Port Harriet area. Instructed to march to Darwin to be ferried to Fitzroy, the company left their positions on Sussex Mountains. After an incident on Exercise *Welsh Falcon* in which equipment went astray during a helicopter move, Lieutenant-Colonel Morgan insisted that the Battalion must never be separated from their equipment. Without the benefit of vehicles, D Company shouldered their load, many Gurkhas carrying their own weight and more, and set off. Twenty miles and thirty hours later, after an extremely difficult march, D Company was dug in north of Goose Green. They then received orders to make their way to the jetty to be ferried to Fitzroy on the *Monsunen*.

The Argentinian forces had seized the 230-ton Falkland Islands Company coaster MV *Monsunen*, after finding it abandoned and adrift in kelp off Lively Island, and used her to ferry supplies to the settlements. Attacked en route from Stanley to Goose Green by HMS *Yarmouth* during the early hours of 23 May, the coaster had been run ashore on kelp near Goose Green and abandoned. On 3 June a prize crew from HMS *Fearless* surveyed the *Monsunen* and found that the kelp had cushioned her beaching. The only problem was a rope twisted around her propeller. 23-year old Janet MacLeod, the daughter of the Falkland Islands Company manager at Goose Green and a qualified skin diver, dived into the chilly waters to unravel it. Her husband, Bob, was the amateur radio enthusiast whose messages had alerted the world to the Argentinian invasion.

Major Robert Satchell, Wilson's senior Royal Engineer staff officer, was placed in charge of the *Monsunen* but Major-General Moore and Commodore Clapp did not relish 5th Infantry Brigade operating her independently and took the vessel under naval command. Lieutenant Ian McLaren and three sailors from HMS *Fearless* and a small group of Falkland Islanders were detailed to crew her as Naval Party 2160 with instructions that she was to sail only at night and requests from Headquarters 5th Infantry Brigade were to be confirmed with Commodore Amphibious Warfare. Although a useful asset from the Brigade's potential transport resources, Clapp's decision made sense. Clapp:

That did not stop it helping 5 Brigade in any way they wanted and the only reason why I insisted the Commanding Officer telling me what he was up to or wanted to do was to prevent blues on blue which would have been certain if left to Wilson and his pirates from past experience.

While 3rd Commando Brigade had Rigid Raiders of the 1st Royal Marine Raiding Squadron to assist its inshore logistic operations, 5th Infantry Brigade had no such resource and was entirely reliant upon a headquarters which also was responsible for unloading ships at San Carlos, so it was no wonder that the move of the Brigade was taking time.

As Second-in-Command, Captain Matt Helm had taken over command of the Headquarters and Signal Squadron on the death of Major Forge. Hampered by the slowness of stores and equipment being brought from San Carlos, he worked hard at improving communications. Daughtrey's rebroadcast station on Pleasant Peak was replaced by Corporal Naylor and his Land Rover-borne radio rebroadcast crew, who were given a short period of rest after re-appearing, having been mistakenly stranded on Verde Mountains, which is north of San Carlos, for three days. The deployment of Naylor's detachment improved communications although the Rover had to be regularly supplied with fuel. Poor weather had precluded flying equipment to Port Pleasant and, on 6 June, Helm instructed Lieutenant Mark Edwards, who commanded A (Radio) Troop, to take eight vehicles by the track to Fitzroy. The convoy left at 11am but such was the state of the track that only fifteen miles were covered in five hours at the expense of two Land Rovers broken down. As predicted, the weather worsened and Edwards returned to Darwin, an event that was reported by the BBC. It is thought by the Squadron that the sources to be Argentinian. It seems that the suspected observation post on Mount Usborne was alive and well but no one knew where it was. Next day Major Keith Butler took command of the Squadron and instructed Lieutenant Trevor Bradley to embark B Troop on the *Monsunen* for a night voyage to Fitzroy and set up Brigade Headquarters. The remainder would follow in a landing craft, which was apparently due in from Fitzroy at last light. Butler had been posted to Headquarters 1st Signal Group and ran Army communications from HMS *Fearless*. Also on board were Kefford's Gurkhas and several dozen 2nd Parachute Battalion soldiers left behind at Goose Green. The total Embarked Force was about 200 men, few with lifejackets or survival suits. At 10pm the *Monsunen* cast off for the four-hour voyage to Fitzroy.

By 6 June Brigadier Thompson believed he had sufficient information for a Brigade attack on Mount Longdon, Two Sisters and Mount Harriet and sent a warning to his commanding officers to assemble at his headquarters in Teal Inlet for orders on 7 June. Before confirming them, he sought assurances from Headquarters Land Forces that 5th Infantry Brigade would be ready to follow through in quick time to take the next objective, go firm and allow his Brigade to pass through and so on until the Argentinian Army had been destroyed. He asked for a battalion, preferably 40 Commando, as a Brigade reserve. However, Land Forces could give no assurances that 5th Infantry Brigade would be ready and neither could a forecast be made. As Thompson succinctly puts it in his book *No Picnic*:

> *Headquarters 5 Infantry Brigade were having to cope with seemingly endless infuriating changes of plan caused by lack of shipping to move their units round to Fitzroy. No sooner had they given orders for one plan than shipping given to them would be changed, as Headquarters at various levels above them were told what they could or could not do with various types of ships available.*

Thompson therefore cancelled his orders for an attack but reminded his commanders of their objectives and that patrolling was to continue. He wanted to get on because he was very concerned about the condition of his men, in particular 42 Commando.

That evening Major Southby-Tailyour joined Captain Green and several of his officers for dinner on board *Sir Tristram*.

7

Port Pleasant – 8 June

As, at about 6.50am, *Sir Galahad* nosed into Port Pleasant, un-announced, and anchored north-east of Pleasant Island about 400 yards east of her sister ship, *Sir Tristram,* there was a mixture of surprise and concern. No one ashore was expecting her and no one knew why she was at Port Pleasant. Brigade Headquarters was apparently unaware what was happening.

When Commodore Clapp learnt that *Sir Tristram* was still off Fitzroy, this indicated that not only had more been loaded than could be unloaded in one day but also confirmed his suspicions that the beaches around the settlement were unsuitable for amphibious operations. The day promised to be bright over parts of East Falklands with the hint of the occasional shower – perfect flying weather. In San Carlos Water it was still overcast, although the cloud base had lifted to allow low-level flying, but he was not aware that the skies over Port Pleasant were clear because no one was keeping his team briefed on weather conditions. Clapp and Lieutenant-Commander Mike Goodman, his Senior Warfare Officer, agreed that if there were clear skies over Fitzroy the omens were not good. Both had learnt the lessons from the tempestuous fighting over San Carlos Water but the head-quarters of Land Forces and 5th Infantry Brigade had both been cushioned by a thick cover of damp, dark grey cloud since their arrival and had no such experience.

Communications on the southern flank continued to be intermittent. Headquarters Land Forces on HMS *Fearless* was still having difficulty speaking to 5th Infantry Brigade because of the land mass of Wickham Heights and because the latter was moving to Fitzroy. As we have seen, Commodore Clapp lacked confidence in Wilson's brigade, but, to his great credit, he knew there were battles to be fought and, against his tactical instinct, had taken a huge risk in sending a ship laden with troops to a lightly defended anchorage. He was unaware that Major Southby-Tailyour had dispatched *Foxtrot Four* to Goose Green. Lieutenant-Colonel Ivor Hellberg, who was now commanding the enlarged Commando Logistic Regiment, had no resources to unload her and since there were no preparations for the arrival of the second ship, unloading *Sir Tristram* continued so that she could return to San Carlos Water next night.

Seeing activity on the stern ramp of *Sir Galahad,* Majors Todd and Southby-Tailyour motored out to her in *Foxtrot One* and, coming alongside on the port side of the stern ramp, to their surprise saw soldiers wearing helmets. Mystified by who they were, Southby-Tailyour singled out two Army majors, who told him that most of the troops were the balance of the two Welsh Guards companies left on HMS *Fearless* the previous evening. When one asked who was responsible for the unloading of ships, Southby-Tailyour told him that it was Todd. When Southby-Tailyour said he would consider the feasibility of their needs, one major replied that while the Rapiers, 4 Troop, 9 Parachute Squadron and 16 Field Ambulance should be offloaded at Fitzroy, his instructions were to join the rest of the Welsh Guards at Bluff Cove, as ordered by their commanding officer. Southby-Tailyour told him that 'Nobody is going to Bluff Cove – unless they walk'; adding that with clear skies and the possibility of air raids, the troops should be landed immediately and that any sea moves would take place that night by landing craft, provided unloading of the two ships was finished. He also said that the stores would be unloaded as soon as *Sir Tristram* was finished and mentioned that, in any event, soldiers milling about in the confined space of the tank deck would hinder the unloading of vehicles and stores – so it would be best to disembark using *Foxtrot One* and Boultby's Mexeflote, both of which were alongside taking stores and equipment, and any helicopters that happened to be in the area. The two officers insisted that their companies be taken to Bluff Cove but Southby-Tailyour again explained that at present there were no landing craft to take them since *Sir Tristram* had to be unloaded. Without landing craft the only other way was on foot via Fitzroy Bridge, a distance of about seven miles, not exactly a long way, and he would arrange for the heavy equipment to be ferried independently. But the officers did not believe that the bridge had been repaired, claiming that Captain Foxley's 4 Troop, which was on board *Sir Galahad*, had been specifically tasked to repair it. They envisaged a difficult cross-country fourteen-mile march around the head of Port Fitzroy by Ridge Camp. In fact, as we have seen, while 1 Troop, 9 Parachute Squadron had specifically been tasked to repair the bridge, Foxley's sappers were needed to support the Brigade Maintenance Area. But there was nothing that Southby-Tailyour could do to persuade the two majors that Fitzroy Bridge was passable.

It seemed to Southby-Tailyour that the two officers were unable to grasp the vulnerability of the anchorage from air attack. He emphasized that despatching *Sir Galahad* in broad daylight to Bluff Cove under the noses of Argentinian observers was out of the question and again tried to convince the two officers to disembark. If they agreed, they would be ashore within twenty minutes and on their way to Bluff Cove within half-an-hour. This was rejected because *Foxtrot One* was half-loaded with ammunition and there was a belief that men and ammunition are not to be mixed on boats. The two officers also said they were fed up with being messed about, as indeed their Battalion had been since it arrived. Southby-Tailyour was unaware of the nightmare of the Welsh Guards' aborted march to High Hill and that the Battalion had been treated, in his words in hindsight, 'like the Duke of York's ten thousand men' since it had landed. Trusting the two officers would acknowledge that as a Royal Marine major and therefore equivalent in seniority to an Army lieutenant-colonel, he gave them a direct order to land their men. This was not the sort of challenge that Guards officers take lightly and was rejected on the grounds they were not prepared to take orders from an officer of equivalent rank. Southby-Tailyour, his patience and perseverance worn thin, warned them that they were staying on board against his advice. Returning ashore, he sought out Major Rolfe-Smith and told that him there were about 300 troops, including two Welsh Guards companies, on board. Rolfe-Smith said that he was mistaken because, as far as he knew, the Welsh Guards had been landed the previous night at Bluff Cove. Southby-Tailyour explained that they had been forced to return to San Carlos, were now back and that it was important they disembark. While he could offer amphibious advice, Southby-Tailyour felt it was Rolfe-Smith's responsibility, as the senior 5th Infantry Brigade Operations Officer then at Fitzroy, to get them to Bluff Cove by the most effective means but it was imperative they must be landed as soon as possible.

On board *Sir Galahad* Captain Roberts rejected the Welsh Guards offer to defend the ship against air attack with machine guns in the belief that the combat air patrol and the Rapiers covered the anchorage. He did not know that there had been a mishap at 'Sid's Strip', which had reduced the combat air patrol loiter coverage appreciably.

'Sid's Strip' had increased the combat air patrol coverage significantly but it had been rendered non-operational again at about 10.50am when the GR3 Harrier flown by the commanding officer of 1 (Fighter) Squadron, Wing-Commander Peter Squires, suffered a mechanical failure on take-off, crash-landed on grass adjacent to the strip and then careered through the runway panels, sending them flying in all directions, all again observed through the gritted teeth of the sappers of 11 Field Squadron RE, who would now have to fix the mess. Combat air patrols and fighter ground attack support reverted to Carrier Battle Group but, since HMS *Hermes* had retired further to the east to maintain her boilers, this meant shorter loitering time over the Falklands. Fate was again conspiring against 5th Infantry Brigade.

Meanwhile the troops on board *Sir Galahad* waited and waited with very little information being circulated as to what was happening. Those who had been at San Carlos knew it was important to be off the ships, particularly on clear days. At about midday a verbal message was delivered from Brigade Headquarters to the unit commanders on board that the Embarked Force was to disembark. A Sea King flew the Rapier Troop ashore. Lieutenant Waddell placed Sergeant Steve Brook's Rapier on Fitzroy. East of him and north of Fitzroy settlement was Bombardier McMartin's malfunctioning Firing Unit. Nearby was Headquarters Company, 2nd Parachute Battalion. South-east of the settlement was Sergeant Pearson and on high ground in Fitzroy Parks was Sergeant Morgan.

The Welsh Guards majors assumed the warning order to move meant that landing craft were being made available to take their companies to Bluff Cove and arranged for the bergens and ammunition to be dumped on ten pallets on the stern ramp. However, a disagreement developed as to who should disembark first. Lieutenant-Colonel John Roberts, commanding 16 Field Ambulance and the senior Army officer on board, insisted his unit should land first. It seems that he realized that the possible absence of a landing craft ferrying the Welsh Guards companies to Bluff Cove would delay his disembarkation and therefore insisted his unit have priority. There was no great urgency to land the medics in favour of infantry. In hindsight, it proved a near blessing. When *Foxtrot One* returned to *Sir Galahad* to collect more troops, after one of its ship-shore-ship trips taking the medics ashore, a fault developed in a hydraulic winch, which meant its ramp could not be lowered. This meant that the ten Welsh Guards pallets would have to be lowered by crane into the landing craft over the port side of the landing ship, which is the normal way anyway. While this was underway, the ramp remained closed.

Meanwhile Argentinian intelligence reports from its electronic warfare units and observation posts on Mount Usborne indicated increased naval and military activity in the general area of Port Pleasant. With 3rd Commando Brigade known to be 'yomping' across the northern plains and in the mountains to the west of Stanley, this had to be 5th Infantry Brigade. 'Over the other side of the hill' Intelligence arrays were available from a large number of sources, one of which were satellites. During the Falklands campaign the Soviets launched twenty-nine during a sixty-nine-day period, at least eight of which were in orbit during early June. They were a mix of reconnaissance and early warning and there is a possibility that the activity at Fitzroy was picked up by the Soviets and relayed to Argentina to add collateral from other sources.

Headquarters Southern Air Force Command at Comodoro Rivadavia rapidly put a plan together for the Skyhawks of 5th Fighter Group and Daggers of 6th Fighter Group to attack Fitzroy and Bluff Cove, while the Mirages of 8th Fighter Group created a diversion of a simulated attack on San Carlos Water to draw the British combat air patrol. Take-off times were calculated so that the faster Daggers would arrive over the target area at the same time as the Skyhawks. At about 11.50am the two 5th Fighter Group flights selected for the attack, 'Dogo' and 'Mastin', each of four Skyhawks A-4Bs armed with 500lb anti-shipping bombs, took off from their operational base at Rio Gallegos. The bombs were high explosive in the conventional sense; they burst open on impact and spread flames.

With its normal base at San Luis, nearly 300 miles from the Atlantic coast, 5th Fighter Group was already the most successful of the Argentinian Air Force squadrons. Flying refurbished McDonnell Douglas Skyhawk A-4Ps and A-4Qs, exported to Argentina as A-4Bs by the United States, it was the largest squadron in the Argentinian Air Force. The single-seat Skyhawk was a versatile aircraft that had seen combat service in Vietnam and the Middle East. Powered by a single Pratt and Whitney turbojet engine, it carried two 20mm wing cannon as standard and could carry a 2,250lb and 450lb bomb on each wing or air-to-air missiles or electronic counter-measures equipment. The naval A-4C variant could launch torpedoes. So far the squadron had sunk HMS *Ardent* on 21 May and dropped the bomb on HMS *Antelope*, which then exploded so dramatically on the night of 23rd. Two days later the squadron sank HMS *Coventry* and damaged HMS *Broadsword* and then carried out the successful attack on the 3rd Commando Brigade logistic centre at Ajax Bay on 27 May. Bombs were still lodged in the refrigeration plant. By the end of the campaign, 5th Fighter Group lost eight pilots killed of thirty-five and ten of the forty-one aircraft with which it had begun operations.

6th Fighter Group flew from Military Air Base Rio Grande. The Argentinian Air Force received its first Israeli-built delta-winged Mirage-5s in 1978 and named them Daggers. Technically in excellent condition, it was a tough, if austere aircraft but lacked in-flight refuelling capability and was weak in electronic warfare systems. The on-board twin 30mm cannon was effective and it could carry a bomb load of 2,000lbs. The Mirages flown by 8th Fighter Group were formerly French Mirage-111Es, which were delivered in June 1972. Primarily all-weather interceptors, they were eventually tasked exclusively for the Falklands theatre, but, without an in-flight refuelling capability, their loiter time was limited. So far, 8th Fighter Group's war had been sobering, with the Mirages easily outclassed by the manoeuvrability of the Sea Harrier and superior training of the Royal Navy pilots. The squadron operated from Military Air Base Rio Gallegos.

HMS *Exeter,* on duty in the San Carlos area, picked up the incoming raid and issued an Air Raid Warning Red, indicating air raid imminent, but it seems that this did not reach the Port Pleasant sector. It was about 12.35pm. What was about to happen was therefore completely un-expected. The aircraft first appeared over the Falklands shortly before 12.45pm when the pair of Mirages simulated a Dagger low-level attack north-west across West Falklands aiming for the San Carlos Water anchorage. Picked up flying at 35,000 feet by HMS *Cardiff,* two 801 Squadron Sea Harriers, which were flown by Lieutenant-Commander 'Sharkey' Ward and Lieutenant Steve Thomas, who were orbiting at the southern end of Falkland Sound on combat air patrol at 20,000 feet, were directed on to the Mirages. They hoped to tempt the Argentinians into a fight but, as they approached them, the Mirages, as planned, broke and fooled the two Sea Harriers into pursuing them for a short period, and then, banking over West Falkland, headed for Argentina. The Mirages had done their job and the Skyhawks and Daggers streaked through the hole in the British defences.

'*Perro*' and '*Gato*' Dagger flights, each aircraft bombed-up with two 1,000lb bombs, had taken off from Rio Grande at about midday. Led by a 1st Air Photographic Group Learjet, it was planned they would join the Skyhawks in a co-ordinated attack. Almost immediately after take-off, First-Lieutenant Antonietti suffered a bird strike and made an emergency landing at base. The remaining aircraft, led by Captain Carlos Rohde, made landfall near Cape Meredith and turned north-east toward Falkland Sound, intending to cross Lafonia and then west to Port Pleasant.

Aware of HMS *Exeter's* air raid warning, the Type 12 frigate HMS *Plymouth*, which was commanded by Captain David Pentreath, was steaming to Chancho Point from San Carlos Water with orders from Commodore Clapp to provide naval gunfire for a Special Forces report of a suspected Argentinian position on Mount Rosalie, which overlooked the northern approaches of Falkland Sound. At about 12.55pm a lookout reported a visual sighting of five aircraft at almost sea level about two miles to the south-west. Helm hard to starboard, the frigate lurched around to the east and, at full speed, headed for the protective air defence umbrella of San Carlos Water.

Seeing the ship and believing he had lost the element of surprise,

Captain Rohde ordered it to be attacked. The Daggers screamed over her to the north and then, hauling their aircraft around in a wide turn and in line astern, the pilots attacked. In the face of intense 20mm fire from ship's secondary armament and the launch of a Seacat missile, the Daggers opened up with cannon and damaged the hydraulic and electrical lines feeding the 4.5-inch main armament. Approaching the ship at high speed they then dropped their bombs. Four hit, one careering through the funnel, two damaging the hoist and handling gear of the anti-submarine spigot mortars and the fourth landing on a depth charge stowed aft, which then started a fire in the Chief Petty Officers' Mess and dining room. All four bounced into the sea without exploding. But as the Argentinian pilots climbed, they saw that HMS *Plymouth* was apparently burning and billowing smoke. With her hull and engines intact and damage control parties fighting the fires, the frigate limped back to San Carlos where a helicopter brought additional breathing and fire-fighting apparatus and evacuated two seriously injured men and three others less so to Ajax Bay. Within the hour the fires were out. Although the naval gunners claimed the starboard Oerlikon had hit a Dagger, none of the aircraft was damaged and the pilots returned to Rio Grande in the justifiable belief they had sunk a ship, which was later identified as HMS *Plymouth*. They had given the British the first bloody nose of the after-noon but in so doing had reduced the Port Pleasant attacking force.

The Mirage diversion and Dagger attack bought the Skyhawks valuable time. While refuelling from a KC-130H tanker midway between the mainland and the Falkland Islands, three of the eight Skyhawks, two of them piloted by the flight leaders, had developed problems and returned to Argentina. The remaining five aircraft, now commanded by First-Lieutenant Cachon on his third combat sortie but first as mission leader, flying through intermittent rain showers in an otherwise bright day, crossed West Falkland and settled down for the final run-in over Lafonia. They were slightly deflected by a Sea King, possibly from 825 Naval Air Squadron, near Choiseul Sound and then, in the vicinity of Swan Inlet House, surprised a Scout flown by Sergeant Dick Kalinski of 656 Squadron, Army Air Corps. Kalinski took cover at low hover behind a hillock over MacPhee Pond, but as he started to climb, the drive shaft to the tail rotor failed and the helicopter spun around and ended up in the four-feet-deep pond. Kalinski and his observer, Lance-Corporal Julian Rigg, paddled ashore using one of the doors.

At about 1.05pm the five Skyhawks, in an arrowhead formation with Cachon leading, flew over the western edge of Port Pleasant and then inspected Bluff Cove, encountering some light low-level air defence fire, which slightly damaged Lieutenant Galvez's aircraft. Seeing no ships,

Cachon decided to return to base. With First-Lieutenant Carlos Rinke as his wingman and Ensign Leonardo Carmona on his left, he heaved the flight to starboard through a 180 degrees tight turn and climbed slightly over East Island. Ensigns Gomez and Galvez, as the number four and five, edged over to Cachon's left and it was then that Gomez excitedly reported two ships in Port Pleasant. The five Skyhawks settled down to attack, with Cachon, Rinke and Carmona aiming for *Sir Galahad* and Galvez and Gomez targeting *Sir Tristram*. A Blowpipe missile whistled between Cachon's and Rinke's Skyhawks but this did not deter them.

At Fitzroy the Rapiers had only just been landed and the Troop had yet to complete the vital tests and adjustments, which were so necessary each time the firing unit was moved. In his book *Operation Corporate,* Martin Middlebrook writes that it was Sergeant Pearson's Rapier that had an optical tracker failure. Pearson's gunner, Gunner Tony McNally, has no recollection of this. He picked up the aircraft visually at low level from the east and pressed the firing button only to hear a systems fault message in his helmet. The missile stubbornly refused to leave their ramps. On Bombardier McMartin's Rapier, Lance-Bombardier Tim Ward, knowing that the unit's command transmitter had not yet been repaired, lined up on the approaching aircraft and pressed the firing button in the hope that the system may work but the missile remained stubbornly on its ramp. As he later commented, 'Can you imagine how impotent we felt watching this disaster unfold before our very eyes? This feeling will remain with me for the rest of my life.'

Cachon released his bombs as he passed over the starboard side of the stern of *Sir Galahad*. One hit the water, another pierced a diesel ready-use tank without exploding, but the other two detonated, causing a savage fireball to funnel through the soldiers waiting to disembark on the narrow tank deck. Following him, Carmona peppered the upper works with his 20mm cannon and dropped his bombs, but missed. His cry of frustration led Rinke to believe that it was his bombs that had been released, but he then realized his aircraft was still laden but it was too late to drop them. Galvez's stick hit *Sir Tristram*, badly damaging her, while those of Gomez fell short.

On Mount Challenger Lieutenant-Colonel Vaux was talking to a sapper about mine-clearing when:

RSM Chisnall seized my arm in a vice-like grip. Such informality from him was so unusual that I knew something must be wrong, even before I heard his urgent direction, 'Look over there, Colonel – down the coastline. Just look at those bastards!' Skimming down the shore were four A4 Skyhawks of the Argentinian Air Force. Even as we watched, helpless with horror, they rose upwards, and then swooped down upon the unsuspecting ships. A myriad of malevolent flashes preceded the great booming explosions, which we were all too familiar (from the days of Bomb Alley in San Carlos). We watched the aircraft make two passes. On the second the left hand ship, Sir Galahad, erupted in flames and billowing smoke. Soon the scene was obscured by oily black smog, which hung like a shroud over the area in which 5 Brigade's troops had been landing. It was obvious they would not now be moving forward for a while, which must delay our advance as well.

The five Skyhawks banked to the south, climbed sharply to 35,000-feet and returned to Argentina without refuelling, in the certain knowledge they had caught two British ships exposed and undefended. It was all over in a few seconds. Only later would they know of the carnage they caused.

Below decks on the *Sir Galahad* most of the troops were in the tall, narrow confines waiting to disembark. Down the centre was the ammunition and equipment on pallets and packs, rifles and webbing. Dispersed against the bulkheads were soldiers occupying time as soldiers know best – playing cards, chatting, dozing. There was very little space to move. The passage of information was almost non-existent so most knew nothing until 'Air Raid Red!' was broadcast on the tannoy. As though ashore seeking shelter in a dip in the ground, the cry went up 'Get down! Get down!' But for many it was too late. As the bombs exploded, a huge fireball charged through the deck and burst through to the upper decks. Thick black smoke prevented breathing and then the ammunition began to explode, blasting bullets and shrapnel into the soldiers. There was very little shelter and most of those killed were in the tank deck. One soldier remembers burning paint pinning a soldier on to a bulkhead. Many would suffer years of painful treatment and permanent disabilities. But military discipline and training held and officers and non-commissioned officers began to sort out the carnage. Twenty years later in an interview with the journalist Patrick Bishop, Lieutenant-Colonel Crispin Black, then a Welsh Guards platoon commander, recalled:

We thought it was time we took our boys upstairs and got them ready to disembark. For some reason, we weren't able to. After several hours, there was confusion about what was going on. Johnny Strutt and I had got to the doorway of the superstructure when my radio operator tapped me on the shoulder, 'Sir, it's Air Raid Warning Red'. Then I heard this roar. It was the loudest noise I have ever heard. Jet aircraft were coming in very low towards us. I remember people shouting, 'Get down! Get down!' For whatever reason I froze. We saw the bombs drop; one of them went right into the tank deck. There was a huge explosion. Johnny was covered in blood but fortunately was only slightly injured. We set about trying to find our men. Luckily, because we'd left before we should have done, most of them were no longer on the tank deck. Our main concern was to look calm, be calm and stay calm. You had to communicate to the casualties that you were staying with them until they were taken off in a helicopter or in a lifeboat. That was all we could do – and give people morphine. Those who died were gone pretty quickly. It was the massive explosion – we had been sitting on ammunition cases. It was the first time I'd seen people without arms and legs. I've always resented people who suggested that we didn't get off because we wanted the ship to take us somewhere else to avoid having to march an extra distance. That isn't true. We wanted to get off because we were infantry soldiers and we wanted to land and do our job. We thought we were safe in the bay. We felt we had protection from the Rapier batteries and combat air patrols. History reveals that there was no air protection that day and the Rapiers could not engage.

Captain Drage, of 4th Field Regiment, commanded one of two Forward Observation Officer parties attached to the Welsh Guards:

At 11.00, seven minutes before first light, the two FOOs were looking at the coastline and dominating high features thinking what an ideal target an observer would have. Talking to the ship's officers, it was clear that there was no plan for unloading the Welsh Guards. We had no orders and it was not known if were to disembark at Fitzroy or Bluff Cove. Shortly before midday members of the surgical teams were told to prepare to move. They went ashore probably at 10.30 on a half-full Mexeflote. During lunch the Welsh Guards were hurried onto the tank deck to prepare to move. There was considerable waiting with all the men and equipment in company groups on the tank deck. We were preparing for the LCU to load the men and stores from the stern ramp. Once contact with the LCU had been made, it passed on the fact that the ramp would not lower and we would have to load over the port side. There was considerable effort required to prepare to load. All stores had to be moved and the top hatches opened. Eventually at 12.45 the Prince of Wales Company began to load onto the LCU. The first group was Company HQ and FOO party. Some equipment, including bergens, was lowered into the LCU. At 13.00, as the first group were climbing down into the LCU, the attack came. There was a roar of jet engines very close and instantly two Skyhawk aircraft dropped their loads and flew over overhead. People in the LCU took cover. It was seconds later when the thick black toxic smoke appeared billowing out of the hold, then an enormous flash that shook the whole ship. Bombs were still landing around the ship; some looked like bomblets. One large bomb went through the stern of the ship just missing the LCU. Two other bombs exploded. There was little time between the Captain giving 'Air Raid Warning Red' and 'Abandon Ship'. The wounded soon appeared and started to climb into the LCU. They were very shocked, many badly burnt and some with body wounds.

In the darkened ship confused soldiers, many of whom were ill at ease on a ship, tried to find their way to the upper deck. Fortunately there was a Royal Corps of Transport Port Operator detachment on board with knowledge of the layout of the ship and they repeatedly guided men from smoke-filled compartments to the upper deck where the rescuing of men

136

from the stricken ships was soon underway. Sergeant-Major Brian Neck, of the Welsh Guards, played a crucial role in organizing the evacuation of soldiers from the wreckage of the tank deck. Lance-Corporal Dale Loveridge and Guardsman Stephen Chapman, also Welsh Guards, repeatedly rescued soldiers from the burning tank deck. All three were awarded the Military Medal. Members of the ship's crew donned breathing apparatus to search compartments. Lance-Corporal Barry Willmore of the 30th Signal Regiment detachment attached to the Welsh Guards was one of those plucked from the sea. He was standing chatting to two soldiers in the tank deck when, without warning, there was a rushing sound, a loud explosion and then a blast of hot air, which burnt his face and hair. Bowled over, in near darkness and in considerable pain, Willmore climbed a ladder to the aft flight deck and, finding himself cut off from safety by smoke and flames, then jumped overboard and was picked up by a helicopter. Second Engineer Officer Paul Henry gave his apparatus to a junior officer who had returned to the Main Control Room and told him to abandon ship. Unfortunately Henry and a colleague, Third Engineer Officer Hailwood, later died at their posts. Henry was awarded a posthumous George Medal. Third Officer Andrew Gudgeon found a severely wounded man trapped by debris near the galley. He tried to find more breathing sets so that he could assemble a rescue party, but, finding nothing, returned to the man to make another attempt. While he was doing so, the man died. Gudgeon had already displayed considerable gallantry when he commanded a ship's boat which rescued several sailors from HMS *Antelope* on 23 May. Gudgeon was awarded the Queen's Gallantry Medal. 9 Parachute Squadron Rigid Raider coxswain Lance-Corporal Bill Skinner, who, with his colleague Sapper Leer, had delivered a couple of Special Air Service patrols behind the Argentinian lines a few days earlier, was on *Sir Galahad* taking a short break in the 'heads' when the bomb hit. Concussed, he nevertheless assisted a dazed soldier to the upper deck, then, finding his way back to his Rigid Raider, ferried casualties to the beach.

The anti-submarine pilots of 825 Naval Air Squadron immediately went to the help of the stricken ships and found themselves in very different conditions to that which they were familiar – billowing smoke, leaping flames and explosions, men in the water and the ever-present threats of another air raid or the ship exploding. Lieutenant-Commander Hugh Clark, the Commanding Officer, had just dropped an artillery survey section at Fitzroy when Cachon's flight attacked. Returning to *Sir Galahad*, he hovered in the dense smoke to take off survivors; he was later awarded the Distinguished Service Cross for his leadership. Lieutenant John Miller had just dropped a Rapier section near Fitzroy when the Skyhawks attacked. Hovering behind high ground during the attack, he flew to the ships and rescued several men. When the wind changed and the life rafts were in danger of drifting back to the ships, he hovered above them and gently shepherded them away from danger. Lieutenants John Boughton and Philip Sheldon, both Royal Navy, were awarded Queen's Gallantry Medals for flying close to masts and rigging to lift shocked and wounded men. Twenty years later Sheldon remembers watching a burning soldier being winched into his helicopter and his frustration about being unable to help him. A Sea King flown by Lieutenant Hughes, of 847 Naval Air Squadron, hovered above a dinghy and manoeuvred the rotor downwash to move it from *Sir Galahad*. There is no doubt that Clark and his men played a significant role in minimizing the casualties by courageous flying. As aircrew more used to anti-submarine warfare, flying at such low level often surrounded by columns of smoke and with the threat of further air raids, this was not a familiar environment for them.

Among a group of journalists invited by Brigadier Wilson to film the build-up of his Brigade at Fitzroy and Bluff Cove was a television crew who scooped the aftermath of the attack and took some of the most dramatic pictures of the war.

Captain Roberts knew his ship was fatally damaged and, with virtually all the Embarked Force still on board, he ordered 'Abandon Ship'. *Foxtrot One*, which was skippered by Colour-Sergeant 'Connie' Francis, was alongside and took off men. The Mexeflote commanded by Sergeant Boultby had just finished unloading a consignment from the *Sir Tristram*. Without hesitation, he manoeuvred his 66-foot craft alongside *Sir Galahad* and, on at least two occasions, ferried survivors ashore. He was awarded the Military Medal for his gallantry. A lifeboat manned by the Royal Corps of Transport Port Operator Detachment on *Sir Tristram* motored to her sister ship, took off men and provided fire-fighting parties. Others lowered the ship's lifeboats and rafts and rowed ashore. Within thirty-five minutes most able-bodied men had been evacuated. Left on board were the ship's officers and several Royal Army Medical Corps personnel treating the wounded, many with ghastly, painful burns. Sergeant Peter Naya, of 16 Field Ambulance, was stunned by the explosion of the first bomb. Another explosion set his pack alight and scorched his head; nevertheless he led a shocked soldier up two flights of stairs to the upper deck and then returned to the shambles on the tank deck where he administered first aid to a soldier who had lost a leg and then organized his evacuation to the forecastle where Naya, as the senior medic still on board, then set up a first aid post, organized triage and arranged infusions. The wounded were gently carried and coaxed from below, including another soldier who had lost a leg. Naya left on the last helicopter to take casualties ashore and was himself evacuated to Ajax Bay for treatment. Three days later he returned to his unit's Advance Surgical Centre in time for the attacks on Stanley. Naya was awarded a well deserved Military Medal. Ashore the wounded were assembled in the Fitzroy Community Centre where all available medics worked hard to treat them. For many, even those who had fought at Goose Green, it was the first time that they had seen such numbers and types of wounds – burns, loss of limbs, the blinded and gunshot and shrapnel wounds, but, as is clearly evident from those television pictures, discipline prevailed. While visiting his parachute sappers erecting a water point near Fitzroy, Major Davies and Squadron Sergeant Major Pete Walker heard the bombing. By the time they had run to their command post, a huge pall of smoke was billowing from *Sir Galahad*. *Sir Tristram* appeared to be unharmed. Already helicopters were flying out to the burning ship. Davies:

I called the Defence Section to grab a stretcher, summoned the second-in-command and sent someone to warn the medical centre, which was close to our position. The first man we took off the helicopter was Chinese. He was crying with pain and burned flesh hung off him. I assumed the bomb must have hit the galley. Then another helicopter appeared with more suffering Chinese crewmen. The third helicopter brought blackened and singed men in Army uniforms. It was only after a couple of loads that the enormity of the tragedy began to dawn on me; there had been soldiers on the ships after all. I lost count of the men we took from the helicopters to the medical centre, which rapidly filled to overflowing. We had to take screaming, bleeding, badly burned men off stretchers and put them on the floor to free more stretchers for yet more wounded. The sights, sounds and smell of burning flesh were horrific. Thankfully the brain can delay the realization of such horror and we ran with our smouldering loads, doused them with water and fitted intravenous drips with a vague oblivion. Before long the medical centre overflowed. Those who had walked up from the shore stood around outside shocked and dazed. Many who had burns on the hands stood with them in drums of cold water; others walked around in silent pain with arms raised like prisoners. Some soldiers I took off the helicopters spoke to me as if they knew me. They were so blackened I did not recognize them. It was only when I saw their Royal Engineer stable belts that I realized 4 Troop must have been on board.

Inevitably some people found it all too much. I found a medical officer in an agitated state just when the activity around the helipad and the medical centre was at its height. He was saying how terrible it was, how the second-in-command had been killed and most of the medical stores lost. Since a RAMC staff sergeant was getting on with the task, I led the officer outside and told him to keep out of the way until he could do something useful.

When Davies instructed his Signals NCO to ask Brigade Headquarters for more helicopters, the Operations watchkeeper, divorced from the drama, no doubt juggling with requests for this valuable resource and probably unaware that the Argentinian Air Force had dealt the British a devastating blow without any interference, asked, 'How many?' Davies, close to the trauma on the shore, was not best pleased to be told that, unless he could be more precise, he would not get any. His actual response is not recorded but more helicopters were diverted to help with the rescue. Many of those who had dealt with the casualties returned to their positions, subdued but amazed at the quiet discipline of the survivors. Davies took stock:

> 4 Troop had effectively been written off, with Corporal Andrew McIlvenna and Sapper Wayne Tarbard killed and eight wounded. As we reflected on the day's events, we recalled the horror, the excitement and, incredibly, the humour. For example the diminutive figure of Lieutenant John Mullins, who commanded Support Troop, came stomping up the track. He was shocked and could only speak in a whisper and kept saying, 'It was terrible, terrible, David Foxley's dead, 4 Troop's gone.' I sat him down and asked someone to make him a brew. Shortly afterward Foxley appeared, a bit singed but otherwise unhurt. He had obviously been deafened for when he spoke he yelled. He was all right and he was going to look after his troop – and the whole world could hear him.

Other Royal Engineers began to re-appear. Lance-Corporal van der Kraan, who was employed in the 9 Parachute Squadron Stores and was on board *Sir Galahad*, did excellent work in helping to load casualties into helicopters and boats. Minus all their clothing and equipment except that which they were wearing or managed to salvage from the wrecked *Sir Galahad* and with none to spare from 9 Parachute Squadron, 4 Troop returned to San Carlos. After being refitted out, they joined HMS *Intrepid* as it embarked Sapper Troop and cleared West Falkland settlements of mines and booby traps. Later, when Major Davies went to the sheep sheds to see the 2nd Parachute Battalion and catch up on events, he met a Welsh Guards major who had been a contemporary on a Staff College course and while sympathizing with him was told, 'Well, that's us out of this whole stupid thing; they can't expect us to do anything now.' Davies was shocked by the response. Other survivors were flown to San Carlos to be kitted out on HMS *Intrepid*. Most had lost weapons, equipment and clothing, but such were the shortages after the loss of the *Atlantic Conveyor* that most could not be given everything they needed.

The attack cost the Welsh Guards thirty-two non-commissioned officers and Guardsmen. The Royal Electrical and Mechanical Engineers lost a Corporal and a Craftsman and the Army Catering Corps a Lance-Corporal and three Privates, all killed. Among them was 19-year-old Guardsman Ian Dole and his best man 18-year-old Guardsman Colin Parsons; Dole had been married to his 17-year-old wife Debbie for only a fortnight when he was summoned back to his Battalion after honeymooning in Tenby. Lance-Corporal Christopher Ward had been married only a month when he left for the South Atlantic. His wife, Diane, was in the Women's Royal Army Corps. The brother of Sergeant Clifford Elley later said that, although his brother had done three tours in Northern Ireland, he was looking forward to some 'real soldiering'. Maria, the wife of Guardsman Nigel Rowberry, was four months pregnant when her husband lost his life on the ship. 16 Field Ambulance lost much of their equipment and had suffered three fatalities, including Major Roger Nutbeem, the Second-in-Command. There is a brass memorial to him in the Territorial Army Centre at Keynsham, which is near Bristol. The blue-bereted 4 Troop, 9 Parachute Squadron, lost two killed and eight wounded. On the *Sir Galahad,* two Royal Fleet Auxiliaries officers and three Chinese were killed and two officers and nine wounded, while on *Sir Tristram,* two Chinese were killed. Forty-six men were evacuated to Ajax Bay with serious wounds and others sustained minor wounds and injuries, most of whom were treated at Port Pleasant.

At the Land Forces Main Dressing Station at Ajax Bay Surgeon-Commander Rick Jolly was treating injured and wounded from HMS *Plymouth*, Goose Green and subsequent operations when a helicopter-crewman rushed in with a message: '*Galahad* hit before surgical teams unloaded. Many burn casualties'. As evening drew into night, Jolly was faced with at least 170 wounded and shocked soldiers, some horribly burnt, others missing limbs. The immediate priority was to sort out those who needed immediate treatment from those who could be patched up and transferred to ship sick bays by landing craft for further treatment. He was later struck by the Welsh Valley stoicism of the Welsh Guards as each man seemed to know someone worse off and that he should be treated first.

Lieutenant-Colonel Rickett was visiting Number 2 Company, which was commanded by Major Christopher Drewry, with Regimental Sergeant Major Tony Davies (22), when the Skyhawks appeared. After taking cover, they then noticed a thick column of smoke coming from one of two ships. No sooner had they reached the first position than the platoon commander's radio operator told Rickett that he was required urgently at Battalion Headquarters. Rickett's assumption that his missing companies were on board the ship that had been worst hit was confirmed. He was then informed that when he returned to his headquarters a helicopter would be waiting to take him to Fitzroy. Rickett:

I remember well seeing two ships in the distance coming into Fitzroy harbour but nobody thought very much about this. What the Navy did was none of our business! Although it seemed somewhat strange to see them in the clear light of day. None of us had any idea that the balance of the battalion was on board one of these ships, certainly nobody at Brigade HQ told us anything. I had already made contact with Nick Vaux, CO 42 Commando, who was my flanking unit, the previous day and had volunteered to secure his Start Line for his forthcoming attack on Mt Harriet and help in any way we could. My Recce Platoon was already in fairly close contact with the Argentinians and we were getting to know the area as quickly as we could.

Together with the RSM and the Padre, Peter Brook, we set off for Fitzroy where a scene of indescribable chaos awaited us. We were still of course under constant air attack and there were groups of kitless Welsh Guardsmen everywhere. I remember saying, 'Stick close to me as I am lucky,' and we took cover as best we could. Soon afterwards I can remember the Company Sergeant Majors calling the roll in a sheep shed, but it was impossible at that moment to ascertain who had been killed and who, amongst the wounded, had been taken off direct from the stricken RFA Galahad by helicopter. With a heavy heart I returned to Battalion HQ, assuring Guy Sayle and Charles Bremner that I would get back to see them all as soon as I was able. I remember clearly that neither of them wanted me to leave them, but we had to get on with the war. From that moment I was determined that none of us would look backwards on these tragic events but instead concentrate our minds on the tasks before us.

Elated with Cachon's attack and determined to slow the British advance along the southern flank, Headquarters Southern Air Force Command decide to press home its advantage over Port Pleasant and ordered two more sorties before night fell, the first by 5th Fighter Group, on an anti-shipping strike, and the second by 4th Fighter Group flying A4-C naval Skyhawks on an anti-personnel sortie. Top cover was again to be provided by Mirages of 8th Fighter Group.

So far 4th Fighter Group's war had been frustrating. Its base at San Julian was rudimentary and communication was a problem. It had taken casualties during the battle for San Carlos Water. One of its pilots, Lieutenant Ricardo Lucero, had become the focus of attention on 25 May when his aircraft was shot down over San Carlos, his Skyhawk cartwheeling in massive spray. His knee injured, Lucero was picked up by a HMS *Fearless* boat crew and was fortunate not to be shot when he suddenly produced a knife. Whisked on to the tank deck of the ship, he was filmed by a television crew while a medical team treated his wounds. Taken to the sick bay where, to the irritation of a military intelligence team interviewing him about the mainland bases, members of the ship's company, wanting to see an Argentinian, frequently interrupted the interrogation. One rating declared that he wanted Lucero's ears!

4th Fighter Group's mission on 30 May was probably the most controversial. Headquarters Air Force Command decided to launch its final Exocet mission against the Carrier Battle Group. The plan was for two Super Etendards, one of them carrying the last Exocet missile that Argentinian Air Force had and the other to provide back-up radar cover, to attack one of the aircraft-carriers. Four Skyhawks were added, almost at the last moment, to follow the Exocet and bomb the ship that had been hit. Visibility was reasonable but interrupted by rain showers, which blanketed both sides' radars. Using good radio and flight discipline and with the Skyhawks frequently refuelling from the two KC-130H tankers, the force approached undetected just as the Carrier Battle Group was deploying for night operations. Popping up for a second radar scan, the Argentinians were detected and three ships escorting HMS *Invincible* turned to meet the threat. Vice-Commodore Francisco, piloting one of the Etendards, fired the Exocet at what he believed to be a firm target and then he and his wingman broke, leaving the Skyhawks to follow the missile. Two Sea Harriers were ordered to intercept. Peering through their salt-splattered windscreens and seeing smoke pouring from a ship, the four Skyhawk pilots settled down into an attacking profile. First-Lieutenants Juan Vasquez and Castillo quickly fell to Sea Darts fired by HMS *Exeter*. The remaining two aircraft pressed on to a ship they took to be HMS *Invincible,* straddled it with bombs and left the scene at high speed. On returning to their base the two surviving pilots, First-Lieutenant Ureta and Ensign Isaac, claimed the Exocet had hit the carrier HMS *Invincible* and that she was on fire.

In fact, no ships were hit. The ship attacked was HMS *Avenger* and the smoke was, first, the characteristic footprints of accelerating turbine engines and, second, from its 4.5-inch main armament as she engaged the Exocet. Nevertheless the graphic debriefing of the two pilots led Argentina to claim a successful attack on HMS *Invincible*. This belief was strengthened when the ship withdrew from the battle zone to replace an engine and reinforced even more when HMS *Invincible* returned to Portsmouth sporting fresh paint on her hull. Indeed when a member of the 3rd Commando Brigade Intelligence Section searched Menendez's headquarters in Government House, he found that a cross had been drawn over a picture of the carrier along with other British ships sunk. In any event, satellites would have picked up damage to a ship of such political importance and it would have been impossible for Great Britain to keep her sinking a secret. The attack had a significant undertone because it was the last Exocet that the Argentinian Air Force had and, although she searched for more, British counter-intelligence operations and the speedy conclusion of the war meant that she was unable to buy any more.

Using the pall of smoke over Port Pleasant as his beacon, First-Lieutenant Bolzan, the 5th Fighter Group *Mazo* flight commander, led the second attack on Port Pleasant. In spite of the predictions of Southern Air Force Command, the British were anything but demoralized; in fact they were angry not only at being caught out but also at the amount and state of casualties being brought off the two ships. Sergeant Pearson's Rapier was fixed ten minutes after the first raid and, as the aircraft approached at about 2.30pm, the raid was met with a blistering barrage of small arms and machine-gun fire and Blowpipe and Rapier missiles, but the Skyhawks escaped serious damage. Reports of crashing aircraft were more likely the missiles hurtling into hillsides. The Scots Guards had a well-organized air defence profile and fired over 18,000 rounds. Major Davies managed to loose off several shots at the aircraft, later jokingly claiming a 'head shot', such was his anger at what he had seen. Staff-Sergeant McLean, of 4th Field Regiment, was seen firing his Sterling, the gun in the crook of his left arm and a large black mug of steaming tea in his left hand, while he pulled the trigger with his right forefinger. Captain John Russell, the 4th Field Regiment battle adjutant, was not so canny. He was going to his trench to finish making a cup of cocoa when Bolzan's aircraft screamed overhead. Diving into a trench occupied by Bombardier Nicholson, he spilt most of his precious drink. 'What service, Bombardier, chocolate served in an air raid!' With the stolid humour typical of the Gunners, Nicholson replied, 'But, sir, you've drunk most of it!'

Bolzan cleared the area and led his aircraft west looking for targets. At the mouth of Choiseul Sound he saw a landing craft loaded with jeep-type vehicles. It was Colour-Sergeant Johnson's *Foxtrot Four* en route to Port Pleasant.

As we have seen, *Monsunen* and *Foxtrot Four* had arrived at Goose Green at about 8am. Six Land Rovers of Brigade Headquarters and the Signal Squadron, including two with cryptographic equipment vital for providing Brigade Headquarters with secure communications, and nine soldiers were loaded. Appreciating the importance of his load, Johnson decided to make the trip to Fitzroy in broad daylight, in spite of Southby-Tailyour's instructions not to do so. He raised the ramp, backed off the beach and then set a south-easterly course down Choiseul Sound. The six Army drivers and three others sheltered from the wind and rain in their vehicles and caught up on sleep. The landing craft crew confined themselves aft and thus their single machine gun was not manned. At about 2.35pm, about one mile south of Johnson Island, the alarm was raised when two Skyhawks were seen levelling out in an attack profile and, although the Royal Marines managed to man the machine gun, the landing craft was caught by surprise as Bolzan and his wingman, Lieutenant Vasquez, dived, leaving First-Lieutenant Hector Sanchez and his wingman. Lieutenant Arraras, as cover. Bolzan was unable to line up on the landing craft, but Vasquez bracketed it with one 500lb bomb falling about twenty metres astern, but his second scored a direct hit on the stern and wheelhouse, blowing it off and killing Colour-Sergeant Johnson, three other Royal Marines and two Royal Navy engine room artificers. Marine Quigley was badly wounded as was Airtrooper Mark Price, the Australian driver of the officer commanding 656 Squadron. He had just borrowed a book from a colleague and was blinded when he was bowled over a trailer by the blast and hit his head.

The attack was spotted by two 800 Squadron Sea Harriers orbiting at 10,000 feet on a dusk deck-landing training exercise being conducted by Lieutenant Dave Smith for a recently arrived RAF pilot, Flight-Lieutenant Dave Morgan. Too late to intercept Bolzan and Vasquez, Morgan fired a Sidewinder, which impacted on Arraras's Skyhawk. Sanchez, seeing the attacking Sea Harriers, shouted a warning to Vasquez and they both broke to the south over Middle Island. Morgan's second missile smashed into Vasquez's Skyhawk, splitting the aircraft in two. The pilot baled out, his parachute in flames. Bolzan dived to the north but was attacked by Morgan with cannon. Smith fired a Sidewinder, but, before it connected, Bolzan's aircraft careered into sand dunes at Rain Cove, off the northern shores of Lafonia, killing the pilot. Sanchez unloaded all his stores, including his fuel tanks, and sped from the area. Running out of fuel over Falkland Sound, he made contact with the supporting KC-130H tanker but, since his Skyhawk was not fitted with radar, he had difficulty in finding it. Realizing Sanchez's predicament and in spite of the threat from the British combat air patrols, the tanker captain flew to West Falkland leaving a long condensation trail as a marker. Sanchez saw it and coaxed his near-empty aircraft on to the fuel drogue. The top cover Mirage escort took no part in the fighting and left the scene at about 2.55pm.

Meanwhile 4th Fighter Group's alert 'Yunque' flight left Military Air Base San Julian at 3.00pm with orders to attack troops in the Port Pleasant area, the third attack of the day. The weather was still clear but the sun was setting. The flight, also known as 'Tigre', was led by Captain Mario Cafaratti, the squadron commander, and was also guided by the orange glow and high pall of black smoke billowing from Sir Galahad. At about 4pm the four Skyhawks A-4Cs came in from Choiseul Sound in a line astern attack and were met with a hail of ground fire that damaged them all. Cafaratti believed his aircraft was so badly damaged that he broke south ready to eject into the sea until he realized that his controls were working satisfactorily. He eventually had to descend to below 20,000 feet when his oxygen supply malfunctioned. Ensign Codrington broke north and, passing over Mount Kent, met more heavy fire from 42 Commando, which badly damaged his fuel tanks. First-Lieutenants Paredi and Zattara broke south after suffering extensive damage to their aircraft. Codrington and Zattara met up with the supporting KC-130H tanker and remained attached to its drogues until they reached San Julian. The same tanker crew had just rescued the 5th Fighter Group pilot, Sanchez. The return of 'Yunque' flight was the last combat mission of 4th Fighter Group. During the six weeks it had campaigned, sixty-five sorties were flown at a cost of eight pilots killed and nine aircraft shot down.

Near the mouth of Choiseul Sound the crippled *Foxtrot Four* was wallowing in ocean currents and listing to starboard, the remains of her stern awash. Rudderless, without engines, shocked by the severity and suddenness of the attack and knowing that a Mayday had not been sent, the soldiers, in the gathering darkness, with absolutely no knowledge about the landing craft and not knowing how long it would be before rescue arrived, took measures to keep it afloat. Using vehicle fire extinguishers, the fires were tackled. Quigley and the blinded Price were given first aid and kept warm with sleeping bags. To lift the stern in the confined space of the well deck the Land Rovers vehicle and trailers were manoeuvred for'ard with some difficulty. It was then found that one of the two life rafts had been damaged beyond repair. In case the landing craft had to be abandoned in a hurry, the second life raft was thrown over the side, but this snagged on a jagged piece of metal and punctured. Sergeant Alec Turner and Corporal Bob Taylor disposed of the cryptographic material and then, while Taylor set about improvising a raft from inflated lifejackets and a tarpaulin, Turner collected rations and water. Shortly before the attack, Colour-Sergeant Johnson had fortuitously shown their position to Captain Carel Bouwens, a Royal Engineer staff officer with Brigade Headquarters. This was passed as a Mayday message to Headquarters 5th Infantry Brigade by Lance-Corporals Mair and Davison, who had persuaded a Clansman radio to work. Two 656 Squadron helicopters sent to find the sinking landing craft failed to see the signal lights. No oil slicks and no flotsam and jetsam were seen. A Sea King commanded by Lieutenant Miller, fresh from the rescues off Fitzroy, then found the landing craft and over the next thirty minutes winched everyone and the only working radio on board. Price regained his sight within six days.

Meanwhile the *Monsunen*, en route to Fitzroy, was also searching for *Foxtrot Four*. During the late afternoon she had loaded a mixed bag of 180 Gurkhas from Headquarters and Support Companies and some other soldiers, all under the command of Major Bill Dawson, the Battalion Second-in-Command, to be ferried from Goose Green to Fitzroy. Hanging around the jetty, agitated and impatient, was Brigadier Wilson, who told Lieutenant-Colonel Morgan that as soon as the troops were loaded the coaster must sail. With the Argentinian Air Force alive and well, Morgan and Dawson objected to sailing in broad daylight and a brief debate developed. Eventually Morgan discreetly told Dawson to slow things down so that by the time dusk fell the *Monsunen* would be ready to sail.

Reports then emerged that *Foxtrot Four* had been abandoned but since there was still concern that the cryptographic material on board would be compromised if captured, Wilson instructed Dawson to find the landing craft and tow it to Fitzroy. Lieutenant McClaren, the naval officer in command of the *Monsunen*, then arrived with a completely different set of orders from Commodore Clapp's staff and for a time confusion reigned until it was agreed that the landing craft must be found. As the coaster cast off Dawson was angry that his soldiers' lives were being placed at risk. After several hours the abandoned landing craft was found off Lively Island, wallowing in choppy seas and drifting to the south-east. The *Monsunen* managed to connect a towrope to her but, as the coaster took up the strain, another rope snagged in its propeller. While some on board watched the flashes and heard the crumps of British artillery shelling Argentinian positions on Mount Harriet, Mount William, Two Sisters and Moody Brook, one-time survival suits were broken out and several Gurkhas disappeared beneath the waves to free the rope but, since the suits are designed to be buoyant, this was not entirely successful. With his soldiers becoming wetter and colder, Dawson decided to break radio silence, but, when he found the frequencies given to him by Headquarters 5th Infantry Brigade were incorrect, he contacted Headquarters Land Forces. The duty Operations watchkeeper was astonished when it emerged that he knew nothing about the attempt to recover the cryptographic settings. It seemed to be another 'Wilson Special', as one officer put it.

Meanwhile HMS *Yarmouth* was steaming due south from the Stanley gun line when, at about 1am, she picked up radar contacts ahead. Commander Morton sent his Wasp helicopter to investigate. The contacts turned out to be the sinking *Foxtrot Four* and crippled *Monsunen* and since no one had advised him of the attempted tow, Morton was as surprised to see *Monsunen* as those on board the coaster were surprised to see his frigate. It could have easily turned into another 'blue on blue' involving the loss of troops at sea. Morton despatched navy divers to free the propeller. Dawson was not sure exactly where he was in relation to Stanley Common and instructed the coaster's skipper to return to Goose Green, which they reached soon after dawn. The Gurkhas were then squeezed into the Chinook and joined their battalion at Fitzroy.

Foxtrot Four eventually sank, taking with her the valuable radio vehicles and the 4th Field Regiment Artillery Intelligence Land Rover. For Brigadier Wilson the loss of the vehicles was inconsequential, but the loss of the radios was a serious setback because he lost his ability to have a second Brigade Headquarters and was now reliant upon his lighter Tactical Headquarters. A memorial to the men killed on *Foxtrot Four* was later erected on Lively Island.

The raids over, Major Davies and his commando sappers went back to the grim task of evacuating the casualties from the two landing ships:

By this time we had improvised an 'in' and 'out' system so things began to go more smoothly. However, many men were so badly injured that I could not believe they would survive the flight back to San Carlos Water. Incredibly all of those who we placed in helicopters lived. Youthful resilience and prompt first aid combined to ensure that every casualty who reached the shore survived.

The Falklands campaign was a unique war of the 20th century. There were no atrocities and both sides respected the rules of war governing the treatment of prisoners-of-war and of casualties. A problem faced by both sides was the management of the wounded and their quick return to hospital treatment for recovery. While the Task Force had converted the *Uganda,* a P&O liner on an educational cruise in the Mediterranean, to a hospital ship, Argentina assigned ships previously used as naval transports. When the *Bahia Paraiso* arrived off the Falklands, painted white and displaying a large Red Cross on the flight deck hangar, the British, always smelling a rat and knowing she had been used in the attack on South Georgia in April, insisted on searching her. However, they found she was 'clean' and she proceeded first to Fox Bay to collect sick and wounded and then delivered medical supplies to Stanley and took away casualties. She then met with the *Uganda* in the 'Red Cross Box' to the north of Falkland Sound to cross-deck Argentinian prisoners wounded at Goose Green. The British used three survey ships, HMS *Hydra, Hecla* and *Herald,* as ambulance ships to transfer casualties from *Uganda* to Montevideo to be taken to their home countries. The severity of some *Sir Galahad* and *Sir Tristram* casualties needed specialist attention only available on the *Uganda*. In spite of the Junta's protests that she was delivering war stores and equipment, she sailed into San Carlos Water to collect the wounded. After stabilizing treatment they were then cross-decked to the logistic support ships taken up from trade *British Test* and *British Trent* for the passage to Montevideo and flown to the United Kingdom in VC-10s with aeromedic teams attending to their needs. The Junta's protests were feeble considering Argentina had used its Finnish-built icebreaker, the *Almirante Irizar*, as an assault ship during the 2 April landings and then painted it white as a hospital ship during the latter stages of the campaign.

One observer later commented, 'Half their air force was shot down that day if the claims were correct.' Research contained in *Falklands – the Air War* and in Ethell and Price's *Air War South Atlantic* suggests that, while aircraft were hit, none were shot down over Bluff Cove and Fitzroy on 8 June. It had definitely been Argentina's day. Southern Air Force Command had scored a significant success and might have achieved more had they not miscalculated the character of the British to bounce back under adversity. Equally, the British had again mis-calculated the commitment of the Argentinian pilots to press home attacks, as they had so courageously shown during the battles for San Carlos Water. The Argentinian Air Force was not yet beaten.

Recriminations soon started flying about and scapegoats being identi-fied for a misfortune that could have been avoided had not five Skyhawks appeared over Port Pleasant. Writing in his diary that night, Rear-Admiral Woodward 'could strangle' Commodore Clapp after being told not to put HMS *Intrepid* into Fitzroy. In fact, he hadn't. He later recalled that he wished he had told Moore and Clapp not to land at Fitzroy and Bluff Cove. As the Carrier Battle Group commander, it was not his deci-sion. In a radio conversation with Admiral Fieldhouse the following day both managed to avoid agreeing that Major-General Moore bore the ulti-mate responsibility. This is less than fair. The facts are that the ground forces had been condemned to marching or using ships after the loss of the *Atlantic Conveyor*'s helicopters. The hijacking of the landing craft by 2nd Parachute Battalion meant that the rendezvous with HMS *Fearless* was not made. Until the Rapiers could be landed, Port Pleasant was vulnerable to Argentinian Air Force interdiction. The absence of a warship rather exposed the anchorage to air attack. Fitzroy was within range of the Stanley-based Exocet and fear of it tended to govern naval operations at the expense of active support to the military operating ashore in freezing conditions. Although Woodward claims, with some justification, that the loss of three warships was collectively more serious than the military losses on board the two logistic ships, he misses the point. 5th Infantry Brigade was now expected to attack with a battalion strengthened only by weakening the defence of San Carlos at a time of increased risk. The Navy had won their battle at the expense of several ships. But now a weakened brigade was being expected to fight a battle markedly different in nature, time and conditions than anything experienced at sea.

A Board of Inquiry convened by Commander-in-Chief Fleet into the losses of the *Sir Galahad* and *Sir Tristram* was presided over by Captain Morse several months after the Argentinian surrender. Several officers, including Major-General Moore and Commodore Clapp, gave evidence. At least one witness found it quite hard to differentiate between answers being given off the record and those given on the record. Another officer was unable to answer questions and came across as incompetent. In fact he had very little to do with the events and therefore couldn't contribute. An officer closely involved in the decision-making process was not even called. In any event the conclusion, which has yet to be made public, reached by the Board was that the naval commander, that is Clapp, had assessed the needs of ground force priorities and had taken a justifiable risk in sending the two logistic ships to Port Pleasant. Nevertheless, within a few years Michael Clapp left the Royal Navy, still a Commodore. He has never really been given the credit due to him in making a major contribution to speeding up the military advance and hastening victory.

Was the attack a military blunder? Blunders usually follow one or more failures of a personality, technology, equipment, Intelligence, organization or to appreciate the enemy. There is no doubt that Wilson's bold move to Fitzroy was a high-risk operation but it stalled because not everyone liable to be involved was invited to contribute. In Clapp's view, if the military had included the Royal Navy in its planning, as opposed to expecting support when things went wrong, events might have been different. As it was, five Skyhawks appeared on a clear day and two logistic ships sent to Fitzroy to rescue the military situation were badly damaged.

The Rapier Troop came in for considerable criticism, particularly from 2nd Parachute Battalion who spent some of the war telling others how they should perform. A Parachute Regiment major, who was not aware of the command transmission problem, lambasted Bombardier McMartin's men and threatened to send them back to the United Kingdom. He wasted his breath and it was none of his business. When told of the systems failure, he said he would have a replacement component within two hours. It didn't arrive and McMartin's Rapier spent the rest of the war without a command transmitter. Systems failures are hardly the fault of the gunners and yet these young gunners were heavily criticized. T Battery was credited in the Government White Paper entitled *The Falklands Campaign: The Lessons* with fourteen 'kills' and six 'probables' of the seventy-two 'kills' and fourteen 'probables' claimed, although this does seem a little excessive and may have been included to boost marketing opportunities. The Naval Historical Branch credits the Battery with one direct kill and a 50% share in another, a statistic borne out by Ethell and Price, who claimed that the only confirmed Rapier 'kill' was a Dagger on 29 May. However, in frenetic air defence battles, with so much ground fire, it is often difficult to credit confirmed kills. But the Rapiers were not the only air defence of Port Pleasant – there were twelve .50-inch Brownings of the three infantry battalions, a Blowpipe section from 43 Air Defence Battery and countless General Purpose Machine Guns, and let us not forget that *Sir Galahad* had one 40mm Bofors and her Captain had refused an offer from the Welsh Guards to line her decks with machine guns. So why did this weight of fire not engage Cachon's flight? Maybe it was because the air defence of Fitzroy was unprepared.

Did the Argentinians know? It seems inconceivable they did not. On clear days Port Pleasant can be seen from Mount Harriet. However, for the previous week the weather had been bad. The observation post on Mount Usborne would also have had difficulty in seeing. Most of the Argentinian radar, such as the Westinghouse AN/TPS-43, was in Stanley but it was unable to see 'over the hill' to Fitzroy. The most likely explanation is communication interception. While Argentinian electronic warfare capability lacked the sophistication of the British resources, Argentina was aided, albeit discreetly, by the Soviet Union. 10th Infantry Brigade had its tactical electronic warfare company and they most probably listened to the radio chatter in the area of Fitzroy, quite apart from anything picked up by listening posts in Argentina.

Within days of the attack the Ministry of Defence carried out an initial inquiry and it emerged that the journalist Michael Nicholson had filed a preparatory tape with Independent Television News in which he referred to an operation 'which I can only describe as extraordinarily daring which until completed cannot be revealed'. If the Argentinians were in any way doubtful about the role and deployment of 5th Infantry Brigade, the combination of an intercepted comment such as this and simple Intelligence analysis will conclude that, with 3rd Commando Brigade advancing north of Wickham Heights, 5th Infantry Brigade would be to the south and the 'operation' might well be a landing somewhere along the south coast of East Falkland. A glance at a map shows the best place to land in terms of beach, shelter from the weather and access to a track was at Fitzroy. Nicholson's report, sent in 'clear' language to

London, may have been picked up by the Soviets and therefore there is the possibility that it might have ended up in Buenos Aires. To their credit Independent Television News placed a forty-eight hour embargo on the scoop.

So far as the British were concerned, there was no specific Intelligence that Argentina was going to attack Port Pleasant. However, her Air Force and Naval Air Command had shown they were prepared to fly whenever possible, which generally meant in good weather. There was also still a fear among some senior naval officers that the Argentinian Navy might sally forth. At this stage of the campaign it was most unlikely, particular with nuclear submarines lurking somewhere. But by this time the Royal Navy had lost four warships and a transport.

So, were the events off Fitzroy a blunder? Probably not although, in hindsight, there were errors of judgement, which may not have occurred if some individuals were not so tired. The fact is five Skyhawks took advantage of clear weather to attack weakly-defended British positions. However, it was a shock to the British to read the longest casualty list in a single day since the Korean War and watch those dramatic pictures on their television sets.

Argentinian monitoring of British communications that evening led Brigadier-General Menendez to consider attacking Port Pleasant. Arriving at Stanley House during the evening, Lieutenant-Colonel Soria, whose 4th Infantry Regiment was defending Two Sisters and Mount Harriet, found Brigadier-General Jofre in a fighting mood: 'New Commando units are waiting for the Air Force Chinooks and are ready for deployment to the British rear.' Evidently he believed the day's action at Fitzroy to be a significant victory and that the British were now in a suitable position to be attacked. All he needed was for Menendez's Chief-of-Staff, Brigadier-General Daher, to return from Argentina with confirmation that a counter-attack was feasible. Menendez certainly had sufficient troops to carry out a destabilizing attack on 5th Infantry Brigade. The road was weakly held by the Welsh Guards. A quick attack by his two armoured reconnaissance units would have probably bought time for a political conclusion.

The 181st Armoured Reconnaissance Squadron troop, from 5th Army Corps, and 10th Armoured Recce Squadron, and 10th Infantry Brigade, were similarly organized. The four Troops were normally equipped with one jeep and three French AML-90 four-wheeled armoured cars. Crewed by three, a commander/gunner, driver and loader/radio operator, its 90mm main armament packed a useful punch. Menendez could have made life difficult for the British had he used them as motorized artillery to dominate the motorable track between Stanley and Goose Green, but he chose to hold them in reserve in Stanley. That he did not use them to bolster the defence of Goose Green was also remiss.

On 25 June *Sir Galahad* was towed out to sea south-west of Stanley and torpedoed by the submarine HMS *Onyx*, the only diesel-electric British submarine to go south. *Sir Tristram* was refloated and towed to Stanley where her tank deck was used for accommodation. In 1984 she was eventually brought back to England and reconstructed.

Meanwhile the Royal Navy and Royal Artillery continued to soften up the Argentinian regiments on Mount Harriet, Two Sisters and Mount Longdon. In an interview with the *New York Times* the following day, Brigadier-General Menendez was upbeat and said that the conscripts 'remained in excellent condition, physically and spiritually,' and remained prepared to 'confront and rout the colonial invaders'. No doubt he hoped that the word 'colonial' would strike a chord of sympathy for him with an American audience.

8

5th Marine Infantry Battalion

Mount Tumbledown stretches about 2,000 yards east to west and is 800 yards east of Goat Ridge. It rises sharply from the south through peat and crags to 800 feet at its centre summit. About 700 yards east of the centre is the eastern summit at 750 feet. In between the saddle dips to 700 feet. The terrain is peat, rocks and crags. Mount Tumbledown and Mount William are the gateway to Stanley. Capture them and Stanley is invested. Defending the feature was 5th Marine Infantry Battalion.

The Argentinian Marines Corps, with whom 5th Infantry Brigade would soon be fighting a pitched battle, are no strangers to the British. This is brought home to tourists every 19 November when Marine Corps colour parties march past the monument to Lieutenant Candido Lasala at Retiro, Buenos Aires. This statue commemorates the Battle of Plaza del Mercado in Buenos Aires on 5 July 1807 in which Lasala was a member of a hastily assembled naval infantry battalion, who, in sky blue jackets and white trousers, fought 2,000 British redcoats under Brigadier-General Robert Crauford for a whole day and forced them to withdraw. Lasala was eventually killed directing artillery fire and has since been regarded as the first hero of the *Cuerpo de Infantries de Marina Argentina*.

The Marine Corps can trace its origins to 1806 when marines joined the hastily assembled force of Argentinian-born inhabitants to contest the advance of 10,000 British redcoats commanded by Lieutenant-General Whitelocke, who had landed at Montevideo, crossed the River Plate and advanced on Buenos Aires with the intention of seizing the town as a trade outlet. But the British had not reckoned on the Argentinian demand for liberation from Spanish occupation and the deeper that Whitelocke advanced, the more resistance he encountered. Eventually, on 5 July, he was forced to surrender after taking heavy casualties. This was the second surrender of British troops to Argentinians within the year. The Argentinian resistance became known as The Defence. When Argentina's war for independence from Spain began in 1810 marines were attached as gunners on the ships of Admiral Guillermo Brown, a feature that is also evident in the history of the Royal Marines and United States Marine Corps. The anniversary of the Argentinian Marine Corps is taken from

19 November 1879 when the Marine Artillery Battalion was formed. A Marine Infantry Battalion was formed the following year. Ironically, the Marine Corps saw action in Buenos Aires again nearly in time for the 150th anniversary of The Defence in June 1955. During an insurrection to oust President Juan Peron, the Navy sided with the rebels and Marine units based at Buenos Aires were instructed to seize the Casa Rosada, the presidential residence. But the defenders, which included the Army, were ready and, as the marines advanced along the broad Buenos Aires boulevards, the soldiers caught them in crossfire from rooftops of government buildings and showered them with grenades and mortar bombs. Over 1,000 servicemen were killed or wounded in the chaotic confrontation, which was followed by the Naval Air Arm's bombing of an Army tank regiment. The Army struck back against the dissident Marine Corps. But the famous *Revolucion del 55* precipitated Peron's departure from government.

5th Marine Infantry Battalion was formed on 26 June 1947 and took as its motto *Pugnams Pereror Per Patriam* (Fighting I Die For The Fatherland). The shoulder patch is a Germanic sea serpent coiled around an anchor with the Sun of May in the centre. In 1982 it was part of the 1st Marine Force Fleet and based in Rio Grande in Tierra del Fuego and thus well suited to the cold of the approaching winter. The 49-year-old commanding officer, Lieutenant-Colonel Carlos Hugo Robacio, was a Malvinist and, when warned for deployment to the Falklands, prepared his Battalion with speed and enthusiasm. As with the Royal Marines, US Marine Corps and countless other marine units, the training endured by the 5th Marine Battalion has become legendary. Private Jorge Sanchez recalls:

We trained hard with infantry and anti-tank weapons. The training consisted of carrying all sorts of gear over tortuous terrain, learning to dig camouflaged mountain hideouts. I'll tell you one thing. There are some bloody big hills in Tierra del Fuego and I couldn't imagine a colder or more uncomfortable place. The fierce south-western winds which sweep over the Andes needed great dedication to combat. The battalion was responsible for the entire Route 3 highway between Rio Grande and the Chilean town of Porvenir. We took part in a number of anti-tank exercises during this period near Rio Grande and near the north-western border with Chile in northern Tierra del Fuego and were joined by a number of Marine ERC-90 Panhard armoured cars. And the battalion's German Shepherd Dog Platoon often joined the companies during the exercises.

The Battalion was one of four that contributed to the campaign. 1st Marine Infantry Battalion had been involved during the capture of South Georgia on 2 April, the 2nd Battalion had landed at Port Stanley next day and the 3rd Battalion sent H Company to guard naval facilities. Lieutenant Ricardo Marega's 1st Platoon garrisoned Naval Air Base *Calderon* on Pebble Island from 26 April until the Argentinian surrender. It put up limited resistence to the Special Air Service raid on 14/15 May largely because a fire was thought to have damaged the aircraft and not explosive charges. 2nd Platoon remained in Stanley on internal security duties and had a quiet war. 3rd Platoon defeated the Special Air Service raid on the Cortley Ridge fuel dump during the last night of the war.

5th Marine Infantry Battalion arrived in the Falklands on Thursday 8 April 1982 and deployed straight to 'Sector Bronze' covering Mount William and Tumbledown Mountain and the southern beaches where Malvinas Joint Command was expecting landings to be made. Landings were most feared from the direction of Berkeley Sound and so 7th Infantry Regiment on Mount Longdon and Wireless Ridge were in the front line, with 5th Marine Infantry Battalion holding the left rear flank. Robacio suggested that his unit should be the airmobile reserve but his superior in Stanley, Rear-Admiral Edgardo Otero, told him, more or less, to shut up and get on with his job of obeying Brigadier-General Jofre and ensuring that the Battalion was dug in. Robacio repeated this suggestion to Jofre after the British landed at San Carlos in order to screen the British breakouts from the beachhead.

The 700-strong 5th Marine Infantry Battalion order of battle was standard. The three rifle companies each had three fifty-strong platoons, each bayonet section consisting of two rifle fireteams of five men, each commanded by a non-commissioned officer, and a support section with a 7.62mm *Mitrailleur a Gaz* (MAG) machine gun and a M20 3.5-inch Bazooka anti-tank rocket launcher. Support platoon consisted of two MAGs capable of being fire in the sustained fire role and two 81mm mortars. Platoon firepower was forty 7.62mm *Fusil Automatique Legere* (FAL) automatic rifles, eight of the Belgian-developed MAG machine guns and two Bazookas. Support Company consisted of a platoon of six 120mm mortars, an Anti-Tank platoon of six 105mm recoilless rifles, a Heavy Machine Gun Platoon of four .50-inch Brownings, an Air Defence platoon of two Blowpipes and a Reconnaisance Platoon of four jeeps each equipped with a .50-inch Browning. Additional resources included RASIT ground surveillance radars loaned by the Army, but these were withdrawn after being found to be ineffective.

By comparison, the average British infantry battalion, which included 2nd Scots Guards after adjustment from their Royal Duties organization, was three rifle companies, Support Company and Headquarters Company. A rifle company consisted of three platoons based around three sections of eight men, usually commanded by a Corporal, and a single 7.62mm General Purpose Machine Gun. At platoon level, total firepower came from about twenty-five 7.62mm Self Loading Rifles (SLR) and six General Purpose Machine Guns. Support Company included Reconnaissance Platoon, a platoon of six 81mm mortars and an Anti Tank platoon usually equipped with a mix of Wombat anti-tank guns and/or Milan missiles. As we have seen, the three 5th Infantry Brigade infantry battalions had converted their anti-tank platoons into Machine-Gun Platoons.

Both sides used 7.62mm calibre rifles developed by the Belgian defence manufacturer *Fabrique Nationale*. With a long barrel and a fixed butt, the SLR was not really an assault rifle but designed as a defensive weapon to pick off the enemy. With a twenty-round magazine, it was semi-automatic, i.e. single shots had to be fired, although reloading was automatic. The FAL had very similar specifications as the SLR but, as an automatic and variants having a shorter barrel and folding skeletal butt, it was more suited to attack.

Battalion Headquarters was located 300 metres to the east of Felton Stream. On call was B Battery, Marine Field Artillery Battalion, equipped with six 105mm Pack Howitzers. The headquarters of Major Luis Menghini's 1st Amphibious Engineer Company was co-located with Battalion Headquarters. The Battalion was under operational command of 10th Infantry Brigade but had its own administrative tail to Argentina. In depth on Sapper Hill was Captain Rodolfo Cionchi's M Company defending the key to Stanley. Whoever held the hill dominated the approaches to the town. Captain Eduardo Villarraza and his N Company were dug in on Tumbledown and Mount William with Second-Lieutenant Carlos Bianchi's 1st Platoon on Mount William. On the saddle between Mount Tumbledown and Mount William was Second-Lieutenant Marcelo Oruezabala's 2nd Platoon. On the north-east shoulder of Tumbledown overlooking the north cliff face was First-Sergeant Jorge Lucero's 3rd Platoon and on the highest point was Second-Lieutenant Daniel Vasquez's composite 4th Platoon, which was assembled from a number of unemployed marine infantry in Stanley. Vasquez was joined by First-Lieutenant Hector Mino's 5th Amphibious Engineer Platoon. Captain Ricardo Quiroga's O Company was dug in on Mount William and was later reinforced by elements of 602 Commando Company. Another platoon of Menghini's Engineer Company would later be slotted into a blocking position between Mount William and Pony Pass.

The men of 5th Marine Infantry Battalion were proud to be members of the Argentinian Marine Corps. Their navy-blue beret was distinctive and had been earned after rigorous training. Their equipment was generally good. The company commanders rotated their platoons, when possible, to positions in or very near Stanley Hospital in order to rest the marines. Off duty, they could buy from the Stanley shops. Occasionally the soldiers were able to use the 10th Infantry Brigade bath unit where troops were issued with a clean uniform after showering. The battalion enjoyed decent postal, telephone and telegram services, often addressed to *Conscripto de Infanteria de Marina, Camp 8113, Islas Malvinas Argentinas* by an unknown well-wisher, student or schoolchild. One such letter was found on Mount William in 1983, a year after the war. Frances Waring, partner to Captain Baxter, who commanded 1st Raiding Squadron, Royal Marines, during the campaign, has translated it. It is from Roxanne Maria, a 20-year-old student who lived in the Banfield District of Buenos Aires. Declaring herself an ardent Argentinian, she wrote:

> *I imagine that many of you are my age and, like me, have illusions and dreams. I am in touch with your nobility. This is all about my country and our integrity and in a major part the effort from all of you, the youth of Argentina, who wish our country to be in peace. But, if there is one thing that saddens me, it is the British sailors. They come from such a long way, suffering great torments, all for the sake of a crazy woman like Thatcher. Has she thought about the course of events? What is worse, it saddens me that they defend their country (or that is what they say), for a wage. They get pushed to do it, whilst you are integral noble people. The whole country is waiting that very soon you can all come back, once again be back in your homes with the same joy as ever (because nothing awful has happened). I do not know what your thoughts of God are, but if you think of the religion, I think that all of you should bear in mind that He is very just and He will help us so all can be normal once again, in order to continue working and living in peace. As for the English, do not worry. If they wish to return 150 years to colonial times, then we can also do it and cover them with oil again and goodbye!!!*

The reference to the wage is interesting. The implication is that the British were mercenaries. While the Argentinian servicemen were indoctrinated about the justification of invading the Falklands, the British were professionals and therefore patriotism was not necessarily a top priority. But Roxanne was probably right – few British had strong feelings about the crisis. Apart from the Royal Marines, few had even heard of the Falklands, let alone the 150-year disagreement over its sovereignty.

For six weeks 5th Marine Infantry Battalion did little but react to alerts. At 3.45am on 8 May Brigadier-General Jofre was alerted by Lieutenant-Colonel Davido Comini, the Commanding Officer of 3rd Infantry Regiment on Stanley Common, that sixteen launches were closing fast on the beaches at Port Harriet and within fifteen minutes landings were expected. Robacio placed his Battalion on full alert and jabbered out a few staccato sentences in slang on his radio to show the British that the Argentinians were alert. A 601 Commando Company patrol deployed to the area and found the alert to be a false alarm. It is not clear why Comini should believe that landing craft were approaching. The two British assault ships were still 3,000 miles to the north and there was no British naval activity that night off the south coast of Stanley Common. It may be that it was a 'spoof' message as part of the British psychological warfare campaign, which included leaflet dropping.

When the British offensive began on 1 May 5th Marine Infantry Battalion was largely left alone but could obviously hear and see the naval bombardment and air raids. Occasionally Sea Harriers would fly over their positions. British activity was intensified after 3rd Commando Brigade landed and the battalion found themselves subjected to frequent night naval bombardment from such ships as the three frigates HMS *Yarmouth, Alacrity* and *Avenger* and the destroyer *Glamorgan*, all frequent visitors to the gun line. Robacio recalls the naval bombardment:

> *The 4.5-inch naval gunfire was extremely effective. Some may differ but I can assure you it was accurate. I lost one killed, Private Daniel Cabiglioli, and seven wounded on 1 May. The rate of fire was most impressive. One must be well hidden to escape injury. We were hidden well enough, but if we so much lifted our heads, we would have been decapitated.*

Nevertheless, the British did not have everything their own way. Lieutenant-Colonel Robacio insists that on 7 June M Company shot down a Harrier and registered the claim with the 10th Infantry Brigade war diary. Argentinian Marine Corps records quote the serial number of the aircraft to be XZ 989 and that it had been brought down by ground fire over Sapper Hill at 4.30 pm. In fact, the fighter was the one flown by Wing-Commander Squires, which crashed into the San Carlos metal runway with engine failure the following day and therefore the claim is discredited. The matter is further confused, so far as Argentina is concerned, when Robert Scheina, in the chapter of 5th Marine Infantry Battalion in his *Latin American Navies*, claims the battalion shot down this same Harrier on 30 May. In fact, on that day GR3 Harrier XZ 963 was one of four RAF Harriers that took off from HMS *Hermes*. Two were tasked for a laser-guided bomb mission on a Stanley Common target, which was aborted when contact could not be made with the Forward Air Controller. Squadron-Leader Jerry Pook and his wingman, Flight-Lieutenant John Rochfort, were then tasked to attack the 601

Combat Aviation Battalion helicopter operating base at the Racecourse. They also beat up a column of Argentinian troops, who put up substantial ground fire, and then attacked an artillery position. Flying back to their aircraft-carrier, Rochfort noticed that Pook's Harrier was leaking fuel. Both climbed but the leakage worsened and Pook was forced to eject into the sea at 10,000 feet and was rescued within ten minutes by a Sea King from HMS *Hermes*. It is thought that the column of troops who caused the catastrophic damage was Second-Lieutenant's Llambias-Pravaz's 3rd Platoon, C Company, 4th Infantry Regiment, which was on its way to Mount Harriet. Its loss reduced No 1 (F) Squadron's combat effectiveness to three aircraft. In total, the squadron carried out 130 attack sorties and lost four aircraft, three to ground fire and one while landing.

Any euphoria that Argentinian conscripts may have enjoyed over the Junta's military adventure quickly evaporated when it became clear the British were on their way. Enforcing the Total Exclusion Zone soon meant that supplies decreased and the Argentinian soldiers soon helped themselves to meat on the hoof. Soup with pasta and meat was generally served at dawn and sunset from mobile kitchens and was supplemented by a few luxuries such as chocolate bars. Nevertheless the young soldiers often went hungry. The more enterprising shot sheep; more than a hundred are estimated to have been rounded up and butchered by C Company, 7th Regiment, on Murrell Heights. A 3rd Parachute Battalion patrol, which was accompanied by the Falklands Islands Legislative Councillor Terry Peck CPM, bumped into a 7th Infantry Regiment foraging party. Peck had managed to escape from Stanley and when the British landed he was adopted by the Battalion and proved a useful source of intelligence for 3rd Commando Brigade. He would be awarded the MBE for his contribution to the defeat of the Argentinians. At Malvinas Joint Command, when it became apparent that conscripts were stealing food from the Stanley depots, 601 Commando Company was instructed to help 181 Military Police Company to maintain military discipline. The few who were caught were returned to their platoons where a few were apparently given a field punishment of being staked on the freezing ground. One 5th Marine Infantry Battalion conscript, in the 4th Platoon on Tumbledown, alleges he was made to crawl through rotten sheep entrails. Robacio attacked the morale problem by contacting amateur radio operators in southern Argentina every night and persuading them to pass messages to and from his men's families. He also appealed on the battalion command radio net to his marines' sense of courage and loyalty, reminding them that their predecessors had defeated the British invaders in 1806 and again the following year. It seems everyone in the battalion tuned in to Robacio's one-sided conversation and called it Radio *Pavada* (Radio Nonsense).

A unit that would play a significant role in the battle for Mount Tumbledown was B Company, 6th *General Juan Viamonte* Infantry Regiment, which was commanded by the Regimental Operations Officer, Major Oscar Ramon Jaimet. He was an Army commando who had fought against the People's Revolutionary Army in Tucuman province during the 'Dirty War'. Thoroughly professional and a dedicated soldier, he expected high standards and exercised rigid but fair discipline. It was to Jaimet that Brigadier-General Jofre turned when he wanted a heli-borne company. B Company, 6th Infantry Regiment, soon became a highly motivated unit. It originally had patrolled Stanley and provided working parties to unload supplies at Stanley wharf until it was relieved by C Company, 4th Regiment.

By mid-May B Company, 6th Infantry Regiment, was located at the bottom of Mount Kent in the area of Murrell River. Above them, on flat ground, was the forward operating base of 601 Combat Aviation Battalion, safe from the British bombardment of Stanley Common, or so they thought. They were unaware that the Special Air Service patrol led by Captain Wight had them under almost constant surveillance since the beginning of May. Rumours about Special Air Service patrols were common and on the night of 18/19 May a sentry heard the rustle of boots moving along the spine of The Saddle and fired a couple of rounds. Major Jaimet ordered the Mortar Platoon to fire flares into the night sky and two machine guns opened up for about ten minutes. Nothing was seen. Next morning, 21 May, the day the British landed at San Carlos, four 801 Squadron Sea Harriers attacked the helicopter base. Jaimet was liter-ally thrown from his camp bed as twelve bombs whistled through the low cloud base and exploded. Without air defence weapons, Jaimet and his men had felt particularly vulnerable to air strikes. Fortunately Jaimet had an influential friend, Major Carlos Doglioli, who was an adviser of special warfare and airborne operations at Malvinas Joint Command and the company received several Soviet SA-7 *Grail* portable anti-aircraft missile launchers.

Early in the night of 25/26 May Major-General Garcia telephoned Brigadier-General Menendez and advised him that the British were building up their strength at San Carlos Water. He ordered Malvinas Joint Command to attack using 10th Infantry Brigade. But Menendez was in a dilemma. Convinced that 5th Infantry Brigade might land near Stanley, he disagreed and shocked Garcia by threatening to resign if 10th Infantry Brigade was committed to battle. They were ill-prepared, he said, and there were not enough rucksacks for his troops. However, he suggested using Combat Team *Solari*, which was then on Mount Kent protecting the support helicopter base, to harass 3rd Commando Brigade. But Brigadier-General Parada, who had responsibility for the areas outside Stanley, was not prepared to risk the company. Jofre, a more flexible and imaginative brigade commander than Parada, offered his heliborne reserve and at 6pm B Company, 6th Infantry Regiment, was brought to twelve hours' notice to move to Mount Simon for possible operational tasks at Port San Carlos.

Malvinas Joint Command might have considered using the 5th Marine Battalion but did not do so. Indeed Robacio, like several other commanders, was critical of the static role allocated to his battalion. Lieutenant-Colonel Seineldin's 25th Special Infantry Regiment of conscripts and experienced regulars was another formidable unit. But by choosing to defend Stanley against the threat of a landing by 5th Infantry Brigade, Brigadier-General Menendez allowed the British to gain a firm foothold at the San Carlos beachhead from which they eventually attacked Stanley.

9

3rd Commando Brigade – 10 to 13 June

The bombing in Port Pleasant forced the slippage of Major-General Moore's timetable of the assault on the Stanley defences by at least a day, if only to give the medical teams time to clear the sick bays, casualty reception areas and field hospitals of the casualties. In order to set the operations of 5th Infantry Brigade in context, we need to briefly examine some activites of 3rd Commando Brigade as it prepared to attack Stanley.

Since 3rd Commando Brigade had landed on 21 May the short spells of sun were interrupted by snow or rain, not the comparatively gentle precipitation of an English winter, but stinging curtains that swept across the bleak moors driven by chaotic katabatic winds that ripped shelters aside. When it was not raining, a clinging, foggy, damp mist would leach itself on to uniforms and seep through to attack the body. Sometimes a harsh overnight frost would herald a few hours of precious warmth from a weak sun. Major Rod MacDonald, who commanded 59 Independent Commando Squadron RE, later wrote:

It was at this stage we started to compete with 5 Brigade for the limited helicopter assets to bring up guns and ammunition for our advance forward as well as resupply, for our forward troops who were living in the worst conditions I have ever experienced, and that includes Norway.

And this from a member of a unit that frequently spent three months on winter warfare training in Norway, often ski-ing for hours and then sleeping under the cold Northern Lights, and highly practised at survival in extreme conditions.

Of all its units, 42 Commando, exposed on the wind-battered mountains, had faced the stiffest test of survival. When Lieutenant-Colonel Vaux had arrived on Mount Kent, his manpacked command post 'looked like a shipwreck'. Eventually his BV 202 Bandwagon struggled across the appalling terrain to join them on Mount Challenger and life for Commando Headquarters became a little easier. After leaving San Carlos, the Commando had not received a ration resupply for five days and was without bergens or sleeping bags. In winter the Falkland

Island 'camp' water table is virtually on the surface and consequently almost the entire place is sodden with brackish water. As in the muddy parts of Flanders, digging creates pools. Except for that captured from streams, drinking water is almost non-existent and usually had to be delivered from special ships in plastic jerrycans and flown to the troops.

In spite of the need to divert resources to support 5th Infantry Brigade, the 3rd Commando Brigade logistic chain from San Carlos Water through Teal Inlet to the units was holding up. When supplies did arrive at unit forward echelons, it was usually during the late afternoon. This was always a difficult time for Quartermasters to organize the distribution with minimum lights. Companies would then be called forward to collect the supplies for a wearying load-carry back to their companies. For the soldiers, this reduced their strength and increased fatigue. More often that not the rations dished out to the Commando Brigade were the dehydrated Arctic type of 5,000 calories, which required at least nine pints of water for a decent meal. . The brackish water lying around in pools was not fit even to be boiled and consequently diarrhoea and dehydration were not uncommon. The demoralising cold and constant damp of wet clothing, sodden sleeping bags and soaking ground weakened those who were suffering even more. Keeping feet healthy in these inhospitable conditions became a top priority. Virtually any boot was accepted, provided it was of a military standard, i.e. leather and black, and thus a proliferation appeared, ranging from ankle-length issued demarcated sole (DMS) boots covered by cloth puttees to military skiing boots protected by canvas gaiters to comfortable German parachute boots for those lucky enough to have served in West Germany. A Royal Marine is pictured wearing Wellington boots. In much the same way that Captain Ian Gardiner of 45 Commando later waxed lyrical about his sleeping bag, Lieutenant-Colonel Vaux eulogizes about socks:

> But no matter the footwear, we all had soaking feet almost all the time. On the move blisters and abrasions usually followed from wet boots. But protracted immobility on sentry, or in an ambush, reduced circulation and could cause cold weather injuries, which became so painful that in extreme cases an individual could not walk. The antidote was to dry and powder the feet whenever possible, before cherishing them in a dry pair of socks inside a warm sleeping bag. These last critical conditions became increasingly hard to sustain, although everyone appreciated their importance. That precious pair of dry socks was only worn at rest, and then carefully protected from getting wet until the next time.

Vaux had officers, warrant officers and non-commissioned officers who kept their troops as fit and healthy as possible and, while shaving was not always possible, they were able to carry out their bodily functions. Vaux, crouching over a crevasse backside leeside, imagined 'General Galtieri was down there at the bottom'. Brigadier Thompson offered to bring 42 Commando out of the line to recuperate, but such was their enthusiasm to get on with the job that the offer was rejected. The operational administration of bringing it back to, say, Teal Inlet, would have been significant. Although Thompson was relieved, he was exceptionally keen to bring the combat-fit 40 Commando back from the drudgery of guarding the divisional supplies dump at San Carlos Water.

Vaux had known in early June that his objective would be Mount Harriet. The question was how it should be attacked – direct from the south-west or from the south. Considering the natural strength of Mount Harriet, he initially concluded that even with the British expertise in night fighting, the natural approach would be along the axis of the Darwin to Stanley road. For anyone defending the mountain, it was the expected approach, and therefore tactically the least satisfactory. The seizure of Fitzroy rather forced him to opt for a deep right-flanking attack and therefore finding a secure start line and a relatively quick ascent to the top of the objective was critical. Patrols were despatched to gather information and also dominate the ground with a particular emphasis from the south.

Vaux badly needed his third company and on 2 June, while the 2nd Parachute Battalion was seizing the Port Pleasant, J Company rejoined 42 Commando from Goose Green. J Company, which was commanded by Major Mike Norman, was hybrid. Company Headquarters and 9 Troop was made up of former Naval Party 8901, which had surrendered to the Argentinians in April and then been repatriated to the United Kingdom but without having to give their parole that they would not fight in the war. Lieutenant Bill Trollope was the Troop Officer. He and Norman had both been captured in April. 10 Troop was formed from 42 Commando Defence Troop and was commanded by Lieutenant Tony Hornby, 42 Commando's Assistant Training Officer. He was killed when the Chinook, containing key intelligence personnel from Northern Ireland, crashed. 11 Troop was raised from Milan Troop and was commanded by Lieutenant Colin Beadon.

On 3 June Lieutenant Mawhood and two sections of Reconnaissance Troop, a forward observation party and a Royal Air Force forward air controller advanced through the bone-chilling, clammy fog that was blanketing the 'camp' to set up an observation post in rocks on the lower eastern slopes of Mount Wall. Visibility was next to nothing. Concealed in rocks, the patrol listened for the scuffle of boots across rocks.

Argentinian intelligence had scented the British presence on Mount Wall and Lieutenant-Colonel Diego Soria, commanding 4th Infantry

Regiment, tasked Second-Lieutenant Jimenez-Corvalan's 3rd Platoon, B Company, on Mount Harriet, to investigate. In support, on the road in two trucks, was Second-Lieutenant Marcelo Llambias-Pravaz's 3rd Platoon of C Company from Two Sisters. By about 11am Jimenez-Corvalan was near Mount Wall and in order to cover more ground quickly, he split his patrol, sending one group in a curve to the north while the other probed at Mount Wall. The Royal Marines saw the movement and Mawhood ordered 'weapons tight'. But some of his troops were understandably nervous about live enemy moving very close to their positions and, insisting they had been seen, opened fire at a range of no more than fifty yards with everything they had. Mawhood's position was effectively compromised and a firefight developed. Two Argentinians were quickly killed. After the initial shock, the Argentinians returned fire and were supported by Second-Lieutenant Mario Juarez's 4th Regiment Heavy Mortar Detachment on Mount Harriet, who dropped 120mm mortar bombs around the Royal Marine position. Meanwhile while the forward observation team moved up to high ground to improve the communications with their battery headquarters, Llambias-Pravaz's lorry-borne platoon appeared and threatened Mawhood's rear. When Mawhood ordered his sections to withdraw, the Forward Air Controller prudently put a bullet through his heavy laser rangefinder, in accordance with very strict orders that it should not fall into enemy hands in one piece. Captain Nick D' Appice, the Forward Observation Officer:

We were separated from our heavy bergens with the radios and all our gear. The patrol was spread over quite a large area, with lots of shouting, noise and firing going on. The Royal Marines abandoned all their equipment, and although no one told us, it became clear that we were to withdraw. With no information, and the likelihood of having to fight our way out, Dave Greedus and I decided to abandon our equipment, destroying as much as we could. The HF and UHF radio sets were tough enough, but the HAZE unit of the laser target marker was designed to withstand the weight of a tank!

Lieutenant-Colonel Vaux was on his way to meet with Brigadier Thompson but had left his Tactical Headquarters and its comprehensive radio links behind. Consequently there was very little he could do to influence Mawhood's predicament. Vaux was angry with himself:

It was a most unfortunate development. Suddenly we had lost an invaluable vantage point, which the enemy now is expected to seize in strength. A much-needed and expensive piece of equipment for directing accurate air strikes had also been destroyed. Last, but very damaging from our points of view, half of Recce Troop and two fire control teams had lost most of their kit.

The Argentinians briefly occupied the observation post. Brigadier Thompson, succinct as ever, suggested to Vaux, 'I should like you to get back there as soon as J Company is established.' Next day 10 (Defence) Troop re-occupied the Mount Wall observation post against no opposition. Mawhood's Troop was evacuated to Teal Inlet to be re-issued with equipment and the patrolling now fell to Captain David Wheen's L Company.

That night, in foul conditions, a 4 Troop patrol, led by Acting-Lieutenant Ken McMillan, set off from Mount Challenger to check a culvert across the Stanley track and, if possible, capture an Argentinian from one of the working parties known to be working in the area. The same night the Welsh Guards aborted their march to High Hill. The patrol came across a small shack and Lance-Corporal Garry Cuthell, covered by Marine Mark Curtis's machine-gun team, checked it. Nothing was found, but, as Curtis crossed flatter ground, he stepped on a mine which wrecked his right instep and left his toes hanging by a thread of skin. Cuthell crawled over to him, administered first aid and then carried the 15-stone rugby player to safety where Leading Medical Assistant Hayworth treated him. The weather prevented helicopter casualty evacuation and it took seven hours to carry Curtis, in agony although drugged on morphine, up Mount Challenger to safety. It was a further eighteen hours before he was evacuated to Ajax Bay. After several operations, Mark Curtis was discharged in January 1984. Vaux would later complain that the absence of a lightweight stretcher was a serious omission.

As we have seen, during the evening of 5 June, Major-General Garcia warned Brigadier-General Menendez that 3rd Commando Brigade was about to carry out a major heliborne attack on the Stanley defences during the night. Menendez placed his forces on immediate alert and instructed Brigadier-General Jofre to send out Special Forces fighting patrols to disrupt British operations. On 4 June a 4th Infantry Regiment patrol had established that the Mount Wall observation post had been re-occupied. Next night Captain Ferrero's 3rd Assault Section, 602nd Commando Company, was tasked to raid it and take prisoners. Ferrero:

At about 4 in the evening on the 5th, we moved up to First Lieutenant Carlos Alberto Arroyo's command post on Mount Harriet. Major Aldo Rico commanded the patrol. We were as glad to see Arroyo as he was to see us. Dirty, bearded and a little thinner, he gripped Rico in a bear hug. A gallant Commando, Arroyo volunteered to go with us to Mount Wall. Several conscripts came to see us. There was a lot of laughter, some of it nervous, perhaps adrenalin-driven. We had a chance to get a scrumptious and – let us be honest here – very fatty barbecue going and look at the enemy positions at Bluff Cove Rincon and tried to pinpoint the

*observation post on Mount Wall. A 4th Regiment patrol had been out in the area
the night before. Distances were deceptive. In the thin air Mount Kent seemed
close at hand. In nearly every other direction arose outcrops of limestone. Their
slopes were not sheer; rather they spread themselves, rugged and inhospitable. It
was a very humbling place. We watched 155mm fire falling on the British para-
troopers at Bluff Cove Rincon. The weather was appalling, cold and wet with high
wind. Few people are aware that we also had the ugly experience of being shelled
by the 3rd Artillery Group at one point. It was human error.*

*The plan was to take Mount Wall from the rear. Two artillery batteries were
on call, because our route up the feature was very open – a perfect killing ground.
By 4pm it was almost dark and the temperature had sunk. Moving past shell
craters and remnants of cluster bombs to the base of Mount Wall, we lay up among
boulders while First Lieutenant Lauria cleared a path through the minefields.
Altogether it must have taken three hours to get there. It was a bright moonlit
night and cold. I lay there frozen, not moving. Argentinian Artillery fire started
coming down on Mount Wall at approximately 10.30pm. Crouching in silence we
waited for the fire to end. Some shells fell only 150 metres from us. Then – sudden
silence. It ceased and Major Rico screamed to us to go and we advanced uphill
through the rocks. A fit commando, if anyone was going to get to the mountaintop
first, it would be Lauria but as he swept round a boulder, he came across a straggler
or so he thought. It was Major Rico. Who says age slows you down? On the way
up we passed the body of a 4th Regiment conscript. Captain Hugo Ranieri knelt
down to examine the body and removed the rosary from the young soldier's neck
before moving on. We found a laser target designator and several rucksacks. It
was the first indication we'd had of how well they had been equipped. There was
even a 42 Commando beret.*

Strangely, the Argentinians did not occupy the position. Within
support weapon range from Mount Harriet and covered by the 105mm
Pack Howitzers of 3rd Artillery Group, the occupied Mount Wall would
have been a thorn in the side of 3rd Commando Brigade. Some of the
fruits of this incursion have been displayed in Buenos Aires Army
Museum. The Argentinian journalist Nicolas Kasanzew later wrote that
the aggressive patrolling by the Commando companies was equal to the
British in Malvinas'. Group-Captain Ruben Moro was equally praise-
worthy of Argentinian patrolling:

*The activity of the Argentinian troops, as intense and risky as it was, was no
less so than that of the British, for each side made every attempt to infiltrate
behind enemy lines in order to reconnoitre their position, layout, units, and any
other intelligence that would prove vital to staffs in planning the battle that was
to come.*

Brigadier-General Menendez also praised the patrolling of the
Argentinian Commandos:

We were able to follow the British advance through the reports from our patrols. We had a good idea of where they were more than likely to attack and the possible placement of their artillery and reserve units. But we could not exploit this knowledge because of our limited transport capacity. The truth is that our commandos operated well and brought in a lot of intelligence, capturing enemy equipment and codes, which also helped. We could not prevent the British attack but we had enough information to prepare ourselves.

It is worth noting the emphasis on the Army Commando. Most Argentinian patrolling was carried by 601 and 602 Commando Companies simply because they had the experience. Apart from Mount Wall, the infantry usually protected mine-laying activities. All night the Argentinians had waited for the expected heliborne assault, but when it failed to materialize Jofre stood down his regiments from the high alert with orders to continue working on the Stanley defences. During the morning he visited the 6th Regiment's 'B' Company and its platoons. Speaking to the officers, he reminded them of the long history of 10th Brigade, particularly when it was commanded by General Julio Roca during the War of the Desert against the elusive and hostile Araucanian Indians of Patagonia, who had broken through the ring of forts defending Buenos Aires.

Next day Second-Lieutenant Llambias-Pravaz escorted a Marine Amphibious Engineer Company detachment which had arrived the previous night with a jeep load of mines to lay them on the western slopes of Two Sisters, but he was ambushed by Lieutenant Chris Fox's 45 Commando Reconnaissance Troop near Murrell River. Although platoon Sergeant Ramon Valdez led a counter-attack, Llambias-Pravaz was unable to win the fire fight and withdrew, having lost three amphibious engineers and two 4th Infantry Regiment conscripts, Privates Jose Romero and Andres Rodriguez. Following this action, a local truce was arranged so that the Argentinians could recover their dead. Lieutenant-Colonel Vaux called on Captain Adrian Hicks and his 2 Troop, 59 Independent Commando Squadron RE, to help clear routes. At the same time as Ferrero was patrolling against Mount Wall, Hicks joined L Company:

Our first recce was arranged on our arrival, so, after a quick meal, I took C Section, with Corporal Brown and a section of Assault Engineers under Sergeant Daly RM to rendezvous with 5 Troop, L Company. They were to act as our protection and guides and led us eastwards along the ridge through thick mist and drizzle. The aim of the recce was to establish a safe route from Challenger-Wall saddle south down to the Stanley road. We had been advised that a fence or track could be followed, but, as neither existed, I decided to take a bearing from a large dump of

Argentinian 105mm shells and clear along that. Protected by 5 Troop, an Assault Engineer and Royal Engineer team worked side by side to clear a mine-free path about four metres wide. The mist began to clear and a bright moon illuminated the patrol with frightening clarity. It made our task easier, but, as we were well forward of friendly troops, it raised some heartbeats as we approached the white, surfaced road, a distance of 500 metres. Fortunately there were no incidents and the patrol returned along the safe route to the final RV before making its way back to the company base.

By 6 June, the day the Scots Guards arrived at Bluff Cove, 3rd Commando Brigade was ready to attack the Outer Defence Zone, but, since 5th Infantry Brigade had not consolidated on the southern flank, Moore postponed it until the 9th. Before moving his headquarters from Teal Inlet on to Mount Kent Brigadier Thompson sought assurance from Moore, that whenever he attacked, 5th Infantry Brigade would follow through into the heart of the Argentinian defences.

During the night of 6/7 June Sergeant Neville Weston, the Troop Sergeant commanding 5 Troop in the absence of the Troop Commander, Lieutenant Jerry Burnell, who had hypothermia, took a fighting patrol south of the road. Accompanying him was a K Company recce patrol of Sergeant Tom Collins and three Royal Marines. Their task was to look for routes to Mount Harriet. Leaving Mount Challenger after dark, the patrol moved along the route cleared by Hicks. Soon after crossing the road Marine Kevin Patterson stepped on a mine which blew off his left foot. He was carried back to the patrol base where Medical Assistant Collins administered first aid. A small party, including Collins, set off to rendezvous with a helicopter. A smaller man than the rugby-playing Curtis, Patterson was carried some of the way, but the terrain was sufficiently hostile that sometimes he had to hop, supported by his colleagues. By a mixture of good luck and determination, Captain Nick Pound RM, of 3rd Commando Brigade Air Squadron, collected Patterson in his Scout and took him straight to Ajax Bay. Like Curtis, his foot was amputated and Patterson was discharged in June 1983.

Vaux was now faced with a dilemma. For the second time in three nights Royal Marine patrols without Royal Engineer support had run into minefields. Every time a mine exploded it compromised his strategy of attacking Mount Harriet from the south. Determined to explore the southern option, he told Sergeant Collins that, in spite of the risks, a route must be found through the minefields and any other obstacles to the southern flanks of the hill. Leaving Sergeant Weston at the patrol base, Sergeant Collins led his patrol south of the road and, while probing the western flanks of Mount Harriet, was spotted by a large Argentinian patrol. Covering each other, the Royal Marines rapidly withdrew and then Collins fell into a small peat pond of freezing mucky water. The other three, believing he had found cover, followed and tumbled in on top of him. Dripping wet, the four Royal Marines then waited to be attacked. The Argentinians also went to ground and after about an hour, perhaps uncertain whether they had seen anything, noisily marshalled on the road and returned up Mount Harriet. Collins carefully plotted their withdrawal and gained Vaux valuable intelligence. Suggestions that the Argentinians may have been from Captain Fernandez's 2nd Assault Section, 602 Commando Company, who were then helping O Company, 5th Marine Infantry Battalion, to dominate the area from Pony's Pass, seem unlikely. The Argentinian commandos were generally professionals in their own right and would have probably followed up Collins's hasty withdrawal.

Royal Engineer Sergeant Thompson and two of his men accompanied a K Company reconnaissance patrol investigating the area around two 155mm craters on the Stanley road for mines and examined a minefield found on the south-east corner of Mount Wall. Desultory mortar fire, the odd burst of small arms fire and flares bursting overhead caused a few problems. However, Thompson and his sappers recovered packing from an anti-personnel mine box and a leaflet for an anti-tank mine. The finds would prove most useful three nights later.

Major-General Moore had firmed up his strategy that breaching the Stanley defences would be a three-phase operation – a punch on the outer defences by 3rd Commando Brigade striking from the north and west, followed by an uppercut at the inner defence by 5th Infantry Brigade from the south and the *coup de grace* by 3rd Commando Brigade advancing from the high ground west of Stanley safe in the knowledge that, if they were faced with stiff opposition, they could call upon strong British reserves of the 5th Infantry Brigade. It would be important that the momentum of the three phrases be kept and, once reeling, the Argentinians should be given no time to regroup.

Phase One – 11/12 June

3rd Commando Brigade assault on the Outer Defence Zone.

- *3rd Parachute Battalion to seize Mount Longdon.*

- *45 Commando to attack Two Sisters.*

- *42 Commando, with the Welsh Guards in reserve, to attack Mount Harriet.*

Phase Two – 12/13 June

5th Infantry Brigade attack the south Inner Defence Zone

- *The Scots Guards to attack Mount Tumbledown.*
- *1/7th Gurkha Rifles to seize Mount William.*
- *1 Welsh Guards as brigade reserve.*

3rd Commando Brigade attacks north Inner Defence Zone.

- *2nd Parachute Battalion attack Wireless Ridge.*

Phase Three – on completion of Phase Two

3rd Commando Brigade

- *Break on to Stanley Common and capture the town. (The Commando Brigade intelligence staff had already prepared information for fighting in Stanley.)*

Soon after arriving at Bluff Cove on 8 June Lieutenant-Colonel Rickett had flown across Wickham Heights to liaise with Lieutenant-Colonel Vaux and agreed inter-boundary operational tasks. When the Welsh Guards learnt that the battalion was to come under command of 3rd Commando Brigade for the attack on the Outer Defence Zone morale lifted enormously because an opportunity existed to get to grips with the Argentinians. Regular supplies of rations, ammunition and a BV 202 Snocat, driven by Marine Brown, arrived! Rickett appointed Regimental Sergeant Major Tony Davies (22) to act as Quartermaster, as his echelon at San Carlos was now totally out of the picture. He, together with Company Sergeant Major Jack Hough and six others, ran it most successfully and with great skill until the end of hostilities. To replace the Prince of Wales Company and 3 Company, both lost on the *Sir Galahad,* A and C Companies, 40 Commando, commanded by Captains Sean Cusack and Andy Pillar respectively, joined the Battalion at Fitzroy, bringing it back up to strength. As it is always difficult initially to absorb new units under command, particularly when they are so different in culture and outlook, Rickett was careful to get to know the new arrivals and create mutual confidence in each other's procedures and methods of doing things. Rickett:

Both were very good and their companies were very well trained. However, I had to make sure that everything was carefully spelt out to avoid any unnecessary

misunderstandings; I couldn't afford to take any short cuts in my orders or instruc-
tions which I could have done with my own Company Commanders who were
totally in my mind. Also I was conscious of spending more time and effort with
my new companies, chatting them all up and trying to get to know them at the
expense of the rest of the Battalion, but there was no other way round this if we
were to achieve the aim and finish the job.

The two 4th Field Regiment forward observation parties, which had been on the *Sir Galahad,* returned and a detachment from 30 Signal Regiment arrived with rear link communications. With 9 Parachute Squadron, Royal Engineers, now reduced to two troops, 1 Troop, 59 Independent Commando Squadron, which was commanded by Lieutenant Bob Hendicott, joined the Battalion from 3rd Commando Brigade. He was very impressed by the welcome given to his men – rationed, issued signals instruction and generally looked after. He also learnt that there is only one sergeant major, namely the Regimental Sergeant Major. The rest are 'com'ny sergeant majors'. Retaining a small headquarters, he attached his three sapper sections to the three rifle companies. Each was equipped with satchel charges, Bangalore torpedoes to breach wire and field defences, and the impedimenta for mine clearing.

The arrival of the Royal Fleet Auxiliary helicopter support ship *Engadine* at San Carlos on 9 June with four helicopters gave the ground forces much-needed support helicopter reinforcement. Superbly maintained under difficult conditions by their naval ground crews operating in uncomfortable conditions, they joined the other helicopters flying in guns, ammunition, rations, fresh water, which was scarce in the hills, bergens and the eagerly-awaited mail from home, as well as flying out sick and wounded.

3rd Commando Brigade, virtually unaffected by events at Port Pleasant, continued to probe the Argentinian defences and prepare to attack the following night, 8/9 June. Lieutenant Mark Townsend and his 1 Troop, K Company, 42 Commando, led an important patrol. Probing the north-west slopes of Mount Harriet, his men clashed with Second-Lieutenant Lautaro Jimenez-Corvalan's 3rd Platoon, C Company, 4th Infantry Regiment, killing two Argentinians. Return fire allowed his men to pinpoint Argentinian positions. Of this action *The New York Times* ran a feature in which Argentinian Army High Command said that British forces lost up to thirty soldiers from 3rd Parachute Battalion and 42 Commando in one of the heaviest battles yet. The 4th Regiment revelled in the belief that they had evened the score at Goose Green. One officer is quoted, 'We are going to clobber the British so hard they will not know what hit them.' Vaux's claim that his men killed six Argentinians is unsubstantiated. Unknown to the Argentinians, Townsend had created sufficient confusion to enable two four-man Mountain and Arctic Warfare Cadre patrols led by Lieutenant Fraser Haddow and Sergeant Desmond Wassell respectively to establish an observation post on Goat Ridge, not far from the track connecting Two Sisters and Mount Harriet. Sitting back-to-back Haddow and Wassall then spent the next day sketching the dead ground to the east, including to Mount Tumbledown, plotted a command-detonated mine buried in metal barrels and acquired a mass of information about Argentinian activities on the eastern slopes, unseen by 3rd Commando Brigade. After dark on the 10th the two patrols returned to 42 Commando and were then sent to Headquarters 3rd Commando Brigade for a detailed debrief. This patrol was probably one of the most significant of the war. Carried out by a relatively new unit, it gathered very useful tactical information on Argentinian activities and dispositions and certainly eased the planning of the attacks on Two Sisters and Mount Harriet and consequently led to fewer casualties.

During the same patrol Sergeant Michael Collins, Lieutenant Beadon and three Royal Marines found potential Milan firing-post sites at a track junction south of Mount Harriet to deal with any armoured approaches by the Argentinians from Stanley during the assault on Mount Harriet. Collins then found the fence selected by Lieutenant-Colonel Vaux for his start line. Sergeant Collins was deservedly awarded the Military Medal for his patrolling.

On 10 June Thompson summoned the commanding officers to Headquarters 3rd Commando Brigade on Mount Kent and issued his orders for Phase One on the basis that, if the Argentinians folded, the momentum of the attack must be maintained.

- ❒ *3rd Parachute Battalion to seize Mount Longdon and exploit to Wireless Ridge.*

- ❒ *45 Commando to attack Two Sisters and then exploit to Mount Tumbledown and Mount William.*

- ❒ *42 Commando, with the Welsh Guards in reserve, to attack Mount Harriet and be prepared to support 45 Commando on its drive to Mount Tumbledown.*

Vaux was not too happy about the Welsh Guards securing his start line because he felt that the introduction of a new unit complicated his plan, particularly as he did not know the men and they did not know the ground. It was 42 Commando that had found the back door to Mount

Harriet. Lieutenant Beadon and Sergeant Collins knew the ground well. Communications were also unreliable. Since this seems to have been a decision imposed on Brigadier Thompson by Headquarters Land Forces, Vaux had no alternative but to agree and despatched Lieutenant Tony Allen RM to be his liaison officer with the Guards.

Convinced that attacking along the Goat Ridge – Mount Challenger track was impractical, Lieutenant-Colonel Vaux opted for a deep right hook from south-east of Mount Harriet. As he commented, nearly twenty years later, 'One of the prinicipal preoccupations we had was to try and achieve surprise by stealth, diversion and – above all – by attacking as far as possible around the rear of their positions on Harriet.' His plan was for 11 Troop to mark out the route from the assembly area to the start line for the two assaulting companies, K and L Company. Following up was Porter Troop from Headquarters Company with 10,000 rounds of ammunition and ancillary equipment. 9 Troop was to provide a diversionary phoney attack from Mount Wall while 10 Troop protected Tactical Headquarters. In the meantime, the signallers passed phoney messages suggesting no change to locations or logistic requirements. Movement along the intended approach was kept to nil during the day.

On the same day Argentinian Marine Corps Major Raul Cufre, of the Tactical Divers, arrived in Stanley to set in motion Operational Plan SZE-21. The principle of the plan was to destabilize British operations by inserting 601 and 602 Commando Companies and 601 National Gendarmerie Special Forces Squadron by helicopter behind British lines. 603 Commando Company and the 1st Amphibious Commando Grouping would be inserted from the mainland. Two Air Force 7th Counter-Insurgency Squadron CH-47 Chinooks had already been instructed to return to Comodoro Rivadavia from Stanley on 9 June. The flight was difficult and both helicopters landed at Staten Island for emergency repairs. The entire operation was to be supported by a squadron of the 1st *General San Martin* Cavalry Regiment who had been flown to the Falklands during the night of 8/9 June.

During the afternoon the Welsh Guards advanced from Bluff Cove to a position to support 42 Commando and prepare for battle – orders given, ammunition distributed and medics laying out instruments and bandages. At last light on the 11th the Welsh Guards set off to get themselves into position and soon found that crossing the stone runs was a set off in the late afternoon in order to secure the Commando start line. But there was consternation on Mount Challenger when the Platoon, in broad daylight, moved east across the moorland toward 42 Commando's forming up place in full view of observers on Mount Harriet. Inevitably this drew Argentinian artillery fire. Symes was expected to secure the start line after dark and within the fours hours allowed by Vaux for K and L Companies to leave Mount Challenger and reach the start line. Vaux was irritated because the last thing he wanted was the Argentinians concentrating their surveillance south and west of Mount Challenger. He needed to preserve the security of his attack. To complicate matters communications between the two units broke down, even with the intervention of Headquarters 3rd Commando Brigade, and the risk of a 'blue on blue' rose.

Just after 5.30pm, about an hour after dark, 42 Commando left their lair. When Lieutenant Beadon and the advance party from 9 Troop and the Milan team arrived at the start line there was no sign of Symes' platoon and, since they could not be contacted on the radio, he set off to find them. The delay caused some anxiety for the two attacking 42 Commando company commanders and some crisp comments were passed over the radio. After seeking permission from Commando Headquarters, Beadon used his men to secure the start line, but there was real concern. Somewhere in the darkness and shadow below Mount Harrier were the Guards and it only needed for them to stray too far up Mount Harriet, detonate a mine, clash with an Argentinian patrol or bump into 42 Commando for fire to be opened and the entire operation be compromised. Two weeks of hard work and surviving in hostile conditions were now under great risk. Indeed, if 42 Commando failed to take Mount Harriet and thereby dominate the road from Stanley, the strategy to capture Stanley was in jeopardy. Lieutenant Allen could not be contacted at Headquarters Welsh Guards and so Headquarters 3rd Commando was asked to liaise with 5th Infantry Brigade and arrange for the Welsh Guards to be withdrawn from the area. No sooner had Beadon secured the start line than movement was spotted about 200 metres to the east among some rocks and only about half a mile from known enemy positions. Peering through his image intensifier, he saw that the figures were wearing hoods resembling British windproofs, but they were west of the fence line and therefore might be enemy. Guided by their talking and the pinpricks of cigarettes, Beadon cautiously crept closer to the figures and, certain they were British, stood up with his hands in the air. To his relief it was the missing Welsh Guards Reconnaisance Platoon, but there was also considerable annoyance that the attack had been held up and would now have to be made by the light of a bright full moon.

Vaux's earlier concerns about working the Welsh Guards without rehearsal were justified. About an hour had been wasted and, with Symes's platoon now securing the correct fence, Captain Peter Babbington's K Company silently deployed in single file along the start-line and then crossed and padded through the frosty moorland into the deep shadows of Mount Harriet.

The night attack by 3rd Commando Brigade has been told elsewhere in detail. In brief, 3rd Parachute Battalion opened the assault by attacking a 7th Infantry Regiment company group on Mount Longdon consisting of infantry, an army engineer platoon and marine machine-gunners. The fighting was severe, but, as dawn broke the following morning, 3rd Parachute Battalion had overwhelmed the Argentinians, but at the cost of seventeen killed, including Sergeant Ian McKay, who was awarded a posthumous Victoria Cross for attacking a key machine-gun position. Forty paras were wounded. Of the 287 defenders, only eighty-seven withdrew the following morning, the remainder killed, left behind wounded or captured.

On Two Sisters C Company, 4th Infantry Regiment, was defeated by 45 Commando at the cost of three Royal Marines and a Royal Engineer killed compared to ten Argentinians killed, fifty wounded and fifty-four captured. The fighting was as severe as at Goose Green. Second-Lieutenant Llambias-Pravaz's 3rd Platoon, on *Long Toenail,* the south-western feature, opened fire on X Company at 11.30pm and was not dislodged until about 2.30am. Appreciating that the loss of Two Sisters would give the British a virtually clear route on to Stanley Common, Major Jaimet was instructed to plan a counter-attack with B Company, 6th Infantry Regiment and two troops of eight Panhard AML-90s from 181st Armoured Recce Squadron. The armoured cars had just reached a point north of Mount Tumbledown on the Stanley to Estancia track when Z Company, led by Lieutenant Clive Dytor, charged the Argentinian positions on *Summer Days,* the northern peak. Argentinian resistance crumbled and Jofre cancelled the counter-attack. The sector commander, Major Ricardo Cordon, was captured in his command post at about 3am. Brigadier-General Jofre decided that Two Sisters was lost and authorized that it should be abandoned. From the wreckage of C Company, 4th Infantry Regiment, it fell to Captain Carlos Patterson, the regimental Operations Officer, to guide the shaken survivors of the badly wounded Second-Lieutenant Miguel Mosquera's 1st Platoon from *Summer Days* to a blocking position north-west of Mount Tumbledown, which was held by the dismounted 10th Armoured Cavalry Squadron. It was from this position that the Argentinians opened fire on 3rd Parachute Battalion on Mount Longdon. Second-Lieutenant

Llambias-Pravaz and the survivors of his platoon joined M Company, 5th Marine Infantry Battalion, on Sapper Hill. Llambias-Pravaz had been commissioned in April 1982 and for his outstanding courage and leadership during the battle was awarded the Gallantry in Combat Medal. Major Jaimet was instructed to forget the counter-attack and fall back to Tumbledown. Second-Lieutenant Aldo Franco's 3rd Platoon, B Company, 6th Infantry Regiment, also covered the withdrawal by taking up a position on the eastern slopes of the hill and firing on Y Company, 45 Commando.

In what is frequently regarded as a classic night attack, 42 Commando destroyed the remainder of 4th Infantry Regiment by overrunning Regimental Headquarters, B Company, and several other platoons equivalent to a company on Mount Harriet. Two Royal Marines were killed and twenty-eight wounded. The Argentinians lost five 4th Infantry Regiment, one 1st Cavalry Regiment private, three HQ 3rd Brigade Defence Platoon and one sapper killed and about fifty-three wounded. An estimated 300 were taken prisoner, including Lieutenant-Colonel Soria. Second-Lieutenant Oscar Silva's 1st Platoon, A Company, and Lieutenant Mosterin's surviving 12th Infantry Regiment platoon from Combat Team *Solari* joined 5th Marine Infantry Battalion on Mount Tumbledown.

The Welsh Guards Milan detachment played a small part in the battle when they engaged a machine-gun bunker high up on the mountain's eastern shoulder with a well-aimed missile. This drew unwelcome shelling and mortaring and Rickett pulled the battalion 400 yards to the west behind a small lake to the south-west of Mount Harriet. To the north-west of the lake there was a small Argentinian minefield. Major Kefford's D Company, 1/7th Gurkha Rifles, which was searching for guns and a radar position still thought to be somewhere near Port Harriet, collected eighty-four prisoners. Like many others that night, they had watched the land-based Exocet at Stanley hit HMS *Glamorgan*.

The Outer Defence Zone was captured, but the severity of the fighting and the arrival of daylight meant that 3rd Commando Brigade was unable to exploit to Wireless Ridge and Mount Tumbledown. As they had proved at Goose Green, the Argentinians showed that they were prepared to fight hard and then, next day, Argentinian artillery began shelling all three peaks, causing more British casualties. It was fortunate that by the end of the day the Argentinians had used up most of the 155mm ammunition.

10

The Battle of Mount Tumbledown – 12 to 14 June

Lieutenant-Colonel Robacio was reasonably certain that the British would attack along the Stanley-Darwin track. Enemy activity since 2 June seemed to bear this out. He therefore instructed his Operations Officer, Major Antonio Pernias, to move O Company into a blocking position near Pony Pass. This meant that N Company was left to defend Mount Tumbledown and Mount William. High on the centre of the ridge was Second-Lieutenant Vasquez's twenty-six-strong composite 4th Platoon. It was reinforced by Lieutenant Mino's 5th Amphibious Engineer Platoon occupying positions on the south-western slopes of the feature in rocks above and behind Vasquez. On the northern slopes, looking toward Mount Longdon and Wireless Ridge, was First-Sergeant Lucero's 3rd Platoon. On the saddle between Mount Tumbledown and Mount William was Second-Lieutenant Oruezabala's 2nd Platoon. Second-Lieutenant Bianchi's 1st Platoon was on Mount William.

It was with some relief to 2nd Parachute Battalion that on 9 June they passed back under command of 3rd Commando Brigade. One officer's lasting memory of Brigadier Wilson was at an Orders Group at Fitzroy, which was being filmed, standing up and beginning, 'Well, we have suffered some setbacks . . .' After the experience at Goose Green, Lieutenant-Colonel Chaundler was determined to use time wisely and prepare for the next task, which turned out to be in reserve for the Commando Brigade seizure of the Outer Defence Zone during the night 11/12 June and then carry out the only all arms attack of the war on Wireless Ridge two nights later.

In fact, this particular criticism is a little unfair. Always seeking an opportunity to promote his Brigade, Brigadier Wilson had invited journalists to a staged Orders Group on the upper floor of a warehouse. He was sufficiently security conscious not to reveal operationally secret matters. Afterwards, he gave a detailed briefing, but without the media in attendance, that 5th Infantry Brigade must be ready to support the 3rd Commando Brigade attack on the Outer Defence Zone on the night of 11/12th. The Scots Guards, reinforced by D Company, 1/7th Gurkha

Rifles, would provide right-flank protection for the 42 Commando assault on Mount Harriet. At the same time the Gurkhas were to patrol aggressively against Mount Tumbledown and Mount William in the hope that the defenders would surrender. If the two features did not fall, the Scots Guards and the Gurkhas were to attack Mount Tumbledown and Mount William respectively, in a co-ordinated daylight operation from the south on 12th. This would involve a long uphill assault from the predicted direction – the axis of the road to Stanley – through a mine-field and across ground that had not been reconnoitred. At the same time the 2nd Parachute Battalion was to attack Wireless Ridge. Once the two features were secure, the Welsh Guards would seize Sapper Hill to dominate and support the Gurkhas' breakout on to Stanley Common.

By this time key officers in Brigade Headquarters had agreed that the Scots Guards were best prepared to lead the brigade attack. It was well led by Lieutenant-Colonel Scott and, according to one officer, had high quality and aggressive troops. The Welsh Guards had lost over half a battalion and, although reinforced by 40 Commando, were not in a fit state to lead the attack. There was a feeling that, although the Gurkhas were the strongest battalion, they were better suited to jungle warfare. The fact that Gurkhas come from Nepal, a country of mountains, damp fog and cold winter weather, just like the Falklands in June, seems to have been forgotten, but clearly not their role in the Far East. Some Gurkha officers also believed that they did not stand a chance against two Guards lieutenant-colonels.

The two armoured reconnaissance Troops of the Blues and Royals were switched from 3rd Commando Brigade to 5th Infantry Brigade to take advantage of the better going in the south. Leaving Estancia, they crossed the central range of hills and arrived at Bluff Cove six hours later, instead of the expected thirty-six hours, which again discredited the sceptics who did not believe the CVR (T) armoured vehicles could handle difficult terrain. CVR (T) is short for Combat Vehicle Reconnaissance (Tracked). The main firepower of this family of versatile medium recon-naissance vehicles was with the Scorpion, with its 76mm gun, and Scimitar, with its quick-firing 30mm Rarden cannon. Striker has Swingfire anti-tank missiles; Spartan is the armoured personnel carrier, Samaritan the ambulance, Samson the armoured recovery vehicle and Sultan the command post. The two Blues and Royals Troops accompanied the Task Force, each consisting of two Scorpion and two Scimitars and were supported by a Samson. It is a pity that most senior commanders, in particular in the Royal Marines, did not have the con-fidence to use them effectively.

Returning to his headquarters at Bluff Cove, Lieutenant-Colonel Scott held a planning conference with his company commanders, the Intelligence and Operations Officers, his Battery Commander, Major Gwyn, and Lieutenant Peter McManners RE, whose 3 Troop, 9 Parachute Squadron, Royal Engineers, was supporting the Battalion. His brother, Hugh, was serving with 148 Commando Forward Observation Battery and later became a television personality on survival skills. The major obstacle was the minefield. When Scott asked McManners how long it would take to breach it and take the whole Battalion through, McManners told him all night. Major Bethel commented that, in the current plan, if there was a delay in breaching the minefield, both battalions could therefore hit their objectives piecemeal and in daylight. That night the Scots Guards drew up a plan to attack Tumbledown from 42 Commando's position on Mount Harriet and Goat Ridge, i.e. almost directly from the west across ground that had not been patrolled or examined for mines. The Gurkhas would then pass through and seize Mount William. This was not the axis expected by the Argentinians; however, it would allow the attack to be mounted from a secure base across ground that could be viewed. There would also be immediate direct support from 42 and 45 Commandos. The major problem was inserting the Battalion on Mount Harriet without attracting the attention of the Argentinians. Scott decided he also needed a diversion to keep the attention of 5th Marine Infantry Battalion focused on the south-west. Brigadier Wilson agreed with Scott's proposals.

In preparation for the next phase, Scott terminated Operation *Impunity* and sent a helicopter to recover Captain Scott, the Reconnaissance Platoon commander, from Port Harriet House and also deliver some supplies. Sergeant Roy, a Royal Engineer flying with 656 Squadron, was selected for the task. Just as he was approaching Port Harriet House he came under heavy mortar fire from 4th Infantry Regiment on Mount Harriet which was preparing to deal with the British presence. Roy held his Scout out of range. The Reconnaissance Platoon withdrew toward North Basin under fire, which caused three casualties including Sergeant Allum, and, as Roy moved in to extract the wounded, he flew close to Port Harriet House and was subjected to a Blowpipe attack, the missile passing within twenty-five yards of his helicopter and then smashing into some high ground. With the casualties and Captain Scott on board, Roy returned to Fitzroy where Scott persuaded 3 Troop, The Blues and Royals, to rescue his men. The Argentinians claimed they had defeated a Welsh Guards attack. Roy was later presented with a large chunk of the Blowpipe.

During the night of 9/10 June the Gurkhas moved up from Bluff Cove and, after a very difficult seven-kilometre march over rough, broken ground that tested the resilience of the soldiers, took up a position on the western fringes of Little Wether Ground to protect the 4th Field Regiment gunline and be ready to support 42 Commando's attack on Mount Harriet. However, they were spotted from Mount Harriet and shelled by 155mm artillery. The next day the shelling became far more intense and B Company was the hardest hit, taking four casualties, including Captain (Queen's Gurkha Officer) Dilbahadur Sunwar, the Company Second-in-Command, Lance-Corporal Gyanendra Rai, who was wounded in the shoulder by shrapnel, and Riflemen Balisprasad Rai who had a piece of metal pierce his helmet and penetrate the back of his head. Rushed to the *Uganda*, he recovered. During this incident the Regimental Medical Officer, Captain Martin Entwhistle, was Mentioned in Despatches. Major David Willis, who commanded A Company and was a former Oxford rowing blue, had his trench wrecked and equipment destroyed by a near miss while he was on a reconnaissance with Lieutenant-Colonel Morgan.

By this time 97 Field Battery, which was in direct support of the Welsh Guards, arrived at Fitzroy on 7 June after experiencing its fair share of problems. Commanded by Major C. Jordan, it had landed on 3 June and had suffered from the logistic disorganization experienced throughout 5th Infantry Brigade's landing and was directed to take over from 29 Battery, who were based in a small farm at Head of the Bay House. Everything had to be either flown in, even if it meant hijacking helicopters to do so, or brought in by landing craft. Welcomed like lost brothers by 29 Battery, 97 Battery arrived with only three Light Guns. One gun, brought by a landing craft, became bogged down and was left for two tides before a recovery unit arrived to help. 29 Battery introduced the new arrivals to 'swapping', with one soldier said to have exchanged a kerosene lamp for a motor-cycle. But as one gunner philosophically later wrote in the battery's post-combat report, 'It seemed that nobody was really concerned with helping Blue berets. After all, we were trespassing on an operation to maintain the mobility of the Red and Green berets.' When the guns were flown to Fitzroy Ridge on 6 June, the rear party left at Head of the Bay House had insufficient rations and a bombardier was tasked by Battery Sergeant Major Huggins to bag a few geese from the thirty or so pecking at the ground. As is recorded in the Battery post-combat report, 'Anyone who has chased a pea around a plate with a fork will understand that to get a goose in the right position to humanely despatch it is impossible. It was lucky for our Infantry friends that they were not available to see this demonstration of Gunner marksmanship.' The Royal Artillery lived up to its motto *Ubique* (Everywhere), or more irreverently 'All Over The Place', as the unfortunate bombardier fired seventeen shots at the geese with his Sterling, all of which missed. The task was handed over to another gunner, who strangled the birds.

By 7 June 97 Battery was in a gully on Fitzroy Ridge ready for action and when Bombardier Stewart fired the first round this was a major fillip to morale. The gunners knew everything was back to normal when the Battery Quartermaster Sergeant set up 'shop in his nice warm tent' and sold drinks, chocolate and a few other comforts. During the fourteen hours of darkness it was so cold and wet that sentries were rotated every twenty minutes or so. Just before dusk on the first night Sergeant-Major Wilkinson and Sergeant Aspery were doing their rounds of the sentry positions when Aspery suddenly threw himself to the ground and whispered, 'Argy frogmen – beach attack.' Wilkinson took a look and stood up with tears streaming down his face as he pointed at a pack of seals lounging on the beach. One of the Battery's unsung heroes was Corporal Hughes of the Royal Army Medical Corps. Twice a day he held house calls by visiting every tent and gun position to minimize the risk of trench foot and exposure. When he finished his rounds, he sterilized the Battery's water supply against the upset stomach of 'Galtieri's Revenge'.

12 June dawned bright but cold. During the night, as we have seen, 3rd Commando Brigade had assaulted the Argentinian Outer Defence Zone protecting Stanley. 5th Marine Infantry Battalion had supported the 4th Infantry Regiment defence of Two Sisters and Mount Harriet. Robacio, knowing he would be attacked next, reinforced O Company with 1st Amphibious Engineer Platoon, commanded by Second-Lieutenant Valdez-Zabala. Captain Ferrero's 3rd Assault Section, 602 Commando Company, was moved into an anti-tank position south-west of Mount William. Four platoons had escaped the destruction of 4th Infantry Regiment. Second-Lieutenant Jimenez-Corvalan's men escaped from Mount Harriet and withdrew to Mount William. Second-Lieutenant Llambias-Pravaz left Two Sisters and ended up on Sapper Hill. Lieutenants Silva's 4th Infantry and Mosterin's 12th Infantry Regiments platoons joined Vasquez on Mount Tumbledown, bringing the defenders to ninety-two men. Vasquez had two major problems – too few radios, which meant orders would have to be relayed by runner so he was determined to keep his platoon as near to him as possible, and his position faced south to cover the road from Fitzroy, the expected axis of attack. Avoiding encirclement when Mount Harriet, Two Sisters and Mount Longdon fell, Major Jaimet's B Company, 6th Infantry Regiment, withdrew to the northern slopes of Mount Tumbledown, from its blocking position covering the Estancia track, and was replaced by two troops of 181st Armoured Reconnaissance Squadron, which moved into

low ground east of Mount Longdon. According to a map later recovered from an Argentinian prisoner-of-war, the inter-unit boundary between Jaimet and the Marine Infantry ran along the spine of the central ridge. Major Berazay and A Company, 3rd Infantry Regiment, covered the road to Estancia with orders to support either Mount Tumbledown or Wireless Ridge. The regiment's 120mm Mortar Platoon joined M Company on Sapper Hill.

Released by HQ 3rd Commando Brigade to seek whatever shelter they could before daylight, the Welsh Guards found a hide in broken country south-west of Mount Harriet where they spent an uneasy day being shelled intermittently. Lance Corporal Nicholas Thomas (07) was killed when a shell hit the quad-bike, which had been donated by the Prince of Wales, on one of several journeys taking radio batteries and supplies to and from Regimental Sergeant Major Davies at the Bluff Cove echelon.

It was now the turn of 5th Infantry Brigade to attack and, if they got the strategy and tactics right, the prospect of the prize of entering Stanley first was very real. Brigadier Wilson was under intense pressure to follow through and, according to Major Davies, was keen to do so. The race for Stanley was on. With the British to the west and sea north, east and south, Army Group Puerto Argentina would thus be surrounded and had three choices – fight, swim or surrender. But it also seemed that Wilson fell into the common trap of underestimating the determination of the Argentinians to resist. In his path was a mountain defended by one of the best infantry units the Argentinians had. The Intelligence assessment after the battles of the previous night was also uncertain because 3rd Commando Brigade was slow in selecting prisoners for interrogation and thus no one knew what the Argentinians were doing. Had they gone into dead ground and were waiting to counter-attack the advance of 5th Infantry Brigade or had they left the area completely and abandoned ground to the British? A surveillance drone would have provided the answer but the Task Force did not have a locating battery.

At about 4pm on the 12 June Brigadier Wilson issued orders at his headquarters in Fitzroy for Phase Two. The Scots Guards and 1/7th Gurkha Rifles were to be flown to an assembly area on Goat Ridge and then attack Tumbledown and Mount William that night and be in a position ready for the Gurkhas to break out on to Stanley Common. The advance was expected to begin at about midnight but first a large minefield had to be breached. Wilson was not certain that this could be done in the twelve hours of darkness. The Welsh Guards were assigned as Brigade reserve. Lieutenant-Colonels Morgan and Scott were not too happy. Their battalions were about to be helicoptered into assembly areas in the dark and then expected to advance across ground about which very little was known. Without well-recognized navigation features, a clearly identifiable axis of advance was going to be difficult. There was no opportunity for the reconnaissance, rehearsals and shake-outs that are so necessary in the preparation of an advance to contact. In any event the objectives had to be softened up before the attacks. Lieutenant-Colonel Holt advised Brigadier Wilson that, since the helicopters had spent most of the day resupplying 3rd Commando Brigade, his artillery ammunition had not yet been brought up. Major Davies recalls: 'It would have been madness to expect the Scots Guards and Gurkhas to go virtually from line of march into a complex night attack over completely new ground.' According to an officer at that O Group, Morgan asked Wilson, 'Brigadier, are you sure there is time available?' Scott agreed and suggested to Wilson that he must ask Major-General Moore for a twenty-four-hour delay to give the attacking battalions enough time to prepare for battle. Wilson agreed, in the full knowledge that he would be criticized, which he was, particularly in 3rd Commando Brigade, because Mount Longdon, Two Sisters and Mount Harriet were under accurate artillery fire, which was causing casualties. This irritation was further incensed the following day when Headquarters 3rd Commando Brigade was bombed, forcing a 'crash' move just as 2nd Parachute Battalion was preparing to attack Wireless Ridge. The Welsh Guards were also irritated because they were being accurately shelled by 155mm howitzers. That evening when Major-General Moore told Brigadier Thompson that he had given 5th Infantry Brigade twenty-four hours to prepare for their night attack, Thompson offered Lieutenant Haddow's and Sergeant Wassell's Mountain and Arctic Warfare patrols to guide the two 5th Infantry Brigade battalions to their start lines, which was accepted.

Later that night at Bluff Cove Scott issued his orders for the four-phase night assault on Mount Tumbledown. Precious little Intelligence had arrived from documents or the 400 prisoners being processed at Fitzroy, so he still did not really know what he was up against.

❐ Phase 1.
Major Bethel and Headquarters Company to create a diversion on the expected axis of attack from the south-west.

❐ Phase 2.
G Company to lead the attack and capture the first third of Mount Tumbledown

❐ Phase 3.
Left Flank to move through G Company and assault the summit.

❐ Phase 4.
Right Flank to move through Left Flank and seize the remainder of the objective.

The general axis of advance was directed at the northern end of the saddle between Tumbledown and Mount William. Since the ridge was barely wide enough for a platoon to spread out, fire support was going to be critical:

- ❐ *F (Support) Company, with six 81mm mortars in Mortar Platoon and the six .50-inch Browning machine guns, manned by Anti-Tank Platoon and twelve 81mm mortars, six each from 42 Commando and 1/7th Gurkha Rifles.*

- ❐ *29 Battery on priority call with 7, 8 and 79 Commando and 97 Batteries.*

- ❐ *The Type 12 frigate HMS Yarmouth, which, with HMS Cardiff, had given the Scots Guards such a fright on their landing craft voyage to Bluff Cove, and the Type 21 frigate HMS Active, a total of two 4.5-inch guns.*

Scott ordered that only battle order was to be worn and allowed six sleeping bags per company to keep casualties warm. Helmets could be discarded in favour of berets as an aid to recognition. The password 'Hey, Jimmy' for the Scots Guards and 'Hey, Johnny' for the Gurkhas was adopted because the Argentinians could not pronounce the letter J in English. Rehearsals were also held to familiarize sections, platoons and companies with their role.

13 June dawned bright and brittle with a surprisingly bright sun but little heat. Yellowish snow-laden clouds rushed across the valleys. Patrolling against Mount Tumbledown was out of the question; however, Scott was able to fly his company commanders and key officers to observe it from Goat Ridge and Mount Harriet. Major Bethel saw the diversion that Scott was seeking, the small Argentinian position west of Pony Pass. This was occupied by O Company, 5th Marine Infantry Battalion. Brigadier Wilson moved on to Goat Ridge with his Tactical Headquarters, his Plans and Intelligence officers and a small group of Royal Signallers from A Troop, HQ and Signal Squadron. Throughout the day Sea Kings and the single Chinook lifted the 1,300 troops to their assembly areas south of Goat Ridge where sangars were built and battle preparations carried out amid intermittent shelling from which the Scots Guards lost one man, Lance-Sergeant Billy McGeorge, wounded. Lance-

Corporal Campbell and Guardsman Greenshield were digging a shelter when a shell landed nearby and shrapnel set fire to the phosphorous grenades in their webbing, which they had discarded while they worked. With H-Hour set for 9pm, Scott issued his confirmatory orders at 2pm. Two journalists, A.J. McIlroy of the *Daily Telegraph* and Tony Snow of the *Sun,* were to accompany his attack. Guides and controllers from the forming up place to the start line supplied by Reconnaissance Platoon were to be in place by 7pm.

The British continued to shell Mount Tumbledown and Mount William. Major Jaimet:

> *It was an inferno. The British artillery fire increased in intensity. It went up and down the mountain. The whole mountain quaked and shuddered under the impacts. The rounds arrived like flying kerosene tins filled with hot metal fragments. By pure luck, none hit me, but I saw them hit some soldiers next to me and they just burned through the thickest clothing, winter parka, denim jacket, wool pullover, everything, right through to the flesh. I heard the cries of the wounded. When somebody got wounded he would call out for his mates.*
>
> *The shelling claimed twelve men wounded by the time it was dark. Many looked back with mild regret to the halcyon days before. We thought we were badly off then, but what luxury and comfort compared to this. It was enough to send any young lad out of control. But everyone kept themselves under control and there were no scenes of despair or terror as often happens in some conscript armies. I wonder if the modern conscript can put up with that type of softening-up fire. Our basic training was a lot tougher than what we have today. In Bravo Company there were 168 people and everyone behaved sensibly. Even the conscripts behaved like veterans and many of them were not yet twenty.*

During the morning Wing-Commander Squires, flying from HMS *Hermes*, lobbed two laser-guided bombs on to a suspected company headquarters on Tumbledown. The first bomb failed to detonate, but the second blew a sangar apart in the most dramatic fashion. His wingman, Flight-Lieutenat Hare, followed up with cluster bombs. It is though that this attack was the first laser-guided attack of the campaign and was a complete surprise to the Argentinians who were now faced with being bombed without warning from aircraft they could not necessarily see. These attacks were controlled by Majors Mike Howes of the Royal Regiment of Wales and Anwyl Hughes of the Royal Welch Fusiliers, who commanded 601 and 602 Tactical Air Control Parties respectively and, being located with 45 Commando on Two Sisters, had a good view of Stanley Common. Tactical Air Control Parties were deployed with the ground forces and could communicate directly with aircraft via the *Larkspur* A43 radio set. Although the conscripts must have found the shelling most discomforting, they bounced back with considerable fighting spirit, as we shall see.

Soon after 4pm on 13 June Bethel briefed his men at Mount Harriet House. The diversion consisted of a composite platoon of three four-man sections drawn from Reconnaissance Platoon, one commanded by Major Bethel and the other two by Drill-Sergeant Danny Wight and Sergeant Colin Coull. In support was the Light Machine Gun group commanded by Company Sergeant Major Les Braby from A1 Echelon. The 7.62mm Light Machine Gun had been converted in the mid-1960s from the .303-inch Bren gun and retained its distinctive curved magazine. Sapper support was provided by Corporal John Foran and Lance-Corporal 'Pash' Pashley from 3 Troop, 9 Parachute Squadron, and there was a forward observation bombardier and a battalion mortar fire controller, Lance-Sergeant Ian Miller. Providing heavy fire support was Lieutenant Mark Coreth's 3 Troop, B Squadron, the Blues and Royals. An hour later the platoon clambered on to the armoured vehicles near the 42 Commando rear echelon, which had been set up in an abandoned lorry container beside the track near Mount Harriet House. The moon had yet to rise and a cold wind spilled snow through the darkness. The ground was pitted with peat banks and known to be littered with mines, two types identified so far being powerful enough to wreck light armoured vehicles. At about 6.30pm the infantry dismounted and the Blues and Royals moved into cover to give direct fire support on to known Argentinian positions at H-30 minutes for one hour.

When reports reached Major Rico at Headquarters Army Group Malvinas that British armour were reported to be moving from the west along the Fitzroy-Stanley track, Captain Ferrero's 602nd Commando Company's 3rd Assault Section prepared to meet the threat. In spite of the signals intelligence intercepts indicating an entire Gurkha battalion being no more than four kilometres to the west, the judo black belt engineer First-Lieutenant Horacio Lauria was eager to come to grips with the Gurkhas in the Pony Pass area to show the conscripts that the men from Nepal were human and that he could win a man-to-man contest.

On time, the diversion began. With the two sappers clearing the route, Major Bethel periodically swept the ground with his cumbersome individual night sight on his rifle, looking for signs of the enemy. The approach took longer than expected and by about 8.45pm, after three false alerts, Bethel knew he had to create some sort of diversion to persuade the Argentinians that the attack was coming from the south and help G Company get a foothold on Mount Tumbledown. Making another sweep with his night sight, he saw outlines that suggested trenches about seventy metres ahead. A sentry could also be seen. While Sergeant Major Braby moved right to a fire support position, Bethel cautiously led the three assault sections toward the shapes which were found to be three occupied trenches. When sounds were heard from inside a covered bunker, Bethel signalled Drill-Sergeant Wight to take the left trench while he took the centre and Sergeant Coull attacked the right. The silence of the night was broken when the grenades exploded, wounding two marine engineers. Argentinian positions in depth opened fire almost simultaneously. The 6ft 3in Wight was within about three yards of an Argentinian trench, which was then thought to be empty, when an occupant fired three rounds in rapid succession, killing him immediately. Lance-Corporal Pashley was mortally wounded when he was hit in the throat and four others were wounded. The Argentinian amphibious engineer Sergeant Simon Ponce and Corporals Sanchez, Valdez and Robles and Privates Ayala and Gomez in the forward trenches were not best pleased to find themselves under fire from back and front and Sergeant Ponce shouted insults at Pernias's men to stop.

The fire support of Braby's machine-gun group was neutralized by effective Argentinian fire and they had considerable difficulty in regaining the initiative. Meanwhile four pipers had moved forward to administer first aid. The assault group battled their way into the Argentinian position and attacked several trenches by crawling under-neath the lip of a peat bank and lobbing grenades over the top. Marine First Class Private Jose Luis Fazio was at Pony Pass with O Company:

At about 2230 hours our battalion had its first intensive gun battle with British companies which appeared out of nowhere. I heard Private Roberto Barboza yell, 'The English are here!' And I saw Private Omar Iniguez killed near me in the first exchange of fire. Under covering fire, Privates Rafael Romero, Victor Vital and Oscar Bellavista dashed out, collected two of the wounded, placing them behind cover and won the admiration of all the men. I remember our Operations Officer requested the artillery to assist at 23.00 with starshells. The close-quarter battle was such that the Argentinian artillery was unable to drop shells on to the British attackers. I was shooting, doing my work. I don't know if I killed anyone. We just fired our rifles, that's all. Contact was maintained for over an hour before battalion headquarters ordered Obra Company to fall back. The men took up their fall back positions quietly and efficiently. There Sergeant Angel Quiroga did what was possible for the wounded. The first ambulance came very quickly and took the casualties from the two platoons away. What we did not realize at the time was that at least one of our wounded Marines made his way, about this time, into part of the amphibious engineer platoon position. The Marine conscript hurled a grenade wounding a Major. Simultaneously the British Major opened fire, killing him. We killed and wounded sixty British soldiers for a loss of three of our own men. It was our battle.

It took nearly two hours to fight through eleven positions and Major Bethel only halted when there was no more return fire. With two killed and four wounded, Bethel had three options – to remain where he was, keep up the diversion or withdraw. Learning that Lance-Sergeant Miller had lost communications with Battalion Headquarters, Bethel radioed Coreth to come forward and, after loosing off a couple of Light Machine Gun magazines, returned to the three trenches where the pipers were dealing with the casualties. Bethel was about to withdraw when an Argentinian amphibious engineer survivor in the right trench threw a grenade that exploded, wounding Piper Duffy in the chest and Bethel in the legs. Covered by Sergeant Coull and in the knowledge they could be counter-attacked at any time, the platoon set off, but more mines detonated, wounding in the feet Lance-Sergeants Miller and 'Tic-Toc' McLintock, Lance-Corporal Mitchell and Guardsman David Carruthers, all of whom had been carrying the dead and wounded. The explosions prompted Major Pernias to order First-Sergeant Elvio Cune's 81mm Mortar Platoon on Mount William and the longer-ranged 120mm mortars attached to C Company, 3rd Infantry Regiment with M Company on Sapper Hill to open fire on the minefield and likely withdrawal route of anyone attacking the Pony Pass position. The barrage lasted about forty minutes and more British casualties would have been suffered had not the soft peat absorbed the impact of the bombs; nevertheless debris flew all over the place. Needing to evacuate the wounded, the two dead were abandoned. Using a torch, Major Bethel, Corporal Foran and Piper Duffy carved a path out of the minefield and had some interesting discussions on what was a mine and what was not. Fortunately most were either surface-laid or could be seen underneath the turf when approached from the Argentinian side.

For Coreth the hours ticked by slowly. Nothing was heard from Bethel; indeed, communications with him became progressively worse. He had heard the firing and bark of grenades and, from intermittent radio transmissions it was obvious the Guardsmen were in trouble so he was relieved to be called forward. But just as the armoured vehicles broke cover a flare broke over them and was quickly followed by shelling. Coming across a 155mm crater in the middle of the road, Coreth by-passed it to the left, but his Scorpion had barely moved off the track when it hit an anti-tank mine. Corporal-of-Horse Paul Stretton, in the following Scimitar, later said that the explosion lifted the 8.5-ton vehicle three feet into the air and caused severe damage. Coreth knew that it was vital to provide Bethel's battered infantry with fire support, but the threat of mines confined the Troop to the road. In spite of Argentinian shelling plastering the area, with considerable gallantry he opened fire on Mount Tumbledown and

Mount William. Coreth describes the situation: 'It became a crazy shoot from one vehicle, sitting on the outside, reverse him, climb onto another, bring him forward, fire and so on till the last. There was some excellent shooting by all vehicles.' The next day sappers removed fifty-seven mines from the vicinity of Coreth's wrecked Scorpion, although the turret was in working order. The explosion had severed the engine mountings, shredded both tracks and blew off most of the road wheels. It is probable that it was sufficiently robust to withstand the blast and light enough to absorb the shock of being thrown into the air.

At about 12.45am, just as Major Kiszely's Left Flank Company had their first contact on Mount Tumbledown, Bethel's battered platoon reached Coreth's Troop and were taken back to the 42 Commando A Echelon where the Royal Marines had set up a first aid post in the container. In their book *The Winter War* Patrick Bishop and John Witherow describe how Surgeon-Lieutenant Ross Adley, the Commando Medical Officer, cut away blood-soaked boots and cleaned wounds as best he could by torchlight, for fear of attracting shelling. Within ninety minutes the wounded were on their way to Teal Inlet. Most were then transferred to the *Uganda*.

It was an expensive diversion, with nearly fifty per cent casualties and a Scorpion wrecked, but it kept 5th Marine Infantry Battalion off balance and focused their attention on the Fitzroy track. In many respects it was a decisive action and allowed the Scots Guards to consolidate their attack on Tumbledown but it has not really received the accolades it should have. The Argentinian author Ruben Moro, who flew with 1st (Hercules) Squadron, 1st Transport Group, in the campaign, claims that Coreth's Scorpion was mined before the infantry attack and that the diversion cost sixty men 'littered about the field' as they withdrew to the south. Surprisingly, there were few awards. Corporal John Foran receiving the Military Medal for his gallantry in clearing paths through the minefields. Major Bethel was only Mentioned in Despatches, which, while miserly, reflects the idiosyncrasies and anomalies of the Awards and Honours system. He deserved, at the very least, the Military Cross.

Meanwhile, guided by the occasional shell fired by 29 Battery on to Tumbledown to help navigation, on time at 9pm Major Ian Dalzell-Job's G Company crossed the start line, a wire fence. The objective was two .50-inch machine gun bunkers. Lieutenant Johnson's 7 Platoon, followed by Company HQ, crossed another wire fence and advanced, without incident, across the 2,500 yards of open ground to the western slopes of Mount Tumbledown. Progress was deliberate and interrupted only by the occasional Argentinian flare soaring high into the darkness. To the south the diversionary attack was well underway. Snow showers swept across the bleak mountain. At 10.30pm G Company went firm. 7 Platoon took up positions to cover the southern slopes of Mount Tumbledown. Lieutenant Page's 8 Platoon and Second-Lieutenant Blount's 9 Platoon reached the limit of their exploitation and angled slightly left to cover the northern and southern slopes of the ridge and give Left Flank room to pass through. The company objective was found abandoned but an Argentinian above them shouted. By 10.30pm G Company was firm and undetected. So were the Scots Guards, so far. Phase Two was complete.

Left Flank moved through G Company and took over the advance, its objective being the highest point of Mount Tumbledown. Second-Lieutenant James Stuart's 13 Platoon moved up into crags on the left to support Lieutenant Alasdair Mitchell's 15 Platoon, which was cautiously advancing across the open ground below them in a right hook. Lieutenant Anthony Fraser's 14 Platoon was moving behind Company Headquarters in reserve. Stuart had been commissioned less than two months. On the main feature, about 400 yards ahead of them, Mino's engineers, Vasquez' marines and Silva's and Mosterin's infantrymen watched through their night sights and then opened fire. It was about 10.45pm. The ripple of white flashes split the darkness as tracer carved up the night, bullets cracked and thumped overhead and rock splinters whined into the darkness. Caught in the open, 15 Platoon dived for cover. Lance-Sergeant Tom McGuiness later described the experience:

> Right from the word go when we joined the QEII, we thought in our hearts that we would get down there and there would be no fighting; they would throw their rifles down. We were too confident; I think 50% of us felt like that. There was no real sense of fear but it was a shock when they fired at us.

Lance-Sergeant Ian Davidson took cover behind a small rock but, such was the weight of Argentinian fire striking rocks, that his beret was peppered with stone chips. Guardsman Archibald Stirling was killed and Sergeant Jackson wounded. Mitchell recalled, 'We recovered rapidly and the Argentinians never again put down quite that weight of fire. Even so, our first introduction was slightly shocking. It just showed how much firepower they had.' A quick section counter-attack by Lance-Sergeant Alan Dalgleish was defeated by heavy machine-gun fire, but he managed to shoot an Argentinian, who screamed in agony for about a minute. Major Kiszely shouted, 'Who did that?' No one answered so he repeated the question. Eventually Dalgleish replied that it was he. Kiszely congratulated him. In the rocks above them, 13 Platoon came under heavy fire and suffered badly from good shots. Company Sergeant Major Bill Nicol went forward to supervise the evacuation of casualties and, while pulling the very seriously wounded Guardsman Ronald Tambini into cover, suggested that he might like to push back with his feet but Tambini died, respectfully telling him, 'I've been shot, sir'. Nicol then went to the aid of the mortally wounded Platoon Sergeant John Simeon, who was in considerable pain. As he knelt beside him, Nicol placed his rifle across his body, in the approved weapon-training fashion, when a bullet ricocheted off the barrel and passed through his hand. Possibly the same rifleman shot all three. Lance-Corporal Eyre was wounded and Guardsman Shaw had a lucky escape when three rifle magazines that he had stuffed in his left breast pocket of his jacket stopped a bullet. Nicol had his revenge when Lance-Sergeant McGuinness handed him a Carl Gustav and he fired three projectiles at three sangars. The shock of the firestorm brought the momentum of Left Flank's advance to a virtual halt. Every time after being forced to take cover, the conscript marines and soldiers emerged from their bunkers and returned fire. For the next three hours Left Flank hardly moved. Clouds drifted across the full moon alternately throwing the battlefield into darkness and then spun eerie shadows across the rocks. It was freezing cold and a harsh snow-laden and bitter southerly wind enveloped the summit, which actually proved a blessing by slowing down the body metabolism and enabled the wounded to survive the shock. Lance-Sergeant Davidson later recalled that radio communication was lost and consequently command and control became difficult in the confusion. He and Lance-Sergeant Thomas McGuiness unearthed several Argentinian positions by following field telephone cables. Guardsman James Reynolds led several attacks. Attempts to dislodge the Argentinians with 84mm Carl Gustav and 66mm anti-tank missiles and M79 grenade launchers were only partially successful. Below them Mitchell's 15 Platoon were pinned down by heavy machine-gun and accurate rifle fire.

29 Battery had been firing occasional rounds to guide G Company on to their objectives, but, as soon as Left Flank were pinned down, it and 97 Battery began shelling the Argentine positions at about 11.30pm with Captain Nicol, a Forward Observation Officer, first directing a defensive fire mission in front of 15 Platoon. Making adjustments was difficult because the opposing front lines were often only 100 yards apart and some shells clipped rocks. The 97 Battery Gun Position Officer, Lieutenant Frend, cursed the lack of field artillery computer equipment, which had been left in the United Kingdom with its Land Rover. Each gun had a minimum of 400 rounds, including 250 high explosive. When they were not on fire missions, the gunners quickly cleared the boxes and packaging cluttering the gun positions. Major Gwyn's quiet authority on the radio was compelling.

On Mount Harriet the .50-inch machine gunners were firing at extreme range and then began to run short of ammunition. Major Davies and his Squadron Sergeant Major, Pete Walker, were watching the battle with a Royal Marine sentry when they saw a file of soldiers approaching them. Davies shouted, 'Halt!' There was a scuffle of boots on rocks and then in a Scottish accent, 'Don't shoot!' The group turned out to be from the Scots Guards Machine-Gun Platoon seeking ammunition. Mortar Platoon fought to keep the 81mm mortars on a stable platform, but every time a bomb was fired the recoil drove the base plate deeper into the soft ground and degraded accuracy and distance. After a few rounds, the mortarmen dug the mortar from the mud, moved it to firmer ground and readjusted fire. This all took precious minutes. Several parts broke while firing on maximum charge. For a time only one mortar was operational.

A few Argentinians left the main defensive position to stalk and taunt the Scots Guards, but generally Vasquez and his Platoon Sergeant, Eduardo Fochesatto, managed to keep 4 Platoon and the Army platoons as a single cohesive body. Morale was high. At about 2.00am Robacio pulled O Company back from Pony Pass on to the saddle linking Mount Tumbledown and Mount William. They did not know it but the Scots Guards were now facing three companies – the Marines N and O Companies and the 6th Infantry Regiment's B Company. B Battery, 1st Marine Field Artillery Group, was also shelling Mount Tumbledown, adding to the Scots Guards' discomfort. On the western slopes G Company, which had been giving support to Left Flank, came under artillery and mortar fire and several men in 9 Platoon were wounded, including the Platoon Sergeant, Sergeant McDonald. He refused evacuation from the Company Aid Post until the following day. Twice Lieutenant Blount protected, with his body, wounded Guardsmen. 8 Platoon joined the Company Quartermaster Sergeant's parties from G Company and Left Flank to collect the wounded for the 2,500-yard carry to Regimental Aid Post on Goat Ridge. Some were taken to the Company Aid Post where Piper Rodgers, the Left Flank company medic, was treating the wounded from both sides.

In his manpacked Tactical Headquarters on Goat Ridge, Brigadier Wilson was concerned. Back at Main Headquaters alongside a gorse bush near Fitzroy, Major Lambe was listening to the command radio and heard Wilson, on several occasions over the next few hours, 'chivvying' Lieutenant-Colonel Scott to get on. If the Scots Guards failed to secure Mount Tumbledown then the plan to break out on to Stanley Common by the Gurkhas before dawn was at risk. Scott himself was therefore under considerable pressure and asked Lieutenant-Colonel Chaundler if 2nd Parachute Battalion could fire on Mount Tumbledown from Wireless

Ridge, but Chaundler told that him he had his own problems. He refused an offer of reinforcements from the Gurkhas because the frontage along Tumbledown was just about adequate for a platoon. Captain Spicer, Scott's Operations Officer, recalled:

> Major Roger Gwyn, the Battery Commander, was keen to avoid him [Scott] being killed like 'H' Jones. The Commanding Officer asked my opinion and I advised him not to go up to be seen. He would only be pinned down too. I also told him that we still had confidence in the Company Commander's ability to do the job, and that we should let him get on with it.

Over the radio Lieutenant-Colonel Scott and Major Kiszely planned the destruction of the Argentinian resistance – a short barrage followed by a standard fire and movement infantry attack. Meanwhile Stuart's 13 Platoon slowly edged forward yard by yard using the rocks for cover, at about 3am attacked Mino's Amphibious Engineer Platoon, who, their resolve in tatters, began to leave their positions above and behind Vasquez's 4 Platoon. By dislodging Mino's men and seizing this vital piece of ground Stuart essentially unlocked the defence of Mount Tumbledown. 13 Platoon wormed their way into positions overlooking Vasquez's position and, with the help of Company Sergeant Major Nicol, Stuart divided his men into groups of machine-gunners, anti-tank men and riflemen. Below them Mitchell, now joined by Major Kiszely, lined up 15 Platoon. As Lieutenant Nicol brought down the third artillery salvo, 13 Platoon opened fire, which was the signal for Left Flank to advance. Lieutenant Mitchell:

> We lined up and sure enough the three salvoes came in and on the last one, there was almost a deathly hush in the battle. There was a plaintive cry from me of, 'Is that really the last one?' to John Kiszely and his radio operator said, 'Yes'.

But no one moved. Displaying the same qualities of inspirational leadership demonstrated by Lieutenant Clive Dytor when he charged up Two Sisters at the head of Z Company, 45 Commando, Major Kiszely shouted to his men, 'Are you with me, Jock?' Silence. The Guardsmen were quite naturally happier in the cover of rocks than facing fire. Then the replies began to filter in from the darkness, 'Aye, sir. I'm wi'ye!' Still not certain whether the men would follow, Kiszely told them he was going whether they were with him or not. Breaking cover, he advanced up the hill and with 15 Platoon surged into the enemy positions, bayonets fixed. Mitchell:

> We ran straight into the middle of the Argentinian position, which was only 60 to 70 yards away. Once in there, we started skirmishing through. People dropped

grenades, shooting at close range. Some enemy were bayonetted. In the middle of the enemy position we suddenly felt the resistance crash. It was an intangible thing. Suddenly the Argentinians who had been shouting to us a few minutes before were now streaming down the hill.

As Kiszely charged up the slope he saw a figure coming out of the ground:

I swung around, pointed my rifle and pulled the trigger. I heard a click. What you are meant to do is count your rounds, but of course it doesn't work like that. So there was only one thing to do and, without hesitation, you did it. I struck him in the chest and he fell back into his hole. Looking back on it, it is not something I am proud of at all. I knew he was going to kill me but derived no pleasure from sticking a bayonet into another person.

Left Flank bit deep into the Argentinian defences. Vasquez:

The British soldiers crept up on the platoon position just before midnight. Before long the platoon was completely surrounded and on the verge of being overrun so I decided that the 81 millimetre mortar platoon of Ruben Galluisi should fire on our platoon. At that moment Argentinian mortar bombs landed in the middle of the position, we had no other choice. The British had to withdraw and we started swearing at them. That was how the British were driven out during that first attack. I had up to then lost five of my own men. The British eventually got up and started attacking again. It was now around three in the morning and we had been trading fire off and on for nearly three hours. The British were now amongst the rocks above us. I found out that if I started to give out orders I would draw machine-gun fire and that was the biggest shock to me. I discovered over the radio that they weren't the amphibious engineer platoon. It is a pity. In the dark the platoon came off the position too soon. Of course it was occupied by the British immediately. Finally Private Victor Gasko was able to get a reasonable fix on where this machine gun was firing. Marine Gasko then raked the area with his machine gun and this weapon was silenced by the act of one brave man. I think you have got to have tremendous respect for him. He did that under intense British fire. We then got fire from our own artillerymen, who put down shells all around us. That fire provided a useful breathing space, but it was evident that reinforcements would still be needed to beat the attackers off. In the gunfight that followed five Army personnel and two Marines died. We were alone now, with nothing around except us and the British. It was about then that a bullet hit Second-Lieutenant Oscar Silva of the 4th Regiment in the chest and killed him. What happened was that Silva picked up one of the wounded machine-gunners, taking the Marine to safety through heavy fire. He then returned to the position with one of his soldiers. The Army officer was then killed.

When Brigadier-General Jofre heard that the amphibious engineers had left their positions he was appalled and radioed Robacio and

Lieutenant-Colonel Omar Gimenez, the commander of the 7th Infantry Regiment then engaged with 2nd Parachute Battalion on Wireless Ridge, and warned them both, 'Anyone seen to transmit an unauthorized order to fall back should have their head blown off.' Robacio ordered Major Jaimet to help Vasquez. Moving to the saddle between Mount Tumbledown and Mount William and, leaving his 81mm mortar platoon with O Company, at about 4.30am Jaimet radioed Second-Lieutenant Augusto La Madrid's 1st Platoon and instructed him to counter-attack and relieve some of the pressure on Vasquez. Jaimet was aware that the summit was held but not in what strength. He obviously did not know that a fresh enemy company, Right Flank, was taking over the advance. Had the radios and night-sights of Jaimet's platoons been fully charged and mortar and machine-gun ammunition not been wasted supporting Wireless Ridge, all B Company could have counter-attacked and bought time to allow M Company to be moved from Mount William on to Mount Tumbledown. This missed opportunity probably cost the Argentinians the battle.

Exposed by the withdrawal of Mino's engineers, but aware that reinforcements were being assembled, Vasquez's 4 Platoon conducted an orderly withdrawal. At about 4am Kiszely and seven men reached the summit. There was a violent scuffle in the darkness among the rocks as the last of Vasquez's men were driven off but not before Lance-Sergeant Clark Mitchell was shot dead. Far below, they were amazed to see the lights of Stanley, the ultimate objective. But the fighting was far from over. An Argentinian machine-gunner opened fire on the summit and hit three of the Scots Guards, including Lieutenant Mitchell, who was badly wounded in the legs. Kiszely and three men now held the summit of Mount Tumbledown, but within fifteen minutes several more men from 15 Platoon and Company Headquarters reinforced the position, followed by 14 Platoon, which was almost at full strength. Mitchell's wounds were beginning to hurt and shock was setting in.

Expecting Mino's 5th Amphibious Engineer Platoon to join him at some stage, with his customary enthusiasm and efficiency La Madrid issued quick orders – advance, allow no one to pass and conscript any withdrawing Argentinians to join *his* platoon. Several of his men had helmet-mounted night-vision devices and all were willing, but none of them had seen the ground over which they were advancing. La Madrid:

We moved off through a gap in the rocks; I spread my men out behind the men who were still fighting. My orders were not to let anyone pass, not even Argentinian soldiers. I went forward to make a reconnaissance and could see that the British had two machine guns and a missile launcher in action. I went through

197

another gap in the rocks and was surprised by three men speaking in English behind and above me and firing over the top of me. I could see them with my night binoculars; there were about twelve of them in all. I was anxious to get back to my platoon. I took a rifle grenade and fired at where I had seen the first three men. I heard it explode and some shouts and cries of pain, and the sound of someone falling down the rocks.

It seems likely that La Madrid's 1st Platoon had clashed with Lieutenant Fraser's 14 Platoon, which suffered four casualties, Lance-Sergeant Walsh and Lance-Corporal Coventry both wounded by a rifle grenade and Lance-Corporal Wilson and Guardsman Reynolds both shot. Vasquez:

As dawn approached, I spoke to 'Habana' – that was the battalion commander's call sign – to get reinforcements. Robacio said that no reserves were available, and that fighting was also taking place all around the headquarters of the battalion. At 07.15 sharp I remember I looked out and three British soldiers were up there, pointing their weapons at me. That finished my platoon, but we had lasted more than seven hours of actual fighting, longer than any other Argentinian platoon in Malvinas.

The battle for Tumbledown, so far, had lasted seven hours of hard fighting. Vasquez's stubborn defence had cost the Argentinians seven marines and five army killed, several wounded and others missing, but they had inflicted five killed and twelve wounded on Mitchell's platoon. At about 6am Major Simon Price and two Right Flank platoons, Second-Lieutenant Mathewson's 2 and Lieutenant Robert Lawrence's 3 Platoons, arrived on the summit. Included in the new arrivals was Lance-Sergeant McDermid, who was in 3 Platoon. McDermid later recalled that Right Flank had spent most of the night behind G Company and asking themselves 'What are we waiting for?' It was freezing, but there was no opportunity for a brew in case the Company was ordered to move. He was not aware of the fighting on Tumbledown because the wind was taking the noise to the east. Right Flank then received orders to move and it was only when he saw the wounded and prisoners being brought from the summit did McDermid asked himself, 'What the hell is going on? Someone is fighting up there!' However, he reminded himself he was wearing the three chevrons of a Lance-Sergeant and his section was relying on him.

Kiszely briefed Major Price that an enemy group, including a machine gun, were about 250 yards down the slope to the east and all efforts to dislodge them with Carl Gustavs and 66mm anti-tank missiles had failed. With daylight due in about an hour, time was the essence. Price opted for right hook and instructed 2 Platoon to advance along the southern ridge while 3 Platoon was to move along the left flank. Second-Lieutenant Viscount Dalrymple's 1 Platoon, as the reserve platoon, was to provide fire support from Left Flank's position on the summit. Price's Forward Observation Officer, Captain Miller, then told him he would be unable to register on the target because he had just heard that 1/7th Gurkha Rifles were advancing below the northern slopes of Tumbledown. This was, in fact, correct; nevertheless, without artillery and mortar fire to soften up the enemy, Price was now reliant upon the anti-tank weapons of the platoons for close fire support. In the saddle between the centre and eastern summits 2 and 3 Platoons clashed with La Madrid's platoon with Corporal Marco Palomo's section taking the brunt of Right Flank's advance and holding up 2 Platoon. La Madrid:

> *I ran back to my position and ordered my men to open fire. We stopped them, but they thinned out and came round our flanks; their deployment was good. They also engaged us with light mortars and missile launchers* (author – more likely 66m light anti tank projectiles). *This went on for a long time, and we suffered heavy casualties; we had eight dead and ten wounded. We started to run short of ammunition, particularly for the machine guns.*

3 Platoon, accompanied by the Company Second-in-Command, Captain Ian Bryden, managed to win a foothold on a ledge abandoned by the Argentinians where they found two enemy killed and took four prisoners. The platoon, now in two columns, one led by Bryden and other by Lawrence, attacked three groups of Argentinians. The Platoon Sergeant, Sergeant Robert Jackson, silenced the machine gun that had caused the three wounded to Left Flank on the summit, by discarding his rifle, climbing up rocks and throwing a grenade into its bunker. Jackson and Lance-Sergeant Baxter cleared a particularly strong Argentinian position menacing 2 Platoon and captured a wounded infantryman. Guardsman Andrew Pengelly, his General Purpose Machine Gun slung across his back, also scrambled up some rocks to give covering fire, but was later wounded. Jackson and Pengelly were both awarded the Military Medal. The fighting became fragmented, with small groups of men grenading bunkers and sangars and then following up with rifle fire and bayonets. Lance-Corporal Graham Rennie later described 3 Platoon's advance:

> *Our assault was initiated by a Guardsman killing a sniper, which was followed by a volley of 66mm anti-tank rounds. We ran forward in extended line, machine gunners and riflemen firing from the hip to keep the enemy heads down, enabling us to cover the open ground in the shortest possible time. Halfway across the open*

ground 2 Platoon went to ground to give covering fire support, enabling us to gain a foothold on the enemy position. From then on we fought from crag to crag, rock to rock, taking out pockets of enemy and lone riflemen, all of whom resisted fiercely.

Yard by yard, 3 Platoon, in the rocks on the left, seeped around the Argentinians' right flank and briefly cut La Madrid off from Jaimet. Covered by Palomo's section, La Madrid fell back, but the Scots Guards advanced quickly and the fighting remained close range. Private Montoya is said to have wrestled with a Guardsman but there is nothing in Scots Guards' account about this. La Madrid:

I could see that we were outflanked, with the British behind us, so we were cut off from my company. Some of my men had been taken prisoner. I reorganized and found that I was down to sixteen men. I started to retire. The British above me were firing machine guns, but we passed close to the rocks, actually under the machine-gun fire. I left six men in a line with one machine gun to cover our retreat, but really we were fighting all the time; we could not break contact. They came on us fast, and we fell back; it was starting to get light. The whole hill had fallen by then, and we were on lower ground, just south of Moody Brook. We eventually got through to Stanley, through what I would like to say was a perfect barrage fired by the Royal Artillery. We had to wait for breaks in the firing, but I still lost a man killed there.

The man killed was Sergeant Eusabio Aguilar, a well known and popular drill instructor. In the face of aggressive attacks, the Argentinian defence slowly crumbled. Private Jorge Sanchez, who in Vasquez's 4 Platoon, knew he was being surrounded:

The fighting was sporadic, but at times fierce, as we tried to maintain our position. By this time we had ten or twelve dead including one officer. I hadn't fired directly at a British soldier, as they had been too hard to get a clear shot at. I can remember lying there with all this firing going over my head. They were everywhere. The platoon commander then called Private Ramon Rotela manning the 60 millimetre mortar and Rotela fired it straight up into the air so that the bombs landed on ourselves. At this point I had been up and in actual combat for over six hours. It was snowing and we were tired. Some of the guys had surrendered, but I didn't want to do this. I had only twenty rounds left and I decided to continue the fight from Mount William. I popped up, fired a rifle grenade in the direction of eight to ten British soldiers to keep their heads down, and then ran for 2nd Platoon. I can remember saying some type of prayer hoping the British wouldn't shoot me in the back. Sanchez was a very lucky man to not have been shot by men of his own battalion when Second-Lieutenant Oruezabala, commanding 2 Platoon, instructed his men not to open fire as the soldier, clad in a baggy uniform and camouflaged steel helmet, was clearly a member of the Argentinian Marine Corps falling back from the night fighting.

Lance-Sergeant McDermid recalls that his platoon employed simple fire and movement tactics and every time they came to a stubborn position it was stormed with M79 rifle grenades, rifle and bayonet. 2 Platoon was still having a tough time clearing out Argentinian positions and progress was slow until Sergeant Robertson appeared with men from 1 Platoon and the momentum of the advance increased. 2 Platoon linked up with Captain Bryden and his group from 3 Platoon, who had reached a quartermaster's supply dump on the eastern tip of Mount Tumbledown. Although the Argentinian defence of Tumbledown had been destroyed, there was still resistance. Guardsmen Norton, Harkness and McEnteggart were all wounded, as was Lieutenant Lawrence, who was shot in the back of the head. In the flurry of shooting and with a blizzard sweeping across the mountain, McDermid recalls that Lance-Corporal Rennie shot someone at short range and then, while he and Lance-Corporal Richardson gave covering fire, Rennie dragged Lawrence into cover where the company medic, Pipe-Sergeant Jackie Oates, worked hard to keep him alive. A television drama would later be made about Lawrence's experiences. Right Flank had some trouble reorganizing because platoons and sections had become hopelessly muddled in the final attack, casualties needed to be gathered, ammunition re-distributed and positions taken up for the expected counter-attack, all under long-range and effective machine-gun and mortar fire from Sapper Hill

Throughout the night stretcher-bearers had been collecting the wounded. Sergeant Strettle and elements of 3 Troop, 9 Parachute Squadron, checked captured Argentinian positions for booby traps and mines and helped to evacuate any wounded that they came across. But it was not until soon after daybreak that teams arrived on the summit, which was still being mortared. One bomb landed near the stretcher party carrying Lieutenant Mitchell, and Guardsman Reynolds, who had been wounded in the fighting and was carrying the stretcher, was killed instantly, as was Guardsman Daniel Malcomson. Eight others were also wounded. For his gallantry during the night Reynolds was posthumously awarded a Distinguished Conduct Medal. The stretcher in tatters, Guardsman Findley let Mitchell use his rifle as a crutch and helped him hobble down the slope. As dawn broke, 656 Squadron light helicopters arrived at the Scots Guards Regimental Aid Post on Goat Ridge to fly out the wounded. The evacuation of those on the eastern slopes of Tumbledown would necessitate a long carry by stretcher. Heli-medivac was another option for the more seriously wounded. In the appalling weather of snow and low clouds, Captain Drennan and his observer, Lance-Corporal Rigg, flew forward to collect wounded. However, the evacuations were not without their risks. On at least three occasions a rifleman from Second-Lieutenant Franco's platoon opened fire at the Scout from rocks above the northern cliff of Tumbledown. In the gloom of a snowy dawn locating him was difficult and, although he was constantly moving between shots, the Scots Guards were able to pin him down most of the time. An Argentinian officer prisoner, invited by Captain Campbell-Lamerton, who commanded the Anti-Tank Platoon and spoke Spanish, tried to persuade the rifleman to desist, but failed. Eventually Lance-Corporal Gary Tyler, of Left Flank, landed a 66mm round on the Argentinian's position, which mortally wounded him by blowing off both legs. At the time Tyler was helping to evacuate casualties caused by some desultory mortaring from Sapper Hill. Despite the problems of weather and enemy action, Drennan and Rigg rescued sixteen wounded from front-line positions, including a Gurkha injured by the shelling in front of the minefield north of Mount William through which 1/7th Gurkha Rifles were then negotiating. On occasions Rigg is said to have stood on the Scout's skids to allow a wounded soldier to take his seat. Drennan was awarded the Distinguished Flying Cross and Rigg was Mentioned in Despatches.

It was later suggested that the Argentinians deliberately attacked stretcher-bearers on Mount Tumbledown. A mortar is an area weapon and the Argentinians on Sapper Hill were legitimately bombarding movement on Mount Tumbledown as were the guns shelling Mount Longdon, Two Sisters and Mount Harriet. It is of interest that while Argentinian medical personnel were clearly identified with the Red Cross on brassards and helmets, British medics wore no such insignia.

The cost of the Scots Guards attack was eight Guardsmen and one Royal Engineer killed and forty-three wounded. Headquarters Company lost two killed, including the Royal Engineer, and six wounded in the diversion. G Company lost ten wounded, principally to shelling. Left Flank suffered seven killed and twenty-one wounded, eighteen of whom were hospitalized. Five Right Flank were wounded. Lieutenant Lawrence's recovery was miraculous. Fifty per cent of the dead and wounded were officers, warrant or non-commissioned officers, which reflects the quality of leadership during the night. Such was the inexperience of the British in dealing with the dead that, at Ajax Bay, Lance-Corporal Pashley's identity was muddled with Sergeant Strettle, Lieutenant McManners's Troop Sergeant, who was alive and well. Major Davies later identified Pashley and he was buried at Ajax Bay in a quiet ceremony officiated by the Scots Guards padre, Major Angus Smith, the day after the Scots Guards buried their own men. Pashley was eventually brought back to England and his ashes spread over Hankley Common, a well-known parachute-dropping zone near Aldershot.

For the Scots Guards the action was remarkable. In the eight weeks since the Battalion had exchanged Royal Duties in red tunics and bearskins in London for combat kit, it had sailed south on a three-week voyage in a luxury liner as part of a Brigade with whom it had never operated. The Guardsmen had suffered a ten-hour soaking in four landing craft and, on landing at Bluff Cove, immediately sent out patrols to dominate their area of responsibility. Following the 3rd Commando Brigade assault on the Outer Defence Zone, the Battalion had, after a delay and the briefest of reconnaissances, then attacked Mount Tumbledown and, after nearly ten hours of intense fighting with tenacious marines and infantry, had captured their objective. The Battalion had not experienced such fighting since the Second World War. One of Lieutenant La Madrid's men christened the Scots Guards ' The panthers in the dark'. The capture of Mount Tumbledown was a significant victory and, although it took longer than expected, as most battles do, it signalled to the Argentinian commanders in Stanley that further resistance was pointless. The achievement was down to simple planning, effective fire support and the willingness to be decisive in the attack. An abiding memory of Lieutenant-Colonel Vaux, who listened to the battle in his command post on Mount Harriet, was 'the timeless Oxford English dialogue on the Scots Guards' command net'. It seemed to him that no matter what the situation was, the officers always spoke in those measured polite terms frequently heard at Ascot racecourse, Henley regatta and in the Chelsea Barracks Officers' Mess after Trooping the Colour. It reinforced the history of the British Army and was a marked difference from the crisp, and almost 'chummy', radio transmissions of the Royal Marines and Parachute Regiment.

The 5th Marine Infantry Battalion had also performed well, considering that it was made up almost entirely of conscript soldiers led by inexperienced young officers. In the forty-four days since 8 April 5th Marine Infantry Battalion had suffered sixteen dead and sixty-four wounded. Vasquez's defence had been robust and he lost seven killed. Of the amphibious engineer platoon, Lieutenant Mino was the only casualty. Between them the 4th and 12th Infantry Regiments platoons lost five killed. When La Madrid reorganized to retire, he mustered just sixteen left from the forty-five who had started the counter-attack; several had been captured. He lost five killed. Lieutenant Franco's 6th Infantry Regiment platoon lost three killed. About fifty Argentinians were wounded. Some of these were recovered by the 5th Marine Infantry Battalion Medical Officer, Captain Ferrario, who led a medical party, including Sergeants Angel Quiroga, Victor Palavecino, Miguel Arrias and eight others, back on to Mount Tumbledown during the final stages of the fighting. Most of those they recovered were from Jaimet's infantry company. Vasquez had shown the same commitment as First-Lieutenant Carlos Estaban had shown at Port San Carlos on 21 May and Goose Green and as Second-Lieutenant Juan Baldini did on Mount Longdon. They weren't the only ones. Robacio, who came in for criticism from some British officers for being too sentimental when he was taken back to Mount Tumbledown, had total command of N Company and the Army platoons involved and deserves credit for doing all that was possible to limit British gains. He was one of several senior officers who felt that Brigadier-General Menendez had not reacted aggressively enough to the British landings. Perhaps his wisest move was made before Vasquez's positions fell, when he ordered O Company to move into a position on to the saddle between Tumbledown and Mount William that would allow it to play an active role in the fighting. His defence of Sapper Hill provided a barrier that had to be breached before the British broke onto Stanley Common.

11

The Battles for Mount William and Sapper Hill – 14 June

The nearer the British advanced towards Stanley the more dangerous it became for the residents in the town. John Smith, who later wrote *74 Days,* which is an interesting account of the Argentine occupation, described how the intense bombardment by the ships on the gunline and Harriers ceaselessly attacking Argentine positions on Stanley Common and Sapper Hill caused the whole town to shake. The artillery added to the chaos and several houses on the outskirts were hit. Fortunately casualties among the civilians were low, although three women died when a British artillery shell hit a house.

But the air defence gunners were still resisting. During the early morning of 12 June No 1 (F) Squadron flew three paired sorties against positions on Sapper Hill. In the second, at about 10am, Squadron-Leader Peter Harris and Flight-Lieutenant Murdo Macleod met with resistance and Macleod's aircraft was damaged. First reports suggested a bullet, but an eyewitness indicated that it was a Tigercat missile prematurely exploding near the aircraft, which caused substantial damage to the engine and showered the powerhouse roof with shrapnel. Tigercats were operated by the 1st Marine Anti-Aircraft Artillery Battalion.

The Welsh Guards had spent the previous two days in positions north-west of Bluff Cove. Lieutenant Hendicott shared the opinion of some Guards officers that since 3rd Commando Brigade had been prevented from maintaining the momentum of its attack the British had lost vital impetus. Next day Lieutenant-Colonel Rickett issued a warning order for the attack on Sapper Hill as part of Phase Three. Shortly after dark on 13 June, at about the same time as the Scots Guards crossed their start line, the Welsh Guards advanced towards a suspected platoon position about 2,000 metres south-west of Mount William. Hendicott monitored the 59 Independent Commando Squadron radio net and briefed Rickett on likely minefields.

In preparation, 97 Battery was softening up Sapper Hill with high explosive, phosphorous and smoke to demoralize and disorientate the defending marine infantry. Since Mount Harriet was a better vantage point for spotting, the battery commander, Major Jordan, and a fire direction team supporting 2 Company were flown to a position about 500 metres south of the feature and began the weary climb. No sooner had they set off than 155mm shells shelled the slopes, forcing the group to shelter for the next forty-five minutes. When they reached a suitable observation point, it became clear that the registration of artillery targets for the attack on Mount Tumbledown was not yet complete and, since the Scots Guards were a higher priority, adjustments for the Welsh Guards were discontinued. Jordan returned to Battalion Headquarters just as Lieutenant-Colonel Rickett was issuing final orders for the night's operations – an approach to an assembly area ready to exploit the attack on Mount Tumbledown by seizing Sapper Hill. Since Brigade Intelligence believed that there were three company positions on its axis of advance, Lieutenant Symes was instructed to send three patrols, one to each position, and report on the strength and disposition of the enemy. The patrols were each accompanied by a commando sapper.

At 10.45pm, with C Company, 40 Commando, leading, the Battalion set off in a long single file south of the road to Stanley. Symes' Reconnaissance Platoon led and protected the right flank. 42 Commando on Mount Harriet indirectly protected the left. The night was clear and sharp with a bright moon although sharp, southerly winds would soon bring clouds and snow showers. Like all columns crossing difficult country, it concertinaed backwards and forwards, one minute the soldiers almost sprinting to catch up, the next standing still as those in front negotiated an obstacle or stopped for some reason. A particularly virulent stone run was encountered and then Company Sergeant Major Jack Hough, following close behind in the BV 202, started to attract Argentine shellfire. Rickett later commented:

> This was one of the most unpleasant nights that I can remember in my life, being shelled while virtually trapped in a horribly difficult stone run. Eventually we extricated ourselves from this and continued our advance with the Recce Platoon now in contact with Argentine minefields on the edge of Mount William.

By 2pm the Battalion had advanced only about a mile. In spite of protesting that he should be with Tactical Headquarters and able to advise Rickett, Lieutenant Hendicott and his Troop Headquarters trudged along with Main Headquarters near the rear of the column. He mentioned to his senior troop non-commissioned officer, Staff-Sergeant Smith, that he believed that they were heading very close to an area that he had briefed to be a minefield at the previous evening's Orders Group. In his opinion the ground also lent itself to one anyway, a lake and boggy ground south of the road. His suspicions eased when some white mine tape was found. This was later found to have been used by 59 Independent Commando Squadron to guide 42 Commando to its start line for its attack on Mount Harriet. Royal Marine Lance-Corporal Chris Pretty was a section commander with Lieutenant Carl Bushby's 9 Troop in C Company:

> *After some time we passed around a small hillock and started moving alongside a small re-entrant. In the light of the moon we could see a stationary armoured vehicle across the valley pointing in the same direction as us. Using our infra-red sights, it is one of the Scorpions* [The Scorpion was supporting the Scots Guards diversionary attack on the marine infantry position at Pony Pass.] *Going on a bit further and we are heads down with weight of equipment and supplies but keeping alert as we are not far from the Argentine positions. There was then a quiet 'Whump'. And then a few seconds later, this terrible high-pitched screaming. Somewhere down the back of the column there had been an explosion and we thought it might have been a grenade going off in someone's pouches. Word then came down the line that Lance Corporal 'Mac' MacGregor, in 7 Troop, had trod on an anti-personnel mine, which had blown his foot over the heads of those following him to hit one of the blokes in the face. As soon as we heard the word 'mine', we froze, literally from the cold and also from not moving. The Troop officer, Lieutenant Paul Allen, then walked back down the column to see how things were going with Mac when he also trod on a mine, which also blew a foot off. Apparently he was pretty calm about it.*

The explosions drew mortar and shelling, fortunately inaccurate, and life for the leading platoons became distinctly uncomfortable. Unwilling to move forward, or indeed into cover off the track, the column stopped and sought whatever shelter they could, the soldiers gathering in small groups in areas gingerly thought to be safe. The entire Battalion was stationary in a minefield of unknown size and liable to be late for the 5th Infantry Brigade operations. Rickett sent Captain Julian Sayers back down the column to halt any further movement forward until the minefield had been breached. At the same time a request was made to Brigade Headquarters for a helicopter to evacuate the two wounded Royal Marines, who were being tended by Medical Assistant Black of the Royal Navy. A 656 Squadron Scout did two separate sorties, both times landing in the minefield in an area checked for mines by the Royal Engineers. None were found. A small unidentified helicopter, probably another 656 Squadron Scout collecting casualties from Tumbledown, also flew overhead, which drew Argentine machine-gun fire. It seems likely that the ground was so frozen that the pressure pads of the mines had become stuck but were loosened and gradually pushed down as about thirty Royal Marines walked over them until the final pressures blew off the feet of MacGregor and Allen. In a minefield at night, with casualties and under fire, Hendicott later described the situation as 'not pleasant'.

Lieutenant-Colonel Rickett then radioed Hendicott to breach the minefield. Assembling his three sections, Hendicott moved past about 400 very still Guardsmen and Royal Marines, all very reluctant to move off the track, and reached the danger area. With Corporal Morgan and his section leading, the sappers carved a path through the minefield, laying out white tape behind them. Breaching minefields takes time. A sapper or assault engineer crawls forward and carefully prods the ground with a 6-inch spike. If he strikes something, he carefully clears away the earth to find out what it is. If it is a mine, it is defused and set to one side for eventual disposal. The sapper then carefully gropes for the wire and either lays white tape on the top or, if possible, crawls to the end and neutralizes the device. Behind them, others lay white tape marking the cleared path. Medical orderlies are positioned to deal with casualties quickly. A method to detect tripwires is by lobbing a light thin wire forward and, if the end touches anything, it is investigated as a potential tripwire. It is a long and laborious business, worse at night when raining or cold.

By this time Rickett was becoming anxious that he might not be in a position to exploit 42 Commando's success and was eager to press on. Hendicott advised him that, since the Argentines had not fenced or marked the perimeter, there was no way to tell whether they were still in the minefield. Rickett decided to continue the advance. 9 Troop followed the tape and then came to the end. A few yards further on some commando engineers were seated on the ground. The leading Royal Marines assumed they had breached the minefield and as each man passed them, they said, 'Cheers, lads' to the astonished sappers, blissfully unaware that the soldiers were actually taking a rest from the nerve-wracking business of mine-clearing and that ground had yet to be cleared of mines. Pretty later estimated that the Welsh Guards were trapped in the minefield for about four hours. The Battalion eventually moved into a position in low ground about 800 metres south of Mount Harriet, dug shell scrapes and, in dropping temperatures, watched and listened to the fighting on Mount Tumbledown.

The delay gave Hendicott time to debrief the three sappers who had accompanied the Reconnaissance Platoon patrols. The trio, two commando and one from 20 Field Squadron, reported that they found the same minefield, at different points, that had given Major Bethel such trouble a few hours earlier and had breached it, amidst the occasional mortar fire. One patrol had found the Argentinian positions attacked by

Bethel and captured four Argentinian marine infantry who had been left behind when O Company, 5th Marine Infantry Battalion withdrew to the Mount William area. The bodies of Drill-Sergeant Wight and Lance-Corporal Pashley were also recovered near the edge of the minefield and Rickett instructed that the Argentines should carry them.

Meanwhile on Goat Ridge 1/7th Gurkha Rifles had spent all night in freezing conditions waiting to advance, which they had expected to do at about midnight. As dawn neared, Lieutenant-Colonel Morgan was worried. He needed to be in position on the eastern slopes of Mount Tumbledown to attack Mount William and in the best possible position to break out on to Stanley Common by daybreak. His orders from Brigadier Wilson included entering Stanley and, if necessary, fighting in the town. But the Scots Guards were still fighting on Tumbledown and, theoretically, he could not move until the Argentines had been defeated. Nevertheless Morgan reasoned that if he followed the sheep track running beneath the northern cliffs he would be in cover. But the previous day, while tying up his plans with Lieutenant-Colonel Scott, he had been told by Lieutenant McManners that he risked running into a minefield and that the Argentines were 'bound to have planted mines right up to the rock face'.

Morgan issued quick orders and stuck with his original plan:

❐ *The 9 Parachute Squadron three-man section commanded by Sergeant Hugh Wrega was to lead and breach any minefields.*

❐ *A Company was to occupy the east end of Tumbledown and form a Battalion firebase with its own weapons, the MILANs and all six .50 Browning machine guns.*

❐ *B Company was to seize a small knoll north of the east end of Tumbledown ready to break out on to Stanley Common.*

❐ *D Company was to swing south and seize Mount William.*

Relieved to be on the move, the frozen 650-strong Gurkha battle group filed south of Goat Ridge, crossed to its northern flanks and picked up the sheep track heading east. As Battalion Headquarters, which was the second group in the column, passed the Scots Guards Tactical Headquarters, Morgan had to decline a plea for some help from Lieutenant-Colonel Scott. He needed to be at full strength for Phase Three. About a quarter way along the track, Wrega reported that they had encountered the minefield thought to be covering the northern cliffs of Tumbledown. In the gray dawn, Captain Villarraza's artillery Forward Observation Officer on Sapper Hill, Second-Lieutenant Marcelo De

Marco, spotted the movement and radioed 3rd Artillery Group for airburst and mortar fire. Fortunately the soft peat cushioned the explosions. Nevertheless this was the first time that most of the Gurkhas had been under shellfire and eight were wounded, two of them seriously. Most reacted with stoicism, which was reflected in the comment passed by Captain (Queens Gurkha Officer) Bhuwansing Limbu, the D Company Second-in-Command, to Major Kefford, 'Jolly exciting this, isn't it, Sahib?' Morgan had a choice – go straight through or find a way round. Time being of the essence, Morgan decided to follow the original route and told Wrega to find a way round. Fortunately the Argentines had not laid mines right up to the rock face and the Battalion squeezed through the gap. By the time that the Battalion reached the eastern slopes the fighting on Tumbledown had died and, as dawn broke, A and B Companies were in position and D Company was formed up ready to assault Mount William.

As these manoeuvres were taking place, a lone rifleman opened up from behind them causing everyone to dive for cover. Morgan led his Tactical Headquarters forward to find out what was happening and also came under accurate fire when, while sheltering behind a rock, a shot cracked overhead between him and his radio operator. The 4th Field Regiment Forward Observation Officer with D Company, Captain Keith Swinton, then announced to his bombardier that he believed he had been shot. The bombardier saw that Swinton had been hit in the chest and declared, 'So you have, sir.' Swinton was later evacuated by helicopter to the Regimental Aid Post on Goat Ridge where the doctors put him to one side to be treated later. When Swinton protested that he had a serious chest wound, the medics told him that he would undoubtedly live since the bullet had entered his chest, passed within an inch of his heart, missed his vital organs and exited without causing serious damage. Meanwhile Sergeant Wrega had breached a minefield on the saddle between Tumbledown and Mount William. There was another brief delay as boundaries between the Scots Guards and Gurkhas were sorted out and then D Company advanced and found Mount William abandoned except for the body of an amphibious engineer. Kefford then set about preparing for the Battalion advance on to Stanley Common. For his night's work Wrega was awarded the Military Medal.

The mystery of the lone rifleman turned out to be a member of the Scots Guard Reconnaissance Platoon who was too far forward and had encroached into the Gurkhas' area. Seeing men in the open and not knowing that the Gurkhas were on the move, he assumed them to be Argentines assembling for a counter-attack and opened fire. As we have seen, the Scots Guards had already suffered quite badly from a lone

Argentine rifleman. Another near 'blue on blue' involving the Scots Guards occurred at about the same time when Headquarters 3rd Commando Brigade, after a very difficult and dramatic night, was moving into a position on Mount Kent overlooking Stanley. Its Intelligence Section saw men high on a stony ridge and, since no friendly forces were thought to be in the area, it was assumed they must be Argentines. Covered by the machine gun on their BV 202, the Section skirmished up the hill and intercepted the party, who turned out to be a Scots Guards Forward Observation party. Fortunately no one opened fire.

1/7th Gurkha Rifles were now firm and, when Morgan reported to Brigade Headquarters that Mount William was captured, Wilson told him, 'Stanley is yours'. Morgan was slightly shocked by the order. In front of him were 11,000 well-armed Argentines of three infantry regiments, two armoured car squadrons, seven batteries of 105mm Pack Howitzers and one of 155mm howitzers and several Army and Air Force anti-aircraft batteries with a useful ground attack capability. By any stretch of the imagination, attacking was a daunting prospect, but one factor that Morgan had in his favour was that Argentine morale was declining. Interestingly, he did not have the Intelligence collated in early May by Headquarters 3rd Commando Brigade for fighting in Stanley. 5th Infantry Brigade had not carried out any preparations for the complexities of fighting in a built-up area still occupied by civilians. In his favour, Morgan led the strongest battalion that the British took to the South Atlantic. The Gurkhas, whose status in the British Army had been challenged by the Argentines and whose kukri the Argentine media had insulted, were itching for a fight. But, as Morgan was preparing to issue orders, he was then told by Wilson to go no further forward until ordered.

Learning from Lieutenant-Colonel Robacio that La Madrid's counter-attack on Tumbledown was in trouble, Brigadier-General Jofre's annoyance was magnified when he learnt that Mino's amphibious engineers were again withdrawing without any authority. Jofre therefore ordered his Chief-of-Staff, Colonel Felix Aguiar, to instruct Robacio that he was to break contact and regroup on Sapper Hill. Robacio and Major Jaimet were furious because they believed they were holding the Scots Guards and were in a position to counter-attack. It would be six years before they openly criticized the decision. Robacio:

On the last day of the war, 14 June, at about 6.30am I thought that we were still winning. My unit hadn't suffered any real losses. We hadn't given up any of our positions. All we had lost was a very, very small part of Mount Tumbledown. I knew that we were running out of ammunition, so I asked my headquarters for more. We were concentrating our efforts on Mount Tumbledown because that was the battle that would seal the fate of Port Stanley. Unfortunately we never received the ammunition we needed. At about 7am I received the order to withdraw prior to surrender. Our military code states that for an Argentine military unit to surrender it must have spent all its ammunition or lost at least two-thirds of its men. It was awful to have to ask the units that were still fighting to withdraw. It was a very bitter moment. We really felt defeated. You could see the battle coming to an end.

Jaimet:

Just as dawn was breaking Robacio came up on the air to advise me that he would not come to our assistance and that he had orders to withdraw the companies. I was gutted more than anything because I wanted to use the rest of the company. That was the only thing I was thinking of really. I was a commando and it was a matter of personal as well as national pride to continue fighting regardless of the consequences. I considered Malvinas my paradise. I got through to HQ 10th Brigade and made it clear that my company should be going forward. The orders puzzled and dispirited us. Many looked on the big break of contact as running away and did not like it at all.

With La Madrid's platoon severely mauled, Jaimet had appointed Second-Lieutenant Franco's platoon to cover the withdrawal of 5th Marine Infantry Battalion from Mount Tumbledown. Franco had already successfully covered the withdrawal of C Company, 4th Infantry Regiment, from Two Sisters on 12 June but lost three killed. Robacio again:

The unit withdrew in orderly fashion, under intense enemy fire and with the help of God, because God exists on the battlefield. Then my men prepared to resist on Sapper Hill to the last man, but we were told that our commanding officers had already surrendered and I had to give my units the order to withdraw yet again.

Jofre, in an interview with the mass circulation *Gent* news magazine, disagreed:

Sometime during the morning Robacio came on the air to advise me that his command post, near Felton Stream, was under direct attack. There are varying accounts of the report time, but I am sure it was around 7am. 'We are encircled,' Robacio told me in a hurried call. 'All around us are British forces firing at us; at least 150 troops and more than a dozen tanks. We are not in a good position.' This came as a shock to me. To us it was apparent at the time that Special Air Service personnel dressed in Argentine Army uniforms had mixed in with the 7th Regiment soldiers and under their cover infiltrated to the rear of the 5th Marine Infantry Battalion. Now we did have something to worry about.

212

The British troops and tanks referred to by Robacio were 2nd Parachute Battalion and 4 Troop, the Blues and Royals, who, having destroyed the remainder of 7th Infantry Regiment on Wireless Ridge, had been released by 3rd Commando Brigade to pursue the Argentines into Stanley. There was no truth in the rumours circulating among Argentine troops that the Special Air Service were mingling with them to spread discontent. They had insufficient Spanish speakers although enough men had 'gaucho' moustaches to pass as South Americans. Even if the performance of the Special Air Service during the campaign was open to improvement, their psychological value as 'super soldiers' was helpful. In any event 2nd Assault Section, 601st Commando Company, was ordered to seek out and shoot on sight British Special Forces in Argentine uniforms.

Even as Franco was moving to cover the withdrawal Robacio was preparing to counter-attack in the belief he could retake Tumbledown. With his headquarters threatened by 2nd Parachute Battalion, he telephoned Captain Villarraza to finalize a counter-attack by O Company from Mount William. Jofre was not happy and radioed 5th Marine Infantry Battalion:

When I got back to Robacio I made it clear that he should regroup on Sapper Hill. Apart from re-opened communications in the rear and an abundance of ammunition, there would be a dozen Army radar-guided anti-aircraft guns and 'C' Company, 3rd Regiment to support him. In his earlier reports he had reported a shortage of belt-fed ammunition for the machine guns and pressing requirement for casualty evacuation. It would be very loathsome to somehow suggest that I was a quitter, that somehow I misled and that we did something wrong. That is nonsense. To stay would have necessitated reorganizing our deployment in broad daylight. There was no immediate response to this. Obviously he had more confidence in the situation than I did. I patiently chewed at my fingernails for as long as I could tolerate it. I then got on to battalion headquarters for an explanation and was told that O Company was planning a counter-attack. From my point of view we had already lost too much time and I was anxious to get the companies off Tumbledown and the withdrawal under way while we still had darkness. It was still dark outside. I asked Jaimet if his company could hold out for another hour as we were planning to pull the 5th Marine Infantry Battalion back and up on and around Sapper Hill. Jaimet agreed. Villarraza waited for artillery to open up to signal that he could get away. At 9.45 Jaimet was ordered to withdraw and although hindered by British fire his company was able to break clear. All 5th Marine Infantry Battalion elements had reached Sapper Hill by 10am.

Back at Headquarters 10th Infantry Brigade, Jofre reasoning that British heliborne units were likely to go for Sapper Hill, which would trap the defenders of Mount Tumbledown, selected it to be a strongpoint.

At about 5am he ordered C Company, 3rd Infantry Regiment, to join to Captain Cionchi's M Company on Sapper Hill. Cionchi's force now consisted of Second-Lieutenants Davis's 2nd and Koch's 3rd Marine Infantry Platoons and Second-Lieutenant Marcelo Llambias-Pravaz's 4th Infantry Regiment platoon, which had escaped from Two Sisters two nights earlier. Headquarters 5th Marine Battalion was south of Felton Stream and Battalion Headquarters and C Company, 3rd Infantry Regiment, sat astride the coast road. The Amphibious Engineers were in reserve east of the Marine Battalion Headquarters and elements of 25th Infantry Regiment were creating another strongpoint on the western outskirts of Stanley. The two armoured reconnaissance troops were in the area of the Slaughter House covering the road into Stanley from Sapper Hill. The artillery was gathered on Murrell Heights.

At about 7.30am Lieutenant-Colonel Rickett was advised that the Scots Guards did not require reinforcement. Since his Battalion was in danger from artillery and mortar fire, he obtained permission from Brigadier Wilson to withdraw to the assembly area near the lake where he instructed his Battalion to relax and await further instructions, which he expected from 3rd Commando Brigade and which would be to break out on to Stanley Common. It had been a difficult night, which had tested everyone's fitness and nerve, and all now settled down to a welcome brew. While waiting for further orders, Lieutenant Hendicott instructed Corporal Ayres to breach a path through the minefield to the north-west of the lake to the road. A number of mines were found and destroyed. In recognition of his Troop's work throughout the night Hendicott was Mentioned in Despatches.

At about 9.30am, shortly after visiting A Company, 40 Commando, Rickett received orders from Wilson to attack Sapper Hill as soon as possible and that a flight of Sea King helicopters would be with him soon. Not too happy about an attack in broad daylight, he was assured that the Battalion would receive all the support needed, including the bombing of Sapper Hill by Harriers at the *moment critique*. Additional support included Lieutenant Coreth's 3 Troop, the Blues and Royals, which was down to one Scorpion and two Scimitars, having lost Coreth's own Scorpion during the Scots Guards diversionary attack. Hendicott attached a sapper section each to 2 Company, the Welsh Guards, and C Company, 40 Commando, and kept the third section in reserve with him at Battalion Headquarters. Rickett issued orders over the command radio net and within fifteen minutes the Welsh Guards were ready to move. 9 Troop, C Company was instructed to secure the start line.

The Sea Kings arrived on time and Rickett briefed the pilots to drop his Battalion on the track south of Tumbledown about three miles west of Sapper Hill. Reconnaissance Platoon had previously reported that there was indiscriminate mining everywhere, but not, it appeared, on the track itself. After a very short flight the Welsh Guards were landed exactly where they wanted to be, but the track turned out to have mines on both sides and was an extension of Bethel's minefield. Unfortunately, the two helicopters carrying 9 Troop flew too far to the east and dropped them on the track below Sapper Hill in full view of the defenders. The Argentines watched, with some incredulity, as the two Sea Kings appeared from the west. 'I was so mad; I wanted to shoot both helicopters out of the sky,' recalled Llambias-Pravaz. Lance-Corporal Pretty remembers that it was broad daylight and his helicopter hurtled along at high speed, almost at ground level. He thought the duration of the flight for the expected distance was a little long and then the nose of the Sea King lifted sharply. The Royal Marines braced themselves for a heavy battle landing and rapid debussing. Pretty:

No problem, we would be out and start our work in the normal fashion under the watchful eye of the Gurkhas. Before we had the chance to land properly, the whole of the left side of the helicopter came blasting in with bits and pieces flying everywhere. The noise was deafening. The helicopter thudded onto the deck and the guys started spilling out immediately, trying to find cover and identify where they were. We had landed on a small light-coloured track in the middle of nowhere and the helicopters were still being shot up. Someone suggested it was the Gurkhas on Mount William. The helicopters then revved up and banked over to the south, leaving 9 Troop under heavy fire. Someone said that the road might be mined on both sides but it seemed better to be in the middle of a minefield than in the open without any cover. The Argentines were only a short distance away on a small hill. With the 17-year-old Marine Vince Coombes giving covering fire by spraying the hill with his machine gun from the hip, I stood in the middle of the road and pushed guys off the road into cover afforded by a tiny bank about 8 feet high.

The firefight rolled backwards and forwards as each side opened heavy fire, and then took cover from the inevitable retaliation. Lieutenant Bushby tried to radio for help, but, since he was using a trailing antenna, that is to say a bit of wire as opposed to a whip aerial, he was unsuccessful. Marine Coombes was badly wounded in the arm and a number of Royal Marines wormed their way over to treat him. Another Royal Marine, who was not wearing a helmet, suffered a head wound and another thought that he had been hit in the backside until it turned out that his rear pouches had been shot off. Indeed, several 9 Troop lost webbing in this manner. Koch's platoon attacked 9 Troop's right flank, but this was defeated by heavy, sustained machine-gun fire. The firefight continued with neither side making any headway. The firing gradually slowed down and then the Marine Infantry simply evacuated Sapper Hill. Bushby again gingerly raised the trailing antenna and learnt from C Company that the Argentines had surrendered. At the cost of three men killed Cionchi's force made their way back to Port Stanley and eventual captivity.

The Royal Marines got to their feet, very slowly. No one fired. The whole action had lasted no more than ten minutes. The last shots of the war had been fired. Both helicopters later had to be taken out of service while repairs were completed. Extremely anxious to link up with C Company, the Welsh Guards' advance was fast. Rickett:

> Just as we crossed our Start Line, my Battery Commander held his radio to my ear as Tony Holt, the Gunner CO, wanted to speak urgently to me. Suffice it to say that we were out of communications with 5 Brigade but the Gunners always seem to get through! I was told that white flags were up in Stanley, that we were only to fire if we were fired upon first and that the Brigade Commander wished me to hasten with all speed for Sapper Hill. By this time we could hear firing from the area of the forward troop, which had been dropped too far forward. Captain Pillar duly reported that they were under fire from the Argentine positions on Sapper Hill. He appeared rather reluctant to move his company forward. He wasn't totally in the picture on my last radio transmission with 5 Brigade, so together we all moved at best possible speed down the track, firstly to link up with his Troop and second to get to Sapper Hill fast. I had already summoned the Blues and Royals Troop but it seemed to take an awful long time to catch up with us! Undaunted, we linked up with 9 Troop, where one Royal Marine had been shot. We hurried past them and, at last, the Blues and Royals arrived. Jumping on the lead vehicle with my command group and telling Andy's company to follow on at best speed, we occupied Sapper Hill from the rear, i.e. from the Stanley side, and occupied it. There was no resistance as Argentine soldiers had been withdrawn to Stanley, leaving their dead behind them. The remainder of the Battalion soon joined us and I gave out positions for the companies to man.

Pretty remembers that the rest of C Company was the first to appear on the scene, having run along the road:

> The next thing I know is that there is a Scimitar on the road in front me loaded with Guardsmen. When the tank commander invited me to step out of the way, I told him that we were going to capture Sapper Hill. A ridiculous argument then developed in the middle of the road, which was ended when its Rarden cannon was pointed at me. No point in arguing over a principle and I had to let them pass. This really hurt. However, we formed up in single file and moved off behind the Scimitar on to Sapper Hill.

This accidental heliborne assault on Sapper Hill seems to have convinced Brigadier-General Jofre that further resistance was pointless. He recalls:

As predicted, British helicopter-borne infantry, 40th Commando Battalion, lost no time in following up until checked with a bloody nose at Sapper Hill. After that things went from bad to worse. No sooner had Jaimet reached Sapper Hill than Colonel Dalton, the Brigade Operations Officer, told me, 'Many soldiers are in a strange state and the kelpers are bound to get hurt. One 3rd Regiment platoon has been told to go into the houses by a fanatical lieutenant, who has also ordered the men to kill the kelpers – something awful is happening.'I'll never forget that moment. It was like a lightning bolt had hit me. It was becoming evident to me that I was no longer at the control. 'We've had it. The lives of the kelpers are being risked,' I told General Menendez and he realized that there was no question of fighting any further. Menendez told me that he wished to talk to Galtieri to arrange a ceasefire. I agreed. It was all over. Fighting on Sapper Hill was out of the question.

While the Welsh Guards were reorganizing on Sapper Hill Lieutenant-Colonel Whitehead and 45 Commando appeared from the west and the two commanding officers cheerfully divided the hill between them, Rickett ensuring that the Welsh Guards were on the leeward side, which seems a little ungallant, considering 45 Commando had just spent the last sixteen days exposed to the most awful weather. But all's fair in love and war! At about the same time Lieutenant Hendicott took off from the Welsh Guards helicopter landing site in war and landed several minutes later on Sapper Hill in peacetime after the surrender. His Troop was the first Royal Engineers to reach the hill and later probably wished they hadn't been, after an extremely cold night 'being blown to bits by an Antarctic southerly storm'. Soon after their arrival they were joined by Condor Troop, who had arrived with 45 Commando.

The previous night Major Chris Davies had become aware of the difficulties the Blues and Royals were experiencing with the ground and, knowing that most of his leading sappers were without mechanical support, had ordered Captain Willet to catch them up with a Combat Engineer Tractor. Unfortunately Willet and his 1 Troop were still at Fitzroy, and Fitzroy Bridge, which they had repaired, was still not passable for tracked vehicles. This did not deter Willet and, with a half section of sappers, he followed the tracks of Blues and Royals and, driving all night, fittingly arrived on Sapper Hill just as 45 Commando and the Welsh Guards were reorganizing. Brigadier Wilson arrived soon afterwards and was elated that the Welsh Guards had arrived so quickly. But who was going to enter Stanley, the Royal Marine brigade or the newcomers, the Army?

Argentine command and control was in chaos as Brigadier-General Jofre struggled to stem the British advance. Wireless Ridge and Mount Tumbledown had been abandoned, Mount William was undoubtedly in

British hands and Sapper Hill had just been seized after the expected heliborne assault. That his assessment was a mistake was irrelevant, but it was enough to convince Jofre that further resistance was useless. All the counter-attacks had failed and the army was now in full retreat with nowhere to go. Argentina and Brigadier-General Menendez had no alternative but surrender. As with many defeated armies, ill discipline and disorganization took hold of the defeated troops and 181st Military Police Company and 5th Marine Infantry Battalion Regimental Police Detachment were instructed to restore order and ensure an orderly withdrawal to Stanley.

On Mount Harriet Lieutenant-Colonel Vaux had been watching the fighting when he was called to his command post. The guns stopped firing and, apart from the occasional shot, an eerie silence drifted across the smoking battlefield. Vaux returned from his command post with the news: 'They're falling back from Sapper Hill. There are white flags all over the place.' The news quickly spread. A television crew persuaded the ebullient Major Dawson, at the Gurkhas's alternative Battalion Headquarters, to leap out from his command post shouting, 'There are white flags flying over Stanley. Bloody marvellous. Tee Hee!' But it took several takes before the crew was happy. Dawson actually had other things to do. The Gurkha Regimental Sergeant Major Karnabahadur Rai, out of frame, was less than happy that he had been denied a battle. Standing at about 5'3", and almost as wide and known as 'One Ton', he was thought to be the smallest Regimental Sergeant Major in the Armed Forces. In fact, there were few white flags, but it sounded good, particularly outside No 10 Downing Street, 8,000 miles to the north.

Brigadier Wilson was ordered by Major-General Moore to go firm, while 3rd Commando Brigade advanced quickly through the withdrawing units along the tarmac coast road into Stanley. It was a wise decision, for Wilson's men were in a dominant position to keep an eye on the Argentine units on Stanley Common while Thompson's men went in by the back door and captured Government House – the seat of government. The fighting was finished, but the hostilities would drag on for another three weeks, such was the stubbornness of the defeated Junta.

Negotiations were underway, but no one in Stanley was sure what was happening. The ceaseless firing had been replaced by windy silence. Defeated units streamed into the town and consequently the Argentine military authorities advised residents to stay indoors for their own safety. John Smith was having a cup of tea in West Store when Major-General Moore walked in and, with masterly aplomb and reserve, said, 'Hello, I'm Jeremy Moore and I'm sorry it took us three weeks to get here'. Seventy-four days of occupation were over and one of the most pointless wars of the 20th Century ended. But as a member of the Press remarked, 'Have we come all this way just to see this? The town looks so insignificant.'

The weather was cold, with snow showers and very windy. The units on Sapper Hill spent a miserable night among the wreckage of the Argentine position. However, the British rations were augmented by captured Argentine cigarettes and rations that lay in abundance everywhere, some of which contained small bottles of Scotch whisky. Soon after last light the Welsh Guards received their bergens, courtesy of some deft logistical magic by Regimental Sergeant Major Davies. The next day the Battalion was withdrawn to Fitzroy and linked up with the Scots Guards, the Gurkhas and other elements of 5th Infantry Brigade. Denied the triumph of entering Stanley, at least the Welsh Guards, (or more accurately 9 Troop, C Company, 40 Commando) had the satisfaction of being the nearest to the town when the Argentines surrendered.

Within a week all but about 600 of the Argentines captured in the Falklands had been repatriated. When 160 Provost Company helped in the searching of the prisoners before they were captured, Captain Barclay was instrumental in making it quite clear to Brigadier-General Jofre that the disruption and non-cooperation by certain senior officers to the repatriation process was unacceptable. The 600 were retained ostensibly so that a specialist interrogation team could gather information about the Argentine Armed Forces. In reality they were hostages until Argentina agreed to unconditional surrender. On board the prison ship MV *St Edmund*, Major Charles Bremner's 3 Company, 1st Welsh Guards guarded the prisoners and accompanied the ship to Puerto Marin where the prisoners were released.

Also within the week, most of 3rd Commando Brigade was on the way back on a long therapeutic voyage to the United Kingdom to the spectacular homecoming on 12 July when the *Canberra* docked at Southampton. The parachute battalions were flown back and did not have the advantage of that relaxing therapy.

The departure of 3rd Commando Brigade left 5th Infantry Brigade to provide the garrisons for the Falkland Islands and its Dependencies. Workforces began to clear battlefields, gather the dead and erect memorials, but not without casualties. At Goose Green Lance-Corporal Budhaprasad Limbu, of 1/7th Gurkha Rifles, was killed when his shovel hit a buried unexploded grenade on the lip of a trench he was filling in. Accompanied by a small group of Argentine sappers on parole, 9 Parachute Squadron began to clear important minefields. One of the Argentines was injured in an explosion. In July members of 5th Infantry Brigade Headquaters and Signal Squadron were helping the Welsh

Guards to clear the runway at Stanley Airport when a Harrier skidded on take-off and accidentally jettisoned its Sidewinder missiles, one of which ran into some soldiers and wounded eleven, the most serious being Signalman Davies, who lost his right leg.

Major-General David Thorne took over as Commander British Forces Falkland Islands. When 1st Queen's Own Highlanders and a company of the Queens Lancashire Regiment arrived in mid-July, the Welsh Guards and 1/7th Gurkha Rifles returned home and were followed by Scots Guards at the end of the month. None were given the Sunday afternoon welcome extended to the Commando Brigade, except the Gurkhas, who were greeted by the people of Fleet on 9 August, ninety days after they had left the United Kingdom, half spent on ships. The 5th Infantry Brigade combat and service support units were replaced with new arrivals, unit titles usually being preceded by 'Falkland Islands', such as the Falklands Islands Logistic Battalion. A project conceived in June 1982 came to fruition on 12 May 1985 when His Royal Highness Prince Andrew, who had been a helicopter pilot on HMS *Invincible*, opened a large camp and new runway at Mount Pleasant, not far from where Corporal Daughtrey had found the wreckage of Staff-Sergeant Griffin's helicopter. The new facilities enabled direct Tri-Star flights to the Falklands and the ability for quick reinforcement.

For one soldier the campaign lasted another seven weeks. Guardsman Philip Williams was a Scots Guards stretcher-bearer when he became separated and disorientated during the battle for Tumbledown. For the next three days he survived in the mountains in atrocious conditions and then made his way to Port Harriet House where he found some equipment and rations left behind by his battalion's Reconnaissance Platoon. In spite of intensive searches, Williams was not found and his disappearance remained a mystery. Seven weeks later he walked into Bluff Cove and was quickly flown home. Lieutenant-Colonel Scott obviously had to consider whether Williams should be court-martialled, but after debriefing him decided that the matter should be allowed to rest.

As with all wars there are winners and losers. One of the more spectacular falls was Brigadier Tony Wilson, who retired from the Army on 31 December 1982, six months after leading 5th Infantry Brigade to Stanley. The departure of 5th Infantry Brigade had all the hallmarks of troops going to the Boer War, but it does seem that not everyone knew what was expected of them – garrison or combat – until they landed. They had no amphibious experience and yet were not given much practical support. The move to the air-defenceless Port Pleasant sector was a bold move and, had it not been for the appearance of five Skyhawks, it may well have been considered to be a brilliant tactical move. However, Wilson's Brigade picked itself up and the Scots Guards conducted themselves well along the narrow spine of Mount Tumbledown. But the knives were out for Wilson, even before the campaign ended, much of the criticism centring around the disaster at Port Fitzroy, over which, as we have seen, he had little control. Of the senior commanders, Wilson was denied an award of any sort; however, it is indicative of the loyalty of some of his officers, as well as others not involved in the campaign, that they felt that, although he had been badly treated, he had acted with considerable honour until retirement and since. He has yet to write his version, but, as he wrote to the authors in February 2000, both of whom served in Hong Kong at the same time, 'My conviction is that there may well be a time to daub the eye of the dragon and bring it to life, but it is not, at this juncture, in my calendar.' Major-General Walter Walker, the architect of winning the Confrontation with Indonesia from 1962 to 1966, also experienced similar harmful recognition from the military establishment. But the naval and military establishment has always been cruel.

5th Brigade survived in an infantry and airborne role until 2000 when it was converted to 12th Mechanized Infantry Brigade and lost the role to the newly formed 16th Air Assault Brigade. This, with 3rd Commando Brigade, has rather become the advance guard of British military operations at the expense of the rest of the Army, who are confined to peacekeeping duties. Whereas few are allowed to forget that 3rd Commando Brigade took part in the Falklands campaign, reminiscences about 5th Infantry Brigade are confined to events off Fitzroy. In comparison to the pointless but much-studied engagement at Goose Green, Tumbledown and Sapper Hill barely receive a mention.

Bibliography

Bilton, Martin and Kosminsky, Peter; *Speaking Out;* London; Andre Deutsch; 1989.

Brown, David; *The Royal Navy and the Falklands War;* London; Leo Cooper; 1987.

Burdon, Rodney; Draper, Michael; Rough, Douglas; Smith, Colin and Wilton, David; *Falklands – The Air War;* London; Arms and Armour; 1986.

Clapp, Michael and Southby-Tailyour, Ewen; *Amphibious Assault Falklands;* London; Leo Cooper;1996.

Daily Telegraph; *The Falklands War;* 30 March 2002.

Dingemans, Captain Peter; *Leadership in the Falklands;* April 1983; The Naval Review, Vol 71, Number 2.

Armour in the Falklands; Guards Magazine; 1982.

Field, Richard; *A Vignette of the Falklands as a Watchkeeper, Infanteer and Car Commander;* Guards Magazine; 1982.

Frost, Maj-Gen John; *2 Para Falklands – The Battalion At War;* London; Buchan and Enright; 1983.

Gander, Terry; Encyclopaedia of the Modern British Army 2nd Edition; Cambridge; Patrick Stevens; 1982.

Lawrence, John and Robert; *When the Fighting is Over;* London; Bloomsbury Publishing Ltd; 1988.

London Gazette; *Honours and Awards;* London; HMSO; 8th October 1982.

Middlebrook, Martin; *The Fight For The Malvinas;* London; Viking; 1989.

Middlebrook, Martin; *Operation Corporate;* London; Viking; 1985.

Moro, Ruben O; *The History of the South Atlantic Conflict;* New York; Preager; 1989.

Oakley, Derek; *The Falklands Military Machine;* Tunbridge Wells; Spellmount; 1989.

Ratcliffe; Peter; *Eye of the Storm;* London; Michael O'Mara Books; 2000.

Reed, John; *Commando Logistic Regiment Royal Marines;* Armed Forces; June 1983.

Royal Engineers Journal; *Operation Corporate;* 1982.

Ruiz-Moreno, Isidoro; *Commandos in Action, The Argentinian Army in Malvinas*

Southby-Tailyour, Ewen; Reasons *in Writing;* London; Leo Cooper; 1993.

The Wire (Journal of the Royal Signals); *The Corps in the Falklands;* September 1982

International Defence Review 9/1982.

Thompson, Julian; *No Picnic;* London; Leo Cooper; 1983.

Turolo, Carlos; *Asi Lucharon;* Editorial Sudamericana.

Vaux, Nick; *March to the South Atlantic;* London; Buchan and Enright; 1986.

van der Bijl, Nick: *Nine Battles to Stanley;* Barnsley: Leo Cooper; 1999.

Villarno Amilio; *Batallon 5*; Aller Atucha y Asociados.
Wilsey, John: *H Jones VC*; London; Hutchinson; 2002.
Woodward, Admiral Sandy; *One Hundred Days*; London; HarperCollins; 1992.
www.britains-smallwars.com.
www.noticiaspatagonicas.com.ar/informes/bim.htm (Marine Infantry website).
www.seineldin.8m.com (Colonel Seineldin and his followers).
www.faa.mil.ar (the official site of the Argentine Air force).
www.ejercito.mil.ar (the official site of the Argentine Army).

UNPUBLISHED MATERIAL

Davies, Chris; *A Memoir of 9 Parachute Squadron Royal Engineers in the Falklands Campaign.*
Falkland Island Logistic Unit Battlefield Tour pack for *2 Scots Guards – Tumbledown*

POST OPERATION REPORTS

Post Operation Reports.
   2nd Battalion The Parachute Regiment.
   4th Field Regiment Royal Artillery.
   59th Independent Commando Squadron RE.

ARGENTINE SOURCES

Calvi Report; the official Argentine report into the Falklands campaign.
Castagneto, Mario Luis and Spadaro, Jose Ricardo; *La Guerra de las Malvinas;*: Argentina; Editorial Oriente; 1987.
Jofre, Oscar and Aguiar, Felix; *La X Brigada de Infanteria Mecanizada "General Nicolas Levalle" en Accion en Malvinas*; Buenos Aires; Circulo Militar; 1992.
Kasanzew, Nicolas; *Malvinas: A Sangrey Fuergo.*
Menendez, Mario and Turclo, Carlos; *Malvinas: Testimonio de su Gobernador*; Argentina, Sudamericana-Planeta; 1983.
Rattenbach, Lt-Gen Benjamin; *The Rattenbach Report: The Commission for the Political and Strategic Evaluation of the Conflict in the South Atlantic Report.*
Testimonio de Officiales Superiors y Jefes de la Guerra de las Malvinas; 1988.

Index

226

232